Barbara Korte, Sylvia Paletschek (eds.)
Popular History Now and Then

Historische Lebenswelten in populären Wissenskulturen
History in Popular Cultures | Volume 6

Editorial

The series **Historische Lebenswelten in populären Wissenskulturen | History in Popular Cultures** provides analyses of popular representations of history from specific and interdisciplinary perspectives (history, literature and media studies, social anthropology, and sociology). The studies focus on the contents, media, genres, as well as functions of contemporary and past historical cultures.

The series is edited by Barbara Korte and Sylvia Paletschek (executives), Hans-Joachim Gehrke, Wolfgang Hochbruck, Sven Kommer and Judith Schlehe.

Barbara Korte, Sylvia Paletschek (eds.)

Popular History Now and Then

International Perspectives

[transcript]

Printed with the support of the German Research Foundation (DFG)

Bibliographic information published by the Deutsche Nationalbibliothek
The Deutsche Nationalbibliothek lists this publication in the Deutsche Natio-nalbibliografie; detailed bibliographic data are available in the Internet at http://dnb.d-nb.de

Cover concept: Kordula Röckenhaus, Bielefeld
Proofread and typeset by Barbara Korte and Sylvia Paletschek
Printed by Majuskel Medienproduktion GmbH, Wetzlar
ISBN 978-3-8376-2007-8

Global distribution outside Germany, Austria and Switzerland:

Transaction Publishers
New Brunswick (U.S.A.) and London (U.K.)

Transaction Publishers   Tel.: (732) 445-2280
Rutgers University   Fax: (732) 445-3138
35 Berrue Circle   for orders (U.S. only):
Piscataway, NJ 08854   toll free 888-999-6778

Contents

Popular History Now and Then

An Introduction

BARBARA KORTE AND SYLVIA PALETSCHEK

It is a commonplace by now to state that the popular representation of history is booming.[1] This rising interest in history emerged in the 1980s, and it has been at a peak since the second half of the 1990s. This trend is reflected in such indicators as increasing numbers of visitors to historical exhibitions and museums; considerable public interest in controversies among historical experts;[2] and the prominence of historical topics in new and old media, in documentary and fictional genres, or in performative forms (theme parks, living history and re-enactments). Numerous websites on the internet, articles on Wikipedia, CD-ROM productions and historical computer games attest the phenomenon's expansion into the digital media. We witness these trends all over the world, in the global North as well as increasingly in the global South. In many cultures, representations of history are of major significance for the negotiation of national, ethnic and regional identities. The contemporary re-turn to history helps to construct continuity and orienta-

---

1 For their help in editing this volume, we would like to thank Natalie Churn, Kathrin Göb and Kerstin Lohr.

2 A German instance is the controversy surrounding the *Wehrmachtsausstellung* in the 1990s – an exhibition focusing on the war crimes of German soldiers on the Eastern Front during the Second World War. For Britain, one could name the recent debate about the bicentenary of the abolition of slavery in 2007 (cf. Korte/Pirker 2011).

tion. But engagement with history, particularly through popular display, can also satisfy the need for emotional and aesthetic experience and for adventure, for a risk-free encounter with what is strange, different or ›other‹ and, finally, for relaxation and diversion. At the same time, public and state organisations, social elites and political groups draw on popular images of history to legitimise either the status quo or political change.

However, this peak of historical activity and interest is not unprecedented. This volume therefore looks at manifestations of popular history between 1800 and the present, investigating differences and continuities. Its contributions deal with various social and political conditions for heightened historical interest in the past, looking at a range of periods and cultures in Western and Southern Europe, North America as well as West Africa.

Stefan Berger discusses the borderlines and interrelations between popular and academic history since 1800, concluding with some of the pros and cons of the current pluralisation of history. Billie Melman points out the fascination which a newly discovered, or rather un-covered Assyrian past had for Victorian Britons who were aware of the modernity of their own society but, at the same time, were reminded by archaeology that their own growing empire might one day join the chain of those great realms already destroyed in the course of the ages. An impressive remnant of the Assyrian empire, the Bull of Nineveh, was thus not only admired as a spectacle, but also interpreted as a warning sign. How important a concern history was for Victorian society also emerges from Leslie Howsam's investigation of the presence of the past in the contemporary periodical press. Howsam shows how in the life of a Victorian reader it was almost impossible to escape history, and how these readers were impregnated with historical knowledge from a very young age; in the »life-cycle« of the readers, layers of historical knowledge were continually added to that early foundation and crucially influenced readers' ideas about their nation's past and their own contemporary lifeworlds. Barbara Korte and Sylvia Paletschek also address the flourishing magazine market of the mid-nineteenth century. In a comparison of leading publications for family reading, *Die Gartenlaube* in Germany and *Household Words* and *All the Year Round* in Britain, they demonstrate similarities and differences in the choice of historical topics and forms of representation. While the print market truly popularised historical knowledge, individuals' historical interests were not always easily satisfied. In the nineteenth century, amateurs and professionals increasingly demanded access to archives, but, as Philipp Müller shows for a Bavarian case, the ›opening‹ of the archive was still highly limited when political interests were at stake.

Novels have long been recognised as a popular medium for presenting history; this is also acknowledged in Birte Förster's discussion of how the image of the highly popular Prussian Queen Louise (1776-1810) was continually reshaped and pluralised during the nineteenth and twentieth centuries in accordance with changing conceptions of gender and feminine identity. The role of poetry in inscribing characters and events in the collective memory of a nation is less well researched to date. It is, however, explored in Stefanie Lethbridge's analysis of the canonisation of (war) heroes through the reappearance of certain poems in anthologies of the nineteenth and twentieth centuries.

Historical traditions are always constructed, and in some instances, their basis is not historical fact but purely invented. Such is the case for the barbershop ›revival‹ discussed by Frédéric Döhl. The allegedly ›traditional‹ pre-World War I performance of this style of a cappella singing was actually invented in the 1940s, in nostalgic reaction to the experience of the 1930s Depression and the longing for an ›ideal‹ world. As Antonie Wiedemann shows for Italian society, the experience of an economic miracle could likewise spark an interest in history: In the 1960s, Italy saw a boom of popular magazines on history and art history that seems to have countered an overwhelming concern with materiality in the present. Fernando Sánchez-Marcos presents results from his ongoing study of historical culture related to the figure of Don Juan of Austria, the hero of the Battle of Lepanto. This study spans different media and European historical cultures and reveals the shifting images and reinterpretations of Don Juan according to changes in the zeitgeist, societal and religious norms. Till Förster's case study of historical culture in northern Côte d'Ivoire reveals the interconnections between politics, identity and history in a society experiencing various political upheavals and literally re-painting the image of the past over a stretch of only a few years.

If politics is a major shaper of historical imagery, so is the media. Susan Crane's discussion is devoted to the relationship between photography, visual experience and the presence of images of the past in the long twentieth century. Focusing on photo books, she analyses the paradoxical quality of photography's relationship to historical consciousness: as preserver of the past and producer of presence. Jerome De Groot, in his afterword to this volume, reflects on possible developments of popular history. Taking successful television programmes of the twenty-first century as a case in point, De Groot demonstrates how the media continually come up with new inventive formats that re-create history for international audiences – a history which has to be, according to global markets and media flows, increasingly transnational and transcultural.

Overall, the contributions in this volume suggest certain lines of continuity: Firstly, popular representations of the past have existed since at least the early nineteenth century and are a form of production and dissemination of historical knowledge in their own right, rather than deriving top-down from academic knowledge. They are, secondly, marked by an affinity to lifeworlds in a double sense: an interest in the history of everyday life, and aspects that are important in the producers' and audiences' own lives. They satisfy a fascination with the authentic and factual, but tend, at the same time, to be personalised, emotionalised, dramatised and narrativised.[3] Thirdly, one could claim that popular history has a share in the democratisation and pluralisation of modern societies, while it can also limit our approach to the past because certain periods, themes or historical actors are more easily adapted to present concerns, desires and intentions than others, for example because they fit into existing narratives, because they help to legitimise societal and political aims – or simply because they will entertain and sell. An important question, therefore, is not only what images of the past are generated, but also which ones are neglected at a certain time. Fourthly, how popular history is represented depends on the available media, genres, formats and institutions of a given time. There is a great variety within these media and genres, and a high degree of intermediality.

Despite the visibility and social significance of popular history, its study is still in its early stage.[4] Further research will have to address a number of areas: reception studies, relating to audiences both of the present and the past; comparative approaches, especially comparisons between Western

---

3   Cf. Korte/Paletschek (2009), Pirker/Rüdiger et al. (2010), Schlehe/Uike-Bormann et al. (2010) and Gehrke/Sénécheau (2010).

4   For other recent volumes cf. De Groot (2009), Hardtwig/Schug (2009), Paletschek (2011) and Berger/Lorenz/Melman (2011).

and non-Western, Northern and Southern images and utilisations of the past, as well as comparisons in a historical perspective; the relationship between popular historical culture and the so-called knowledge society; and finally, the history of popular history and lines of continuity in popular representations of the past, a topic which this volume addresses from many different angles.

WORKS CITED

Berger, Stefan/Chris Lorenz/Billie Melman (eds.) (2011): *Popularizing National Pasts: 1800 to the Present*, London: Routledge.

De Groot, Jerome (2009): *Consuming History: Historians and Heritage in Contemporary Popular Culture*, New York/NY: Routledge.

Gehrke, Hans-Joachim/Miriam Sénécheau (eds.) (2010): *Geschichte, Archäologie, Öffentlichkeit: Für einen neuen Dialog zwischen Wissenschaft und Medien. Standpunkte aus Forschung und Praxis*, Bielefeld: transcript.

Hardtwig, Wolfgang/Alexander Schug (eds.) (2009): *History Sells! Angewandte Geschichte als Wissenschaft und Markt*, Stuttgart: Steiner.

Korte, Barbara/Sylvia Paletschek (eds.) (2009): *History Goes Pop: Zur Repräsentation von Geschichte in populären Medien und Genres*, Bielefeld: transcript.

Korte, Barbara/Eva Ulrike Pirker (2011): *Black History – White History: Britain's Historical Programme between Windrush and Wilberforce*, Bielefeld: transcript.

Paletschek, Sylvia (ed.) (2011): *Popular Historiographies in the 19th and 20th Centuries: Cultural Meanings, Social Practices*, Oxford: Berghahn.

Pirker, Eva Ulrike/Mark Rüdiger et al. (eds.) (2010): *Echte Geschichte: Authentizitätsfiktionen in populären Geschichtskulturen*, Bielefeld: transcript.

Schlehe, Judith/Michiko Uike-Bormann et al. (eds.) (2010): *Staging the Past: Themed Environments in Transcultural Perspectives*, Bielefeld: transcript.

Professional and Popular Historians

1800 – 1900 – 2000

STEFAN BERGER

What is a professional historian? Who calls themselves professional historians? Who calls others professional historians? The ancient historians Herodotus, Thukydides, Cicero, Livius and many others would not have used this term, despite the fact that they had already developed ideas about objectivity and truthfulness that professional historians were to later name as major characteristics of professional historiography. Nor would the medieval chroniclers and historians in their monasteries and courts have described themselves as ›professional‹. The humanist historians were men of letters, polymaths and intellectuals, but few of them would have recognised themselves as ›professionals‹. The methodological ground rules of what would, in the nineteenth century, be seen as hallmarks of a professional historiography, i.e. source criticism, objectivity, the desire to consult as many documents and primary sources and to read as much literature as possible to get an approximation of ›how it actually happened‹ (to use the famous phrase by Leopold von Ranke), and the use of auxiliary sciences in the pursuit of this aim – much of this had already been codified by Jean Mabillon, Johann Martin Chladenius and the Bollandist and Maurist historians in the seventeenth and early part of the eighteenth centuries. And would the eighteenth-century Enlightenment historians in France and Scotland, from Voltaire to David Hume, have been referred to as ›professional‹? Hardly – in fact in the British Isles, the most successful and widely read historians looked down their noses at academic history, because there was little that was being produced there that merited attention. The Regius Professorships of History at Oxford and Cambridge, instituted in 1724, remained sinecures until the second half of the nineteenth century, and their incumbents produced little history and in fact rarely even lectured at the university (cf. Horn 1951: 21).[1]

And yet, it is with Enlightenment historiography that we arguably get the first inkling of professional historiography in Europe – namely with the German-speaking Enlightenment, which was, unlike its Scottish and French counterparts, to a significant extent university-based (cf. Reill 1975). August Ludwig Schlözer and Johann Christoph Gatterer at the University of Göttingen (and, to a lesser extent, their counterparts at the University of Halle) not only began to codify the characteristics of a professional historiography, they also were at pains to attempt to write a history which sacrifices literary ambition and merit in favour of ›scientific‹ worth. Combining questions and data on the demographics, economics, social statistics and political systems of a number of countries, the Göttingen historians tried to approach the past both in a ›synchronistic‹ way, by comparing societies at a given moment, and diachronically, by chronologically unfolding events and thematic processes over time. The description of foreign ›states‹ (›statistics‹ in the broader sense of the eighteenth century) and the collection of quantitative data (descriptive statistics in the modern sense) served their purpose well since they wanted to produce useful knowledge for the ›enlightened‹ prince and his administration. That knowledge could only be useful if it was scientific. If that meant sacrificing their ambitions for a literary rendering of history, then so be it (cf. Epple 2010: 86-106). From the time of the Göttingen historians onward, ›scientificity‹ has been bound up with the idea of a professional historiography which must sacrifice literary concerns for the sake of greater truthfulness and objectivity, i.e. more scientificity.

---

1   An excellent summary of the professionalisation of history writing is provided by Thorstendahl (2002), who points out that the global beginnings of professionalisation can be located in China with Sima Qian, born in either 145 or 135 BC, the first historian employed by the court (Han dynasty) with an office and employees, who consistently reflected on the methods of how to write history properly.

In the early nineteenth century, professional German historiography increasingly came to rely on the hermeneutical-philological method of historical research that had been pioneered by philologists and classical scholars, such as Friedrich August Wolf and Barthold Georg Niebuhr. With the appointment of Leopold von Ranke at the University of Berlin in the 1820s, another major step towards the professionalisation of historical writing was taken. Historists everywhere came to regard Ranke as a foundational father figure who embodied the values and lifestyle of a professional historian (cf. Iggers/Powell 1990). Wherever historians subsequently tried to institutionalise and professionalise historical writing, they referred back to the grand old man of historiography and to German historiography in general. After all, nineteenth-century German universities had no fewer than 130 Protestant full professors (plus a sprinkling of Catholic professors) with a strongly developed sense of being a group of professionals (cf. Blanke 1991). They established a set of principles and methods (never uncontested, never entirely unified) which became known as historism. Johann Gustav Droysen, in his *Historik*, made perhaps the most famous attempt to codify these principles and methods (cf. Jäger/Rüsen 1992; Oexle 1996). For the professionalisation of historiography in Europe, historism became a central benchmark against which progress was measured. Take, for example, William Stubbs, in his lectures as Regius Professor of History at the University of Oxford, who sang Ranke's praises: »Leopold von Ranke is not only beyond all comparison the greatest historical scholar alive, but one of the very greatest historians that ever lived.« (Stubbs 1886: 57) And the first edition of the professional journal of English historiography, the *English Historical Review*, carried a long article by the Regius Professor of History at Cambridge, Lord Acton, on »German Schools of Historiography« (Acton 1886). In the emergence of a new species of professional historian characterised by a need to gain social status and cultural capital by claiming exclusive rights to the truthful interpretation of the past, Ranke came to occupy a pivotal position. National historical associations, historical journals, historical networks, historical source editions, historical archives and libraries were among the most prominent institutions, networks and communities underpinning the process of the professionalisation of historical writing in the nineteenth century (cf. Porciani/Tollebeek 2011).

If fifty per cent of the ›professional‹ historian was defined by scientificity, the other half was characterised as genius. The romantic image of the historian as seer and prophet was not necessarily seen as a contradiction to the cool and level-headed scientific image of the professional historian. Rather, in much of nineteenth-century historiography, scientificity and prophecy went hand in hand. Both were vital to the historians' claim of occupying a special status amongst the sciences. The Romantic idealisation of the historian as seer, priest and martyr in the service of history, who resurrects the past through the ›eye of history‹, contributed vitally to the attempt on the part of professionalising historians to set themselves up as the privileged interpreters of the past (cf. Tollebeek 2000). Jules Michelet, in his national history of France, famously identifies so completely with the nation that he suggests that he actually is France: The historian was reliving and re-enacting the fate of the nation. In breathing in the dust of the arch-ives, he was breathing France (cf. Michelet 1869: 614-615). Michelet im-agined that he could actually do what Ranke only wished for – to com-pletely extinguish the self and become one with the past.

If we can talk about the establishment of the figure of the professional historian around 1800 from the spirit of scientificity and the Romantic cult of the genius, then the emergence of the idea of ›popular‹ historians as a counter-image to professional historians also dates from that period. What did this counter-image entail? Popular could mean being widely read and successful, but in this definition ›popular‹ would hardly function as a juxta-position to ›professional‹. Many professional historians were both widely read and successful. As a counter-image to the professional historian, the popular historian was popular in the sense of consciously popularising the results of professional historical research. Behind the notion of the popular historian, in other words, stood the assumption that historical research was too technical and too complicated to be understood by ordinary people. But who was the audience of popular historians? Who were the ordinary people they often appealed to?

Ancient historians, medieval monks, humanists, even Enlightenment historians wrote for a very limited audience and they assumed that this se-lect audience would be capable of understanding them. Hence there was little need for popularisation. This, of course, does not mean that there were no popular histories, in the sense of popular representations of the past. These have always existed. Popular history is clearly more than the popu-larisation of ›scientific research results‹. It is rightly regarded and treated as a genre in its own right, with its own moral, political and entertainment concerns and its own techniques of writing. There are clear differences to scientific history, in particular greater dramatisation, more reduction, more narrativisation and a greater focus on public attention and the market (often on the part of publishers). However, for this paper I would like to concentrate on the popular history that took its benchmark from and remained oriented towards professional history. What I would like to emphasise here is that the polarity between popular and professional only began to work when there was a broadly conceived need for an interface, for translation from the language of scientificity to ordinary everyday language.

Arguably, it was only with the understanding of history as a science that a notion developed which saw history as too complex, too technical, too voluminous to be presented directly to a general audience. Hence there was the need for interlocutors; all the more so as in the course of the nineteenth century we witness the rise of a mass audience and the increasing specialisation of a professionalising historiography. Increasing literacy rates and more widespread compulsory education led to an increasing number of people willing to learn about the past, especially in an age of historism, where the past was often seen as the key to the present and future. Furthermore, a growing amount of free time and a minimum level of prosperity became a reality for an increasing number of people in the nineteenth century – good preconditions for the intensified reception of popular history. For a long time however, professional university historians remained very capable of popularising their own history. Most of the key nineteenth-century national historians were multi-taskers, doubling up not only as scientists in different fields, including literature, ethnology and linguistics, but also as politicians, journalists, speech writers and speech givers. In the latter capacities, professional historians were essentially taking part in popular history writing. In her brilliant discussion of East-Central European historiography, Monika Baár (2009) emphasises such multi-tasking as a crucial characteristic of nineteenth-century national historians of the region. But it was by no means an East-Central European speciality. One only needs to think of Heinrich von Treitschke in Germany, P.A. Munch in Norway or Yrjö Koskinen in Finland to realise how close, in many parts of Europe, the association of professional historians with popular nationalist movements actually was. And in the British Isles in particular, from Thomas Babington Macaulay and W.E.H. Lecky to John Robert Seeley and, in the twentieth century, G.M. Trevelyan, historians refused to cater for the small professional market and instead preferred to write marketable histories for the masses. Up to this very day, many British historians, such as Norman Davies in his blockbuster *The Isles* (1999), write in their prefaces of their desire to remain accessible to the widest possible audience and to write for the people rather than for their peers and students alone. And yet, when John Bagnell Bury gave his famous inaugural lecture as Regius Professor of History at Cambridge University in 1903 under the title »The Science of History«, he signalled that the idea of history as a science, practiced by professionals, had reached the mainstream of historical thought even in England. Scientific history had delineated its own field and self-conception from that of popular history (cf. Bury 1903).

The popularisation of scientific professional history writing had become all the more important as professionalisation went hand in glove with specialisation. More and more types and sub-fields of history were emerging: political history, social history, cultural history and religious history, among others. Specialised research institutes spread, publishing highly specialised monographs and source editions which were of immediate value, above all, to the community of professional historians. The results of such specialised research had to be ›translated‹ to the wider public via popular historians.

Therefore, around 1900, we can observe a certain parting of the ways in many continental European countries: Professional historians began to restrict themselves to writing professional histories for a largely professional audience, whilst popular historians made their works accessible to the masses via newspaper and journal articles. Sylvia Paletschek (2011) has pointed out how the German weekly *Die Gartenlaube* published an enormous amount of history – often related to anniversaries. Such popular history was written by popular historians – there were hardly any professional historians writing for the *Gartenlaube*. But it is noticeable how these popular historians in the *Gartenlaube* and elsewhere were very keen to maintain ›scientific credentials‹. The novelist Gustav Freytag, for example, bent over backwards to ensure that his books, especially his historical vignettes, were based on the latest historical research, and asked his publisher to send him the most recent works of ›scientific‹ history (cf. Nissen 2000: 269-316). Hence we can conclude that the same idea of what defined good history reigned in both popular and professional forms of history writing.

This is confirmed by a sideways glance at the beginnings of labour history. In fact, we find that across Europe, some of the earliest labour history was written by activists of the labour movement – Jean Jaurès in France, Filippo Turati in Italy, G.D.H. Cole in England, Eduard Bernstein in Germany, Robert Grimm in Switzerland and Georgi Plekhanov in Russia – to mention just a few obvious examples. Thomas Welskopp (2011), in his detailed comparison of Eduard Bernstein and Robert Grimm, has shown how their works were primarily works of political pedagogy written out of a political need and for a particular historical moment. Bernstein was keen to demonstrate the sobriety and responsibility of a labour movement which could be entrusted with political power. In addition, he wanted to trace the forward march of labour from the bloody birth struggles of 1848 to the years of martyrdom under the Anti-Socialist Laws and further to the rise of the SPD (the Social Democratic Party) in Wilhelmine Germany. Grimm's overriding objective, after the failed *Landesstreik* and the attempt on behalf of the liberal-bourgeois Swiss state to co-opt the Swiss labour movement into the political system, was to sustain the unity and distinctiveness of Swiss Social Democracy. Both authors are portrayed by Welskopp as organic intellectuals and autodidacts who occupied very similar positions in their party and were political journalists of some renown. They wrote history in order to write the working classes and the labour movement into national history under circumstances where professional historiography had excluded them. Bernstein positioned himself closer to ›scientific‹ history writing by minimising the issue of authorship and setting himself up as a chronicler of the truth. Grimm, by contrast, openly asserted the perspectivity of all historical knowledge and aimed at retelling national history from the working-class point of view, thereby breaking the bourgeois hegemony over national history.

This example of popular history from the labour movement underlines how it could be a reaction against the professional historians' neat and exclusivist division between ›professional‹ and ›popular‹. If the epithet ›professional‹ was to exclude the ›popular‹ as a form of ›amateurism‹, the popular historians attempted to hold their own by demonstrating their own ›scientific‹ credentials.

The exclusivist practices of the language of professionalisation also had major repercussions for women historians. They were excluded from being professional historians because they were not allowed to enrol in universities, to take higher university degrees or enter careers as professional historians for much of the nineteenth century. The history department was a

»masculine marketplace of knowledge« (Smith 1998: 111). Clio herself was female, but the mastering of the historical facts had to be done by men. The situation only began to change towards the end of the nineteenth century. In many parts of Europe, women were admitted to university studies between the 1870s and 1900s. In Sweden, Ellen Fries was the first woman to obtain a PhD in 1883 – and it was a PhD in history. It took sixteen years, until 1898, before another woman, Lydia Wahlström, completed another PhD in history. Anna Hude was the first woman in Denmark to write a history thesis, which she submitted in 1892. In the Netherlands the first woman obtained a PhD in history in 1904: Johanna Naber, one of the leading female historians of her country at the turn of the century, wrote mainly on the women's movement and feminism, but she was also an ardent nationalist and admirer of Queen Wilhelmina (cf. Grever 1994). One of the first Russian women to pursue an academic career was O.A. Dobiash-Rozhdestvenskaya, who obtained a PhD from the University of Paris in 1911. She secured a position teaching history in special Higher Women Courses at St. Petersburg University and went on to become a Professor of History at the University of Leningrad in the 1920s. Billie Melman identified 66 women historians in England alone who wrote a total of 782 books between them in the nineteenth and early twentieth centuries (cf. Melman 1993: 9). The male resistance to such modest advances of women in professional historiography was considerable. As late as the 1910s, P.J. Blok was adamant that the laborious task of the historian required a specifically male form of heroism. It is unsurprising that, of the small number of female history graduates, hardly anyone pursued an academic career. Instead, most became school teachers. There were, however, exceptions to the rule. In Ireland, the first professor of modern Irish history at University College Dublin was Mary Hayden, appointed in 1911. At University College Galway, Mary Donovan O'Sullivan was appointed to a chair in history in 1914. Mary O'Dowd has argued that the relative success which women historians enjoyed before the First World War in the Irish academy was related to the perception of history as having no important status and hence little cultural capital. Once it became more prestigious, women historians were marginalised in Ireland as well. However, if the highly gendered world of historiography excluded women, the notion of popular history allowed women to succeed in the area of ›amateur‹ history. Mary O'Dowd has demonstrated how economically successful many female Irish historians were, and the considerable literature on early women historians in Europe demonstrates the manifold ways in which women engaged with the dichotomy of ›professional‹ and ›popular‹ in diverse national settings (cf. O'Dowd/Porciani 2004; Porciani/Raphael 2010).

Throughout much of the twentieth century, the relationship between professional and popular historians remained an uneasy one – with the former often all too keen to denounce the latter as charlatans. In particular, where popular historians were successful with the public, they often faced stark criticism from professional historiography. Take for example Emil Ludwig, one of inter-war Germany's most successful authors of popular history, and of biographies in particular. Ludwig's biographies of Napoleon, Wilhelm II and, above all, Bismarck, were runaway successes with the public. Politically on the left, he became a pacifist in the First World War, supported the Independent Socialists in 1917/18 and was one of the staunchest defenders of the Weimar Republic. His books were tirelessly attacked by the conservative-nationalist establishment of professional historians as examples of the aberrations of popular and amateur historians. The National Socialists burnt his books as ›falsifications of history‹. A Swiss citizen since 1932, Ludwig lived in his house on Lake Maggiore until 1940, when he left after the Swiss government had told him to reduce his criticism of National Socialist Germany and after he had become the object of an anti-Semitic hate campaign in the Swiss press (cf. Ullrich 2005).

The Ludwig case once again demonstrates how political the heavily policed borderline between ›professional‹ and ›popular‹ was. A good example from the more recent past, again from Germany, is the rise of everyday life history (*Alltagsgeschichte*) in the 1970s and 1980s. Representatives of the new social science-oriented history associated with the Bielefeld school attacked *Alltagsgeschichte* for its alleged lack of professionalism (cf. Lipp 1990). Hans-Ulrich Wehler famously called the practitioners of *Alltagsgeschichte* ›barefoot historians‹ – suggesting that their lack of footwear indicated a shortage of methodological sophistication. But once again, behind the veneer of a defence of professional values lurked the desire to silence a type of history that was politically unwanted. More Marxist in orientation, *Alltagsgeschichte* threatened the optimistic growth-oriented, progressive, Social Democratic master narrative with which the Bielefelders associated themselves. Instead of endorsing the Federal Republic as a pinnacle of historical development, *Alltag* historians belonged to the sharpest critics of specific aspects of the FRG.

The examples of labour movement history, women's history and everyday life history all show how popular history writing was particularly important for marginal groups. Marginality seems to be an important motivation for groups and their representatives to turn to popular forms of history writing. And marginality had a major impact on the framing of those popular histories. They often directly refer to and reference their work as professional history writing, but do so in such a way as to demarcate themselves from professional historiography. In this sense, there are prominent strands of popular historiography which go well beyond the popularisation of professional historical work.

Scientificity had been one of the sharpest weapons in the armoury of historist, Marxist and Weberian social science history throughout much of the nineteenth and twentieth centuries for drawing a firm line between professional and popular history and thereby excluding methodologically, but, above all, politically unwanted perspectives from the hallowed corridors of the arcane, to which only professional historians had entry rights. However, with the arrival of poststructuralism, the professional historians' most effective weapon threatened to become blunt. The foundational texts by Michel Foucault and Hayden White blasted a gaping hole into the armour of scientificity (cf. Foucault 1966, 1969; White 1973, 1978). Foucault's writings on knowledge and power drew attention to the processes by which knowledge is used to achieve power – a strategy clearly recognisable in the professionalising historiographies of the modern age. At the same time he introduced a much more diffuse concept of power, thereby ending the longstanding pre-occupation of historians with states and the international system of states. And White was to cast doubt on the firm genre demarcations that had become the hallmark of history's stranglehold on truth:

»The older distinction between fiction and history, in which fiction is conceived as the representation of the imaginable and history as the representation of the actual, must give place to the recognition that we can only know the *actual* by contrasting it with or likening it to the *imaginable*. [...] it is a fiction of the historian that the various states of affairs which he constitutes as the beginning, the middle, and the end of a course of development are all ›actual‹ or ›real‹ and that he has merely recorded ›what happened‹ in the transition from the inaugural to the terminal phase. [...] both the beginning state of affairs and the ending one are inevitably poetic constructions, and as such, dependent upon the modality of the figurative language used to give them the aspect of coherence. This implies that all narrative is not simply a recording of ›what happened‹ in the transition from one state of affairs to another, but a progressive *redescription* of sets of events in such a way as to dismantle a structure encoded in one verbal mode in the beginning so as to justify a recoding of it in another mode at the end. This is what the ›middle‹ of all narratives consist of.« (White 1978: 99)

Under the impact of the linguistic turn, large swathes of the classical fields of historical writing – political, social, international and cultural history – were reconceptualised. Where those reconceptualisations were most successful, they produced exciting new perspectives, as was the case with the blossoming field of empire history. Where they met with the most resistance, as in the fields of labour and economic history, history research suffered and failed to produce much exciting new work. Younger historians voted with their feet, moving away from fields of history regarded as old-fashioned and towards those fields of historical writing most informed by poststructuralist perspectives, namely postcolonialism, gender history and micro-history.

On a theoretical level, poststructuralist perspectives had placed a big question mark behind the neat demarcation between professional and popular histories. Poststructuralist theorists insisted on all histories being dependent on particular linguistic strategies, metaphors and tropes in which stories could be told. In other words, the exclusivity of the idea of a professional historiography based on a set of principles and methods guaranteeing an approximation of ›what actually happened‹ could no longer be maintained. Thus around the year 2000 the sharp division between professional vs. popular history that had been such a hallmark of the nineteenth and twentieth centuries' historical discourse was de-emphasised again.

A good example of such a blurring of borders between professional and popular forms of history writing is the internet, which is arguably the technologically most advanced popularisation tool and the one which is most popular with younger generations of the general public. Markku Jokisipilä (2012) has shown how representations of national history are among the most typical and popular online forms of historical information: Wikipedia's national history profiles, created by the joint effort of thousands of contributors, rank among the most visited fact-based sites on the Web. Accounts of national histories have also been posted online by a host of other providers such as university history departments, foreign ministries, travel agencies, television stations, newspapers and news magazines. In all of these, scholars as well as amateur aficionados of history are represented – sometimes side by side. Unlike traditional historical scholarship, many of these accounts have not been subjected to peer or any other kind of review before publication. Consequently, the range of quality of online historical information is at least as wide as its scope. By comparing the online representations of three different national histories, namely those of Germany, Britain and Finland, Jokisipilä demonstrates that, in terms of volume and content, scholarly national histories are in the minority on the web. They are comprehensively outperformed by commercial and amateur sites. Furthermore, national histories on the web are often not up-to-date; their references are mostly to older literature and books, whereas cutting-edge research is often absent from the web. Jokisipilä argues that professional historians ignore the web at their peril, and he calls on them to engage more with the possibilities of the web and to present their research on popular sites such as Wikipedia.

By way of conclusion we might ask where this leaves the relationship between professional and popular history today? Across much of the developed Western world, where once the ideology of scientificity had ruled supreme, historians have suffered a significant loss of status and many have been all too willing to retreat to the ivory tower and their specialist historical research. Not a few continue to cling to notions of professionalism, while others feel free to pursue their research whilst ignoring the societal contexts of such research. Historians as public intellectuals have become rare in the West. Self-doubt and a lack of prestige have meant that they increasingly talk among themselves, leaving the field of popular history to others. There are exceptions to the rule, and after what we have said above already, it is perhaps not surprising that many of them come from the UK and the US. With regard to television history in the UK, virtually all of its most prominent representatives, such as Niall Ferguson, David Starkey and Simon Schama, are professional historians with university posts. Andrew Marr, as a professional journalist, is an exception. And until very recently, Tristram Hunt also occupied a university post – before becoming a Labour MP. Reception studies on television histories demonstrate that viewers watch history on television because they are looking for orientation and identity in their contemporary world and hoping that history will provide it (cf. Meyen/Pfaff 2006). Some television history directly alludes to its identitarian mission, for example the series on the 1950s screened on German television in 2006 (ARD) that was subtitled: »How We Became Who We Are«. Historical docudramas on television also have a strong identitarian spin (cf. Steinle 2009). Identitarian concerns in connection with history have also dominated recent debates on curricula reform in the teaching of history in schools (cf. Grever/Stuurman 2007). It would be a pity if professional historians were to leave this field and its debates on the construction of identity entirely to popular historians.

However, in the burgeoning field of popular history it would be true to say that most popular historians received some form of historical training at university. Whether we encounter popular historians in re-enactment societies or living-history performances in museums, in monument societies, in debates surrounding street naming or re-naming, in museum pedagogy, free-lance history, tourism (history sections in tourist guides) or the history workshop movement, in film, television, commercial historical magazines and other print media, or, more generally, as writers of historical novels, as editors in publishing houses, or authors of youth and childrens' fiction, including comic books, or, indeed, as creators of computer games – it is likely that in all these areas of popular history, many of its practitioners received some formal training as ›professional‹ historians, i.e. many of them studied history at university and perhaps even found their first job there (cf. Horn/Sauer 2009; Hardtwig/Schug 2009). Hence they are equipped with a professional self-understanding and most of them practice popular history with some notion of ›scientificity‹ in the back of their minds. So far, one might be tempted to argue, not much has changed in comparison with the nineteenth century, except perhaps that the figure of the autodidact is more of a rarity these days. But today's notion of scientificity is very different from that of the nineteenth century: It has been informed by and partially undermined by poststructuralist reflections on the difficulties of delineating neatly who can and who cannot speak on behalf of the past. This more self-critical and more self-reflexive scientificity has emboldened popular historians and arguably led to a proliferation of popular histories. As more and more constituencies came to look for their pasts – without having to fear immediate exclusion for amateurism, a fate which had befallen labour history, women's history and history-from-below approaches – a market opened up for diverse forms of popular history that are not being dealt with by the community of professional historians. It is well-known that in the literature on the popularisation of science, two models dominate: the diffusion model and the interaction model. Whilst the former argues in terms of a top-down process of diffusion, the latter insists more on communicative and social interactions as preconditions for establishing ›scientific progress‹ (cf. Schwarz 1999; Kretschmann 2003). The latter is more convincing, and with regard to history, we could also perhaps add that in a diachronic perspective, we have moved decisively from a model based more on diffusion (with important counter-cultures of knowledge in the popular realm) to a model based on interaction. Today there is far more interaction between popular and scientific history than ever before, as both now almost see each other on equal terms.

Historians should welcome such a pluralisation of histories and take courage from the fact that the past is now affecting far more areas of life and far more people than ever before. It is activating more people to become historians themselves, as witnessed by the ever-rising popularity of family history and genealogy. But on the other hand it is worrying that such a pluralisation of history seems to have also led to the retreat of professional historians from the public sphere. As they cannot be the gatekeepers to the arcane past any more, does it follow that they have to retreat to the ivory towers? If their special authority and position has been largely eroded, historians will be required to make a greater effort to have their voices heard, to talk about ›lessons from the past‹, and to bring a sense of history to public political debates. They can no longer claim with the same arrogant self-confidence as earlier that they, as professional historians, know best. Greater modesty surely is a virtue, as is the recognition that history is ultimately nothing more, but also nothing less, than politics by other means.

WORKS CITED

Acton, Lord (1886): »German Schools of Historiography«. *English Historical Review* 1, 1-47.

Baár, Monika (2009): *Historians and Nationalism: East-Central Europe in the Nineteenth Cenury*, Oxford: Clarendon Press.

Blanke, Horst Walter (1991): *Historiographiegeschichte als Historik*, Stuttgart: Fromann-Holzboog.

Bury, John Bagnell (1903): *An Inaugural Lecture: The Science of History Delievered in the Divinity School, Cambridge, on January 26, 1903*, Cambridge/MA: Harvard University Press.

Epple, Angelika (2010): »A Strained Relationship: Epistemology and Historiography in Eighteenth- and Nineteenth-Century Germany and Britain«. In: Stefan Berger/Chris Lorenz (eds.), *Nationalizing the Past: Historians as Nation Builders in Modern Europe*, Basingstoke: Palgrave Macmillan, 86-106.

Foucault, Michel (1966): *Les Mots et les choses*, Paris: Gallimard [English translation (1970): *The Order of Things*, London: Tavistock].

Foucault, Michel (1969): *L'Archéologie du savoir*, Paris: Gallimard [English translation (1972): *The Archaeology of Knowledge*, London: Tavistock].

Grever, Maria (1994): *Strijd tegen de stilte: Johanna Naber (1859-1941). En de vrouwenstem in geschiedenis*, Hilversum: Verloren.

Grever, Maria/Siep Stuurman (eds.) (2007): *Beyond the Canon: History for the Twenty-First Century*, Basingstoke: Palgrave Macmillan.

Hardtwig, Wolfgang/Alexander Schug (eds.) (2009): *History Sells! Angewandte Geschichte als Wissenschaft und Markt*, Stuttgart: Franz Steiner.

Horn, David Bayne (1951): »The Historiographers Royal in England and Scotland«. *Scottish Historical Review* 30, 15-29.

Horn, Sabine/Michael Sauer (eds.) (2009): *Geschichte und Öffentlichkeit: Orte – Medien – Institutionen*, Göttingen: Vandenhoeck & Ruprecht.

Iggers, Georg G./James M. Powell (eds.) (1990): *Leopold von Ranke and the Shaping of the Historical Discipline*, Syracuse/NY: Syracuse University Press.

Jäger, Friedrich/Jörn Rüsen (1992): *Geschichte des Historismus: Eine Einführung*, München: Beck.

Jokisipilä, Markku (2012): »The Internet and National Histories«. In: Stefan Berger/Chris Lorenz/Billie Melman (eds.), *Popularising National Pasts: 1800 to the Present*, London: Routledge, 308-330.

Kretschmann, Carsten (ed.) (2003): *Wissenspopularisierung: Konzepte der Wissensverbreitung im Wandel*, Berlin: Akademie Verlag.

Lipp, Carola (1990): »Writing History as Political Culture: Social History vs. ›Alltagsgeschichte‹. A German Debate«. *Storia della Storiografia* 17, 66-100.

Melman, Billie (1993): »Gender, History and Memory: The Invention of Women's Past in the Nineteenth and Early Twentieth Centuries«. *History and Memory* 5, 5-41.

Meyen, Michael/Senta Pfaff (2006): »Rezeption von Geschichte im Fernsehen«. *Media Perspektiven* 2, 102-106.

Michelet, Jules (1974 [1869]): »Preface de l'Histoire de France«. In: *Oeuvres Complètes*, Paris: Flammarion, 11-30.

Nissen, Martin (2009): *Populäre Geschichtsschreibung: Historiker, Verleger und die deutsche Öffentlichkeit (1848-1900)*, Köln: Böhlau.

O'Dowd, Mary/Ilaria Porciani (eds.) (2004): *History Women*, special issue of *Storia della Storiografia*, 45-46.

Oexle, Otto Gerhard (1996): *Geschichtswissenschaft im Zeichen des Historismus*, Göttingen: Vandenhoeck & Ruprecht.

Paletschek, Sylvia (2011): »Popular Representations of History in the Nineteenth Century: The Example of *Die Gartenlaube*«. In: *Popular Historiographies in the Nineteenth and Twentieth Centuries*, Oxford: Berghahn Books, 34-53.

Porciani, Ilaria/Lutz Raphael (eds.) (2010): *Atlas of European Historiography: The Making of a Profession, 1800-2005*, Basingstoke: Palgrave Macmillan.

Porciani, Ilaria/Jo Tollebeek (eds.) (2011): *Setting the Standards: Institutions, Networks and Communities of Historical Writing in Modern Europe*, Basingstoke: Palgrave Macmillan.

Reill, Peter H. (1975): *The German Enlightenment and the Rise of Historicism*, Berkeley: University of California Press.

Schwarz, Angela (1999): *Der Schlüssel zur modernen Welt: Wissenschaftspopularisierung in Großbritannien und Deutschland im Übergang zur Moderne, ca. 1870-1940*, Stuttgart: Franz Steiner.

Smith, Bonnie (1998): *The Gender of History: Men, Women and Historical Practice*, Cambridge/MA: Harvard University Press.

Steinle, Matthias (2009): »Geschichte im Film: Zum Umgang mit den Zeichen der Vergangenheit im Dokudrama der Gegenwart«. In: Barbara Korte/Sylvia Paletschek (eds.), *History goes Pop: Zur Repräsentation von Geschichte in populären Medien und Genres*, Bielefeld: transcript, 147-166.

Stubbs, William (1886): *Lectures on Medieval and Modern History*, Oxford: Clarendon Press.

Thorstendahl, Rolf (2002): »History, Professionalization of«. In: Neil J. Smelser/Paul B. Baltes (eds.), *International Encyclopedia of Social and Behavioural Sciences*, Leiden: Elsevier, 6864-6869.

Tollebeek, Jo (2000): »Seeing the Past with the Mind's Eye: The Consecration of the Romantic Historian«. *Clio* 29.2, 167-191.

Ullrich, Sebastian (2005): »›Der Fesselndste unter den Biographen ist heute nicht der Historiker‹: Emil Ludwig und seine historischen Biographien«. In: Wolfgang Hardtwig/Erhard Schütz (eds.), *Geschichte für Leser: Populäre Geschichtsschreibung in Deutschland im 20. Jahrhundert*, Stuttgart: Franz Steiner, 35-56.

Welskopp, Thomas (2011): »Clio and Class Struggle in Socialist Histories of the Nation: A Comparison of Robert Grimm's and Eduard Bernstein's Writings, 1910-1920«. In: Stefan Berger/Chris Lorenz (eds.), *Nationalizing the Past: Historians as Nation Builders in Modern Europe*, Basingstoke: Palgrave Macmillan, 298-318.

White, Hayden (1973): *Metahistory*, Baltimore/MD: Johns Hopkins University Press.

White, Hayden (1978): *Tropics of Discourse*, Baltimore/MD: Johns Hopkins University Press.

The Bull of Nineveh

Antiquity and Modernity in Nineteenth-Century Britain

BILLIE MELMAN

Austen Henry Layard's rumination on the shipment of the famous ancient Assyrian winged colossi – dug out in the village of Nimrud in north Mesopotamia – to London, is a thoughtfully constructed narrative of the fate of empires. Appropriately, his musings were publicized in his 1849 bestseller *Nineveh and Its Remains*, which popularized antiquity for large audiences:

»I watched the rafts, until they disappeared behind a projecting bank forming a distant reach of the river. I could not forbear musing upon the strange destiny of their burdens; which, after adorning the palaces of the Assyrian kings, the objects of the wonder, and may be the worship, of thousands, had been buried unknown for centuries beneath soil trodden by Persians under Cyrus, by Greeks under Alexander, and by Arabs under the first successors of their prophet. They were now to visit India, to cross the most distant seas of the southern hemisphere, and to be finally placed in the British Museum. Who can venture to foretell how their strange career will end?« (Layard 2005 [1854]: 104-105)

The narrative of the peregrinations of the colossi across time and place makes for a genealogy of power and conquest, by tracing the rise, decline and fall of four ancient empires: the Neo-Assyrian Empire epitomized in the remains of its ancient capital of Kalhu (Nimrud), which was erected by Ashurnasirpal II (883-859 BC) and finally collapsed in 612 BC, the Neo-

Babylonian Empire and its demise about six decades later, the Achaemenid (Persian) Empire and Alexander's short-lived Eurasian Kingdom. The cyclical narrative of ascent to power and its subsequent loss has no definite closure and does not terminate with the rise of the British Empire, whose sphere of influence encompasses those of its predecessors. The ancient empires and the largest modern empire are not without their similarities: Who can foretell their strange career? The Assyrian antiquities are carted across land and transported down Mesopotamia's rivers by exactly the same techniques used by the Assyrian kings to install the colossi in their capitals at Nimrud, Khorsabad (Assyrian Dur Sharru-Kin) and Nineveh (›modern‹ Kuyunjik). The fall of the Assyrian Empires may foreshadow the burden of the modern empire and its future.

The colossi's odyssey showcases at least four characteristics of the multiple reproductions and uses of antiquity in modernity. The first characteristic is the sheer physical dimension of Assyria, the materiality which ancient history acquired in modernity. This materiality characterized the new popular culture of history which emerged in Britain after 1800: Traces and remains of the past became visible to majority publics. The chief mediator between popular audiences and ancient history was archaeology, that distinctly modern branch of enquiry that seeks knowledge about the past through the medium of material things (cf. Thomas 2004). Ancient remains and artifacts acquired what anthropologist Arjun Appadurai has described as ›social lives‹: Unearthed by archaeologists, antiquities moved in cultures and between them, were reproduced in an astounding array of textual representations and replica objects and engendered multiple narratives and meanings (cf. Appadurai 1986: 3-63). An excessive materiality and reproducibility marked not only the new field of knowledge but was also, as Neville Morley has commented in his analysis of Marx's attitude to antiquity, a hallmark of modernity in early industrial capitalism with its capability of mobilizing labor and capital to produce (cf. Morley 2009: 4-7, 21-48). The second characteristic, and related to the materiality of the historical culture, is the diffusion of knowledge about antiquity and the democratization of access to it. A third characteristic apparent in Layard's narrative is the imperial and global stance of the production and consumption of the ancient, and the relationship between them and urban culture. The fates of the colossi are lessons to present-day empires and their own metropolises. The Mesopotamian civilizations unearthed during the nineteenth and early twentieth centuries were urban *and* imperial, hubs of the vastest empire of their time, as was the case with London (referred to in Layard's mention of the British Museum). A fourth characteristic is the intermixture of old images of the ancient past and new forms of historical knowledge as well as new economies and mechanisms utilized to distribute antiquity and new forms of appropriating it. The discovery of ancient Mesopotamia (or Egypt) served to corroborate and illustrate what was already ›known‹ from the Bible and classical discourse on the Near East, but this corroboration was superimposed by new forms of knowledge and new technologies that developed in urban modernity and characterized the new historical culture.

This article, which touches on these characteristics, is about the relationship between antiquity and a particular form of modernity in nineteenth-century historical culture. Antiquity was, and still is, a heterogeneous term which from the end of the eighteenth century denoted temporality, degrees of geographical exteriority (in its relation to the West) and a qualitative difference between the past and the present. Antiquity was pluralized, hyphenated and endowed with a hierarchy. It is widely assumed that antiquity was related to modernity by way of contrast and denoted its opposite (cf. ibid.). I use antiquity here in a narrow sense to describe ancient Assyria as it was discovered, materialized and appropriated in Britain. Assyria serves as an example for the examination of the role of antiquities (in the plural) in what I have described elsewhere as the popular culture of history: the myriad reproductions of slices of the past and their circulation and consumption by various audiences (cf. Melman 2006).

I.

The interest in antiquity during the nineteenth century – in Britain and elsewhere – is hardly an under-researched subject. Although the expanding scholarship on the popular British culture of history has privileged the revivals of periods in the national past that were easily relatable to modernity and were more immediately accessible through written records and their material traces (the Middle Ages and the Tudor and Stuart eras), there has been a growing interest in the discovery of the ancient world and its legacies. Research has focused on the multiple reproductions and forms of consumption of Rome and Greece and touched on pre-classical heritages (cf. Vance 1997; Bradley 2010; Moser 2006). The last decade has witnessed a growing attention to the discovery of Mesopotamia with Assyria, the locus of British scholarly predominance from 1845 until about 1950, at its centre. The discovery of the north Mesopotamian civilization of Assyria, relevant as it is to discourses of imperialism, orientalism and exoticism, has been charted by historians of archaeology, Assyriologists, historians of literature, by students of the theatre and film historians (cf. Reade 1995; Dalley 1998; Larsen 1996; Russell 1997; Holloway 2006; Ziter 2003; Richards: 2009). Assyria's reception has also been probed most fruitfully by art historian Frederick Bohrer (1994; 1998; 2003). The expansion of research reflects shifts in global politics and the politics of knowledge in the post-colonial era, shifts that are apparent in two transitions. One such transition has been the move away from a historicist and biographical approach stressing the exploits of heroic discoverers of antiquity such as Layard, Paul-Émile Botta and Robert Johann Koldewey, to studies of institutions and networks of power and knowledge propagating the study and ›reception‹ of Assyria. Another transition is from an approach which Elliott Colla has described as a narrative of colonial enlightenment, stressing the rescue, by the West, of the history and legacy of antiquity, to nationalist Middle-Eastern enlightenment narratives and to post-colonial narratives of the West's plunder of antiquity (cf. Colla 2007).

The dynamic cross-disciplinary engagement with ancient Assyria is marked by some blind spots which need to be covered to better understand the obsession with antiquity in the new historical culture that emerged during the moment of Britain's intense modernization. One blind spot is the lack of consideration of the relationship between the visual and material aspects of popular history and the urban experience that was at the heart of modernity. There is little discussion of the ways in which Assyria, and more broadly Mesopotamia, became welded into the urban experience and were associated with industrialization. Another blind spot is the separate treatment of traditional forms of knowing about and imagining the ancient East (such as popular biblism), and the emerging fields of specialist knowledge – such as archaeology, philology and the applied arts, notably industrial architecture and design. Yet another blind spot reflects the assumption that the engagement with antiquity was exclusively a western activity that manifested an exercise of imperial power via networks for the distribution of metropolitan knowledge about non-western histories, or by the imperial state vying with other nation states for prestige via archaeological plunder. Thus the discovery/ruin of Mesopotamia is sometimes presented linearly, as leading directly from Layard to George W. Bush (cf. Malley 2008). However, recent studies of antiquarianism, museum-culture and popular history in the Ottoman Empire focusing on its Turkish center and Egypt have manifested a *variety* of appropriations of ancient Egypt, Mesopotamian and Hellenic heritages, including preservation, and the institutionalization of knowledge about antiquity and its display (cf. Shaw 2003; Colla 2007; Makdisi 2002; Gershoni/Jankowski 2002).

I would argue against binary notions which contrast old and new forms of historical knowledge about, and popular appropriations of, Assyria. I would also argue against the assumption that the popular imagination rested on a binary orientalism, positing ancient against modern, as well as the assumption that Assyria's discovery was an entirely western project. The discovery of antiquity was imperial, but it accommodated exchanges and degrees of cross-cultural collaborations. I would contend that new knowledge, new uses of antiquity and new technologies of approaching it were grafted onto or added to, rather than substituted for, traditional ones. The representations and consumption of a particular antiquity tell us a great deal about the particular characteristics of British modernity. I begin by discussing the materialization of Assyria, i.e. the discovery of its physical remains and their circulation in popular culture. Here I expand on the role of illustration as a technique and organizing idea of Assyria's image and status in traditional Biblical culture. I then discuss illustration and the appropriations of Assyria in an urban, colonial and modern context and consider the applicability of antiquity to nineteenth-century modernity.

II.

The emergence of modern interest in Mesopotamian antiquity is conveniently pinned down to the 1840s and the sudden French and British discovery of Assyrian remains. Assyria and Babylon had had a long presence in British scholarly and popular imagination, but this was largely a *textual* presence that drew massively on sources external to it: the Bible and scattered second-hand accounts transmitted by classical authors from Herodotus and Ctesias, the latter reproduced in Diodorus's *World History*, to

Pliny and others. In Judeo-Christian and classical narratives and their medieval, Renaissance, eighteenth- and early nineteenth-century representations, Assyria stood for an ›other‹: exotic in the original meaning of this word, denoting an exteriority placed *outside* Judaism and Christianity as well as the West, and it was represented as powerful, cruel and corrupt. It had a history insofar as it served a role in a sacred Judeo-Christian history of sin and its atonement, and their related lesson about the ascent to power and fall from it. It played a typological role in cosmology: Assyria's history was a lesson for the present and the future. These images had a wide circulation in a popular culture in which, as Leslie Howsam has noted, the Bible was perceived as a necessity and in which a vibrant religious imagery survived well into the early twentieth century (cf. Howsam 1991). Textuality was central to knowledge on antiquity in general. What distinguished Mesopotamian from classical antiquities (Greek, Hellenic and Roman) and pre-classical antiquities, such as that of Egypt, was the total lack of above-ground material remains. Until 1843 Assyria had been an absence, lacking even ruins. It had been disembodied. This absence, acknowledged even in later antiquity (most notably by Xenophon), was repeatedly noted by travelers in the eighteenth and early nineteenth centuries. In the spate of writings published by archaeologists, art and design historians and in the popular press from the late 1840s onwards, the invisibility of Assyria, the disappearance from history of an entire civilization, is continuously and ritually invoked. Any traveler in northern Mesopotamia, remarks Layard, »[i]s now at a loss to give any form to the rude heaps upon which he is gazing. Those of whose works they are the remains, unlike the Roman and the Greek, have left no visible traces of their civilization, or of their arts.« (Layard 2005 [1854]: 6-7) References to burial and its opposite, exposure, became set-pieces, usually opening discovery accounts such as Joseph Bonomi's *Nineveh and Its Palaces*: »[A] thousand miles from the highway of modern commerce and the track of ordinary travel, lay a city buried in the sandy earth, with no certain trace of its place of sepulchre.« (Bonomi 2005 [1852]: 1) The elimination of material traces can be attributed to the building materials used in Mesopotamia: bricks, dried or baked, mud, bitumen, alabaster and gypsum, all contrasting with industrial material and assumed to be perishable. Reference to the huge mounds of debris of bricks and rubbish in northern and southern Mesopotamia is rampant. Bonomi notes the mounds presumed to be the locations of Nineveh and Babylonia. He and

Layard record the impression that these surfaces, which were covered by local flora, grazed on, and sometimes cultivated by the local Bedouin, left on travelers. Vegetation and habitation marked the obliteration of the past and the contrast between its splendors and present decline, but also its recycling: the destruction of history, civilization and man-made artifacts by nature.

The discovery of material remains, begun by Botta in 1843, was viewed in an ambivalent and complex manner as a hierarchical collaboration. Archaeology in Mesopotamia depended on the cooperation of local Arabs, Kurds, Eastern Catholic (Chaldean) Christians and Nestorians, using their labor and drawing on local technologies and knowledge, not to mention degrees of cooperation on the part of the Ottoman authorities. This cooperation decreased in accordance with the development of the Ottoman interest in antiquity. Non-westerners are visible and audible in discovery texts such as Layard's and are far from being represented as passive. They are active participant observers, the first viewers of the monuments and artifacts exposed, and laborers and their lives and habits are extensively surveyed and recorded. Of course, archaeologists' texts consistently reveal cultural arrogance and racial prejudice. Yet unlike earlier descriptions of the removal of antiquities, such as Giovanni Battista Belzoni's description of his 1816 transportation of the giant head of the Young Memnon (Ramses II) from the Upper Nile to Britain, in which the Egyptians are portrayed as passive, Layard refers to local participation and knowledge. Occasionally, discovery is described as, and indeed was, scholarly collaboration. This was particularly the case with Hormudz Rassam (1826-1910), the first Assyrian Assyriologist, a Chaldean Catholic who became a Nestorian, who embarked on a career as archaeologist on behalf of the Trustees of the British Museum, excavating in Nineveh, Khorsabad, Balawat and Babel. He was the actual finder of quantities of clay tablets at the library of Ashurbanipal, including such groundbreaking finds as the clay tablets containing the epos of Gilgamesh, the series of sculptured reliefs of the Assyrian royal lion hunts, and the gates of Balawat (cf. Rassam 1897).

III.

It is against the backdrop of Assyria's physical absence that the impact of its materialization may be assessed. Materialization took on a number of forms, making for a dense grid of representations of the Assyrian Empire, monarchs, everyday life and, following the deciphering of the Akkadian cuneiform in 1857, epics, government and religion. The archaeological finds which flowed into the British Museum derived their power of attraction from their unique status within a hierarchy and classification of antiquity. Assyrian artifacts were not readily absorbed in western aesthetic canons which drew on the classics. In some early and mid-Victorian hierarchical and evolutionary notions of the history of civilization Assyria was graded beneath (or before) Egyptian, Mediterranean and classical cultures and together with Persian and Indian cultures. Later, this last association occasionally classified it as Aryan, and thus as ›advanced‹. Such categorization, which went hand in hand with a linear historicism that characterized the Whig interpretation of history, was particularly manifest in establishment views on Assyrian arts and crafts, as Bohrer (2003) has amply demonstrated. John C. Rawlinson's words to Layard about the Assyrian winged gods not being the Apollo Belvedere immediately spring to mind (cf. Waterfield 1963: 148). Notwithstanding its initial low status in the civilizational hierarchy, Assyria was quickly absorbed into popular urban consumer culture, both in material culture and in the imaginary.

The absorption in modern culture of an antiquity that predated other antiquities is apparent in the circulation of the history of the Neo-Assyrian Empire and the reproduction and emulation of its artifacts. Notwithstanding their rarity, Assyrian remains were reproduced out of their context and copied onto modern urban contexts. As I will show later, reproduction was, more often than not, industrial reproduction and became a staple characteristic of the revival of ancient historical artifacts. Examples are legion: Reproductions of Assyrian jewelry were exhibited at the 1851 Great Exhibition of the Work and Industries of All Nations in the Crystal Palace. Following the dismantling and installation of the palace in Sydenham in South London as a permanent exhibition complex combining display and entertainment, an Assyrian Court was built there which accommodated imitation colossi and reliefs made from casts of the originals at the British Museum and the Louvre. A plethora of accompanying metropolitan spectacles represented episodes from the history of the Neo-Assyrian and Neo-Babylonian Empires, including stage performances known as ›realizations‹ – dramatic visualizations of texts, such as the ›spectacular tragedy‹ *Sardanapalus*, or their printed illustrations (cf. Meisel 1983). Drawing on Byron's famous poem and first staged in 1853 at the Princess Theatre with Charles Kean in the title role, *Sardanapalus* was described as »the most magnificent piece of stage mounting that we have witnessed«. It connected itself, the *Illustrated London News* noted, »with the most astonishing of modern archaeological discoveries« and »placed on the boards the glories of ancient Nineveh [presented in the form of diorama], with the most perfect accuracy of detail« (*ILN* 18 June 1853: no. 628, 493). The realization resurrected Nineveh, the Tigris and Sardanapalus's royal palace on stage. Outside the theatre and the exhibitions, panoramas, dioramas and tableaux featuring the destruction of Nineveh and excavations of the Assyrian capitals catered for audiences in a variety of London venues of popular entertainment (such as the Leicester Square Panorama and Cremorne Leisure Gardens), as well as in provincial cities (cf. *ILN* 28 June 1851: no. 497, 619). Less spectacular but equally consistent were the numerous educational ventures circulating information on Mesopotamian history, archaeology and the deciphering of cuneiform, arranged by the Royal Asiatic Society, the Royal Institute of Architects, the Society of Biblical Archaeology, in local literary and *conversazione* groups and in the plebeian Polytechnic Institutes' ›lectures for all classes‹, such as the Eisteddfod in Cardiff Town Hall attended by artisans (cf. *ILN* 23 March 1850: no. 418, 208; 13 April 1850: no. 421, 245).

At the same time that Assyria became a public display involving collective spectatorship, it was also admitted into Victorian homes and adapted to lower-key and more individualized forms of material and visual consumption. Assyria's domestication is apparent in the production of small-scale objects, including jewels such as 18 carat gold Nineveh bracelets and earrings at an average price of £10 and £2 respectively (cf. *ILN* 13 December 1876: no. 1951, 27), and adaptations of the large-scale finds, designed for spectacle or museum display, for household or individual consumption. Models and replicas of monuments included a ›reduced‹ 20 inch high model of the Nimrud Obelisk, »carefully copied from that sent by Mr. Layard to the British Museum« (*ILN* 10 March 1852: no. 550, 231). Reduction also characterizes the Assyrian-style Staffordshire statuettes, book-ends and vases manufactured by W.T. Copland and Sons and marketed by entrepreneurial British Museum attendants (and thus by the Museum itself), and Nineveh embroideries. Specifically intended for domestic ornamentation, the Assyrian-style objects were not merely imitations but adaptations, translating the standard two-dimensional Assyrian sculpture into three dimensions and transforming linear and flat forms into curved ones. Imitation and transformation also characterizes the adaptation of Assyrian motifs displayed at Sydenham to illustrated albums as exemplified by the Dalziel brothers' *Bible Gallery* (1881), which reproduced illustrations of biblical scenes by Britain's top history painters, in bound and unbound outsize format for domestic viewing. Ford Madox Brown's *The Death of Eglon* is a case in point, with its multiplicity of Assyrian motifs such as cuneiform inscriptions, weaponry, colossi, facial hair, furniture and jewelry applied to a scene that is not Assyrian, thus demonstrating the widespread and eclectic application of Assyria to other ancient cultures.

Fig. 1: Ford Madox Brown: »The Death of Eglon« (Dalziel's Bible Gallery (1981): n.p.).

The materialization and adaptation of Assyria made the ancient visible and tactile, thus accommodating the exotic in private spaces and in the public venues of entertainment that emerged around 1800 and engendered the new technologies of display and spectatorship. At the same time, uses of Assyria blurred distinctions between public and private appropriations of the ancient (jewels were worn in public and private), between different forms of telling about ancient history, between texts and images, and between ancientness and modernity. This blurring resulted from the assumption, shared by the entrepreneurs of Victorian popular culture, that their audiences moved between texts and images and that word and visual image were mutually illustrative. ›Illustration‹ had several meanings and was key to the new popular knowledge about, and imagining of ancient history. Drawings served to explain archaeological finds; but at the same time pictorial matter was accompanied by elucidating, highly-detailed texts, thus doubly visualizing history. Illustration was the tag of one of the urban genres most identified with modern technologies: the illustrated newspaper, notably the *ILN*, which depicted the modernization and rationalization of life, governance and mobility in London with realistic illustrations. Between 1847 and 1875, the *ILN* covered in extraordinary, ›true to life‹ detail the traffic of Assyrian artifacts to Britain, their circulation and reproductions, and created a free-access »catalogue for readers with an interest in history and the Bible«. Excessive illustration virtually embodied the past. One illustration dated 31 March 1849 brought to life a colossal male figure (figs. 2 and 3) sculpted on a bas-relief. Measuring 7.4 inches by 4, the illustration endowed the figure with a physique and an extraordinary richness of detail and the image was accompanied by the following description:

»A young man habited in a long fringed robe, fitting close to the upper part of his figure. Secured around his waist by the tasseled cords is a species of train formed by five rows of feather-shaped fringes, and round his waist is a broad girdle in which are placed three daggers. He wears sandals, armlets, rosettes, bracelets, and earrings; and round his neck is a necklace, and a cord and tassels. Upon his head is the two-horned cap; and in addition to the ordinary crisply curled hair is a long bunch, likewise curled, and bound with cords and tassels. His right hand and arm are raised and the left is extended, holding a wreath of small and large beads placed alternately. The most remarkable features, however, are the representations of four wings, two raised and two dropping; and that suspended from his neck are two bands, from the upper of which depend ornaments consisting of rosettes, surrounded by a ring, and from the lower, four stars likewise enclosed in rings.« (*ILN* 31 March 1849: no. 364, 213)

Fig. 2 (left): »An Assyrian Divinity, The Nimrud Sculptures, Just Received at the British Museum« (ILN 31 March 1849: no. 364, 213).

Fig. 3 (right): »An Assyrian Divinity«, Detail (ILN 31 March 1849: no. 364, 213).

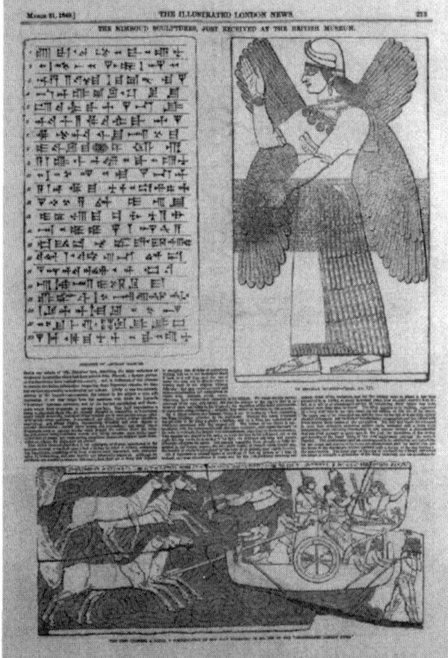

Excess characterizes both the subject matter (the minutiae of hair, jewelry and dress) and the illustrative style and method of the narrative. The excess of ornamentation and Assyrian aesthetics challenged valued canons of classical antiquity concerning aesthetics, gender and the body, not to mention Victorian tenets. The bejeweled and ostentatiously dressed Assyrian men and Assyrian male body displayed on bas-reliefs were a far cry from the Greek image of masculinity and seem to have corroborated the traditional image of the effeminate and lascivious Sardanapalus. But Assyrian masculinity also redefined antiquity, baffling previous definitions of gender, physique and the body. Effeminate Assyrians flaunted middle-class ideals of Christian gentlemanliness, austerity and self-restraint and blurred gendered consumption: Imitations of Assyrian jewelry for men were produced for women. Yet the muscularity of men and animals typical of Assyrian art, profusely copied and commented upon in illustrations and texts, displayed the male physique of kings, soldiers, builders and even eunuchs – all depicted as ruthless conquerors, hunters and slayers of wild animals.

However, illustration as a way of elucidating history *as well as* the materiality of antiquity, which I have located above in modern urban genres and in archaeology, had its origins in an older, vernacular biblical culture that impinged on the status of the new material history of Assyria. Originating in the Reformation and surviving into the twentieth century, British Bible culture had a pull across genders and classes, particularly among plebeian audiences, that did not diminish with urbanization, capitalism and industrialization but was invigorated by them. An arsenal of biblical images of antiquity, biblical chronology and creationism – buttressing beliefs in the recent origins of humanity – persisted in both Victorian popular religion and science (cf. Van Riper 1993: 5-6). The discovery of Mesopotamian civilizations through the medium of material remains corroborated the Bible's status as a history source-book. Moreover, the material past was not merely illustrative; it was tied to the present and interpreted as a lesson for the future.

This religious-illustrative nature of the history of antiquity pervaded the new fields of knowledge about the ancient Orient such as Assyriology, Egyptology, Semitic philology and archaeology and is common in the writings of Layard, George Smith (the decipherer of the eleventh tablet of the Epos of Gilgamesh which contained a late version of the story of the Deluge) and Samuel Birch. Birch, an Egyptologist and inaugural president of the Society of Biblical Archaeology, enjoined its members to »collect from the fast-perishing monuments of the Semitic and cognate races illustrations of their history and peculiarities; to investigate and systematize the antiquities of the ancient and mighty empires of primeval peoples, whose records are centered around the venerable pages of the Bible« (Holloway 2001: 17). Even before his admonition, numerous commemorative monuments and bas-reliefs were interpreted for the illustration of the sacred text. Notable examples include the Black Obelisk of Shalmaneser III (c. 825 BC) showing the earliest surviving picture of an Israelite, Jehu of the house of Omri, or his emissary, offering the Assyrian king a tribute. As the *Illus-*

trated London News put it: »The sacred histories are adventitiously eluci-dated in these investigations [...] those monstrous monarchies [...] are surely no unworthy project of our retrospective contemplation.« (*ILN* 2 April 1853: no. 614, 257) Contemplation included the future as well as the past and the present. Biblical archaeology, which remained dominant until about 1900, bridged the past and the future. Not only *incidents* in Assyrian history, such as the siege of Lachish, the conquest of Israel, Judea or Elam, or Assyria's clashes with the Egyptian Empire, were materially ›proven‹ to have occurred, rather the entire outline of the history of the Assyrian Empire served as a pattern to modern world history and the history of the British Empire. On 27 March 1847, announced as a day of prayer and fast for the victims of the famine in Ireland caused by the potato blight, the text preached in numerous sermons was the third chapter of Jonah, describing the repentance of the Ninevites and their temporary de-liverance. Starvation at the heart of the greatest empire, in the midst of prosperity and progress, was a sign of decline modelled on that of the an-cient empires: »[It] will reduce us [...] like Athens, Rome, Babylon and Nineveh had been reduced, until the name of our exploits and pre-eminence became a tradition.« (*ILN* 27 March 1847: no. 256, 201)

IV.

The multiple secular and biblical illustrations of Assyria's history as well as their circulation and their appropriation evolved in an urban and industrial environment. The discovery of ancient city-empires coincided with one of the most intense phases of urban modernization in Britain, following the end, around 1851, of the First Industrial Revolution (a point in time when urban population first exceeded the rural one). Modernization did not de-velop linearly. Nor, as I have argued elsewhere, was it experienced, or im-agined, as the substitution of the new and modern for the old or ancient (cf. Melman 2009; 2012). Unprecedented intense urban development, particu-larly in London, was inextricable from destruction. Images of metropolitan and imperial might, drawing on imperial supremacy and an optimistic be-lief in progress, intermingled with a sense of urban decay, of the loss of the remains of the old parts of the city and anxieties and fantasies about the metropolis's disappearance, similar to that of the capitals of antiquity:

Nineveh and Babylon. The combined processes of destruction and development occurred both above ground and underground, with the construction of the first subterranean systems designed to facilitate the movement of people, matter and waste: the world's first drainage and sewage system and first underground railway. As David L. Pike (2005) has noted, the construction of man-made space underground, creating a vertical city, was a distinctly modern phenomenon. Excavation and digging in built-up residential and commercial areas became part of the experience of technological progress and a hallmark and symbol of modern urbanization. At the same time, digging destroyed remnants of the unearthed past (cf. Zimmerman 2008; Harvey 2003). I would argue that metropolitan excavation was remarkably similar to the archaeological exposure of the ancient Mesopotamian mounds. In London, indeed in any nineteenth-century modernized metropolis, excavation proceeded by the sinking of low shafts, tunneling close to the surface and digging along the lines of proposed railways, pipes or sewers. This was precisely the technique of early Mesopotamian archaeology practiced by Botta, Layard, Loftus, Rawlinson, Rassam and Place. Moreover, the recovery of the three lost Assyrian capitals and the process of building underground London were represented via the same urban genre: the cross-section drawing, showing at one and the same time surface and depth, materials, artifacts and people above and below ground, construction and demolition.

Fig. 4 (left): »The Metropolitan Underground Railway Works in Progress at King's Cross« (ILN 2 February 1861: no. 1072, 99).

Fig. 5 (right): Robert Clive: »Excavation at Nimroud« (Clive 1852: n.p.).

The cross-section illustration depicting the coeval worlds of the historic and the modern was popularized by the *Illustrated London News* which celebrated metropolitan improvement and archaeology. Archaeology itself, as Julian Thomas (2004) has noted, took shape within the framework of modernity, translating not only practices of exposing lost material objects, but also providing powerful metaphors for thinking about change and structure in history. One of these was the metaphor of surface and depth, which the Victorians used time and again to describe cities. Archaeology made it possible to display duplications of artifacts in the proverbial site of modernity and progress: the first ever industrial and colonial exhibition at the Crystal Palace which hosted over 6,000,000 visitors, and its successor at Sydenham, known as the People's Palace, hosting some two million visitors a year. Its series of courts, forming a museum of the history of architecture, disturbed the narrative of progress ascending from Assyria to the Renaissance: The courts which exhibited ancient civilizations were separated, with the Assyrian court squeezed between the Byzantine and Moorish ones (cf. Layard 2005 [1854]). At both exhibitions, and indeed in all the colonial world exhibitions, display attached to antiquity a commodity value that was not based on exchange, but accommodated a variety of forms of labor (industrial as well as manual) that were partly metropolitan and partly colonial. And as both Marx and Walter Benjamin have noted, the new kind of exhibition made commodities into fetishes to be desired but not purchased, semi-religious objects of pilgrimage (cf. Benjamin 1986 [1935]: 151-152).

Appropriately, artifacts drawing on Assyrian imperial motifs and manufactured in the British Empire were displayed to metropolitan audiences. A quarto-sized drawing features the interior of an ivory-cutting workshop in Berhampoor, India, with the walls covered in life-size sketches of the various parts of animals, and local cutters making ivory artifacts for the Great Exhibition, including »Layard's Nineveh chess sets« (*ILN* 26 April 1851: no. 480, 335). In addition to duplicated artifacts, Assyrian designs and colors were integrated into the design and color scheme of the industrially manufactured building of the Crystal Palace which was made of machine-made, ready-to-assemble iron and glass. The Palace's interior ironwork was painted red, blue and yellow, primary colors taken to represent ancient usages of color, and inspired by Egypt and Layard's Mesopotamian finds. The ancient polychromatic design and color scheme were the brainchild of Owen Jones, superintendent of the building of the Palace (who designed its interior and organized the exhibits), and probably the most influential Victorian design theorist. His *The Grammar of Ornament* (1856) reproduced samples of Assyrian ornamentations from the palaces of Nimrud, Khorsabad and Kuyunjik, samples which suited his definition of a style appropriate to the nineteenth century and modernity. Jones eschewed two of the most popular Victorian revival styles: Neo-Gothicism and Neo-Classicism, both previously described as ›antiquity‹, replacing them with more ancient ones: early medieval Muslim, Egyptian and Assyrian styles that were also non-European. Jones's version of history through the development of a practical aesthetics applicable to the everyday expanded the definition of antiquity and challenged simple progressionism.

The relationship between antiquity and industry is apparent not only in the merging of the ancient into metropolitan sites of modernity and commodification, but also in the circulation and distribution of images of and knowledge about Assyria among working-class audiences. This circulation is characterized, at one and the same time, by the democratization of access to the ancient and the persistence of forms of patronage and hierarchies of class manifest in the cultural entrepreneurship of aesthetes related to industry, who may be described as impresarios of the culture of antiquity. Owen Jones and James Fergusson, the latter an architect and art historian specializing in ancient Mesopotamian, Egyptian and Indian art and manager of the Crystal Palace Company, are two exemplars of this entrepreneurship.

But undoubtedly the most striking example of the mediation between Assyrian history and working-class audiences, between cultural philanthropy and democratization, is the activity of Lady Charlotte Guest Schreiber, née Bertie, and Sir John Josiah Guest. The Guests, owners and co-managers of the Dowlais Iron Company in Wales, at the time Britain's biggest industrial plant, combined conspicuous consumption and collection of Assyrian antiquities with publicizing the archaeology of Mesopotamia among Welsh industrial workers. Lady Guest, patron to her cousin Layard, initiated a collection of antiquities – including a pair of winged colossi – identical to that at the British Museum. Bas-reliefs, smaller artifacts and ivories were supplied to her even as the Assyrian galleries at the British Museum were being supplied. Guest, a linguist and student of Welsh literature, the first translator of the medieval epic *Mabinogion* into English, and a Persian scholar, installed the collection at the Nineveh Porch, designed by Sir Charles Barry (architect of the Parliament buildings) in the

Gothic revival style, with an eclectic interior combining the Gothic and a cluster of Mesopotamian motifs. Entirely conscious of the relationship between industry, democratic display, paternalist philanthropy and social hierarchies, Lady Guest noted in her diary after the inauguration ceremony of the Great Exhibition the need to acknowledge industrial labor: »As the wife of the largest manufacturer in the world I could but feel this to be the most impressive sight.« (Russell 1997: 73) She initiated lectures on Assyrian history delivered by Layard and others to the workforce of Guest's ironworks plants at Dowlais and Poole, to audiences in local exhibitions and to mechanics' classes. In one workingmen's gathering in August 1851, Layard addressed an audience of about 600. Huge folded canvas hangings, featuring paintings of the eagle-faced winged deity incorrectly identified as Nisroch (the god at whose temple Sennacherib was murdered by his sons [II Kings 19:37]), a king and a colossal lion, dropped to full length for dramatic effect, and a model of an obelisk and antiquities borrowed from the Nineveh porch were displayed onstage. The audience listened with »hushed and intense attention« to the lecture and its translation into Welsh by the ministers present, recognizing the biblical stories and allusions (Russell 1997: 74). The lectures preceded the arrival and display at the British Museum of the sculptures from Layard's second expedition.

The Welsh Assyrian revivals may be viewed as remnants of a traditional and rural paternalism rather than as modern urban consumptions of antiquity. But this would mean naively ignoring the distinct industrial framework in which they evolved: Dowlais were the largest steel producers in the world and the manufacturers of capital goods (such as railways), and the factory was located at one of the world's central mining areas around Merthyr Tydfil. Knowledge about Assyria was distributed not just from above, by benevolent industrialists, but circulated via the characteristic organizational framework of workers' self-improvement associationism that developed in the mid-Victorian era. Most notably, the study of antiquity through material things, becoming widely available through the archaeological finds, was grafted onto and added to the cluster of popular images and metaphors which had been prevalent in biblical working-class culture.

V.

The giant two-dimensional image of Nisroch exhibited to an industrial workforce of Bible readers forcefully brings to the fore some complexities and tensions which the multiple productions of Assyria and their circulation in a rich material culture and in the Victorian imaginary present. More broadly, the Nisroch episode, and my discussion, may point to the broadening of the definition and uses of antiquity in a culture that underwent intense processes of modernization. Thus the uses of Assyrian antiquity may tell us a few things about modernity: The first concerns the materialization of the past. Material objects became not only the basis for historical knowledge, but also made ancient history reproducible and transformable into a commodity. However, as we have seen, artifacts did not supplant texts; the evidence they provided was added to biblical texts. A second feature of the popularization of the ancient past is development by accretion. Crucial to accretion was the capacity for duplicating and copying the ancient, which democratized access to it. New evidence, fields of knowledge, technologies and procedures of viewing ancient artifacts were added to, rather than substituted for older patterns. Take for example the emergence and spread of archaeology, critical philology and Assyriology, which were grafted onto biblical culture. The very combination of ›Biblical archaeology‹ and the project of deciphering cuneiform and its immense publicity demonstrate development by accretion. A third complexity is the absorption of antiquity into a colonial and global economy of commodity culture and the relation of the process of discovery itself to the experience of modernity in the metropolis. Oriental antiquity could not be easily absorbed into progressionist interpretations of history which organized the past along a scale of development (increasingly perceived in evolutionary terms), from ancient to modern and from oriental to western. True, views on antiquity projected hierarchical and evolutionary notions of history onto the ancient Orient. However, the repetitious analogy between the decline and fall of ancient empires and the modern world city challenged notions of progress and reflected the anxiety characteristic of urban modernity.

Assyria's history, to paraphrase Reinhart Koselleck (1985), was a »future past«: It served to bridge ancient history and the future via a present. But this was not an optimistic history, as is evident in the abundance of visions of London as a second Nineveh. Take for example the »Bull of Nineveh«, the monologue about the colossus, anonymously published in *House-hold Words* in February 1851 and probably written by W.H. Stone: »[B]oast not, ye vainglorious creatures of an hour. I have out-lived many mighty kingdoms, perchance I may be destined to survive one more.« (*Household Words* 46.8: 468-469) Or consider »An Address from the Smithfield Bull to his Cousin of Nineveh« (*Household Words* 51.2: 589), appearing less than a month later, a caustic critique on the danger of London's meat market, the source of filth and disease and a symbol of the city's malaises. Assyria burst open definitions of antiquity, multiplying them and shifting hierarchies of culture. Assyria challenged narratives of progress, and its discovery manifested forms of orientalism and colonialism that were collaborative and at the same time hierarchical. Assyria was a representation, a style, a commodity, a trope for the present and a prophecy about the end of empires, a manifestation of urban anxiety about over-development, a model for urban dystopia: It was a way to refigure the burdens of modernity.

WORKS CITED

Appadurai, Arjun (ed.) (1986): *The Social Life of Things: Commodities in Cultural Perspective*, Cambridge: Cambridge University Press.

Benjamin, Walter (1986 [1935]): »Grandville or the World Exhibitions«. In: Peter Demetz (ed.), *Reflections: Essays, Aphorisms, Autobiographical Writings*, New York/NY: Schocken Books, 151-153.

Bohrer, Frederick Nathaniel (1994): »The Times and Spaces of History: Representation, Assyria and the British Museum«. In: Daniel J. Sherman/Irit Rogoff (eds.), *Museum Culture: Histories, Discourses, Spectacles*, Minneapolis/MN: University of Minnesota Press, 197-222.

Bohrer, Frederick Nathaniel (1998): »Inventing Assyria: Exoticism and Reception in Nineteenth-Century England and France«. *Art Bulletin* 80.2, 336-356.

Bohrer, Frederick Nathaniel (2003): *Orientalism and Visual Culture: Imagining Mesopotamia in Nineteenth-Century Europe*, Cambridge: Cambridge University Press.

Bonomi, Joseph (2005 [1852]): *Nineveh and Its Palaces: The Discoveries of Botta and Layard, Applied to the Elucidation of Holy Writ*, Boston/MA: Adamant Media Corporation.

Bradley, Mark (ed.) (2010): *Classics and Imperialism in the British Empire*, Oxford: Oxford University Press.

Clive, Robert (1852): »Excavation at Nimroud«. In: *Sketches Between the Persian Gulf and Black Sea*, London: Dickson.

Colla, Elliott (2007): *Conflicted Antiquities: Egyptology, Egyptomania, Egyptian Modernity*, Durham/NC: Duke University Press.

Dalley, Stephanie et al. (eds.) (1998): *The Legacy of Mesopotamia*, Oxford: Oxford University Press.

Dalziel (1881): *Dalziel's Bible Gallery: Illustrations from the Old Testament Engraved by the Brothers Dalziel*, London: Routledge.

Fergusson, James (1851): *The Palaces of Nineveh and Persepolis Restored*, London: Murray.

Gershoni, Israel/James P. Jankowski (2002): *Redefining the Egyptian Nation, 1930-1945*, Cambridge: Cambridge University Press.

Harvey, David (2003): *Paris: Capital of Modernity*, London: Routledge.

Holloway, Steven W. (2001): »Biblical Assyria and Other Anxieties in the British Empire«. *Journal of Religion and Society* 3, 1-19.

Holloway, Steven W. (ed.) (2006): *Orientalism, Assyriology and the Bible*, Sheffield: Sheffield Phoenix Press.

Howsam, Leslie (1991): *Cheap Bibles: Nineteenth-Century and the British and Foreign Bible Society*, Cambridge: Cambridge University Press.

Jones, Owen (2001 [1856]): *The Grammar of Ornament*, London: Day & Son.

Koselleck, Reinhart (1985): *Futures Past: On the Semantics of Historical Time*, Cambridge/MA: Harvard University Press.

Larsen, Mogens Trolle (1996): *The Conquest of Assyria: Excavations in an Antique Land*. London: Routledge.

Layard, Austen Henry (1849): *Nineveh and Its Remains: With an Account of a Visit to the Chaldæan Christians of Kurdistan, and the Yezidis or Devil Worshippers; and an Enquiry into the Manners and Arts of the Ancient Assyrians*, London: John Murray.

Layard, Austen Henry (2005 [1854]): *The Nineveh Court in the Crystal Palace*, London: Adamant Media Corporation.

Makdisi, Ussama (2002): »Ottoman Orientalism«. *American Historical Review* 107.3, 768-796.

Malley, Shawn (2008): »Layard Enterprise: Victorian Archaeology and Informal Imperialism in Mesopotamia«. *International Journal of Middle Eastern Studies* 40, 623-646.

Meisel, Martin (1983): *Realizations: Narrative, Pictorial and Theatrical Arts in Nineteenth-Century England*, Princeton/NJ: Princeton University Press.

Melman, Billie (2006): *The Culture of History: English Uses of the Past 1800-1953*, Oxford: Oxford University Press.

Melman, Billie (2009): *London: Place, People and Empire (1800-1960)*, Tel Aviv: IDF Publications (Hebrew).

Melman, Billie (2012): »The Power of the Past«. In: Martin Hewitt (ed.), *The Victorian World*, London: Routledge (publication forthcoming).

Morley, Neville (2009): *Antiquity and Modernity*, Oxford: Blackwell.

Moser, Stephanie (2006): *Wondrous Curiosities: Ancient Egypt at the British Museum*, Chicago/IL: Chicago University Press.

Pike, David L. (2005): *Subterranean Cities: The World Beneath Paris and London, 1800-1945*, Ithaca/NY: Cornell University Press.

Rassam, Hormudz (1897): *Asshur and the Land of Nimrod: Being an Account of the Discoveries Made in the Ancient Ruins of Nineveh, Asshur, Sepharvaim, Calah, Babylon, Borsippa, Cuthah and Van*, New York: Eaton and Mains.

Reade, Julian E. (1995): *Art and Empire: Treasures from Assyria in the British Museum*, London: British Museum.

Richards, Jeffrey (2009): *The Ancient World on the Victorian and Edwardian Stage*, London: Palgrave Macmillan.

Russell, John Malcolm (1997): *From Nineveh to New York: The Strange Story of the Assyrian Reliefs in the Metropolitan Museum and the Hidden Masterpiece at Canford School*, New Haven/CT: Yale University Press.

Shaw, Wendy M.K. (2003): *Possessors and Possessed: Museums, Archaeology, and the Visualization of History in the Late Ottoman Empire*, Berkeley/CA: University of California Press.

Thomas, Julian (2004): *Archaeology and Modernity*, London: Routledge.

Vance, Norman (1997): *The Victorians and Ancient Rome*, Oxford: Wiley-Blackwell.

Van Riper, Bowdoin A. (1993): *Men among the Mammoths: Victorian Science and the Discovery of Human Prehistory*, Chicago/IL: Chicago University Press.

Waterfield, Gordon (1963): *Layard of Nineveh*, London: Murray.

Zimmerman, Vanessa (2008): *Excavating Victorians*, Albany/NY: State University of New York Press.

Ziter, Edward (2003): *The Orient on the Victorian Stage*, Cambridge: Cambridge University Press.

Growing Up with History in the Victorian Periodical Press

LESLIE HOWSAM

HOW TO STUDY HISTORY AROUND 1882

In the mid- and late-Victorian decades, British people began to learn about the past from a remarkably young age and throughout their lives. Thanks to the little-known genre of ›nursery histories‹ little boys and girls reading books and periodicals had their first introduction to iconic names and events. As children became adolescents they were exposed, both in school and at home, to historical narratives published with their age group in mind. When adults encountered history in a range of books, magazines, journals and reviews, they were building on a strong foundation. A well-delineated story of national heritage had become part of most Britons' consciousness. When a handful of those people adopted history as a profession, that cohort claimed to know better, and to understand more, about the past than did their neighbours. The present article will use the concept of the life cycle of the reader, growing from child to adolescent to adult – and perhaps even to academic historian – as a way of thinking about how the Victorians understood the past of their own country and of the world.[1] The Victorians' consciousness of the life cycle of the growing child and developing adult also shaped their thinking about the appropriate means by which to introduce

---

1   The concept of the »life cycle of the history-book reader« has been developed in Howsam (2009: 3-5).

history into the training of citizens. In studies of the periodical press, the conventional way of working with this sort of discourse has been to analyze the politics, religion or ideology of particular journals as extensions of the views of their editors and proprietors. The life cycle approach, however, moves the focus of interest to the reader, and to specific categories of readers targeted by those editors and proprietors.

A remarkable anonymous essay published in 1882, when matched with other events happening around the same time, serves as a useful moment to begin exploring the British periodical press's treatment of historical subjects. »How to Study History« appeared in the weekly *Girl's Own Paper* on 23 September. The article was intended not for adults, or even for schoolboys, and not for little children at home, but particularly for adolescent girls. The editors and publishers of the periodical could target their audience in this way because each magazine, review, journal or newspaper was aimed at a specific segment of the market, differentiated by class and interests, as well as by gender and age-group. During that period, academic historians in universities were very publicly engaged in asking and answering the question of »How to Study History«, asserting the importance of their discipline among other fields of study, and stressing its scientific character (cf. Soffer 1994: 100-102). 1882 was the year of the foundation of the *Dictionary of National Biography*. The Oxford University Press had just published a translation of Leopold von Ranke's *History of England*, and J.R. Green's *Short History of the English People* had been a surprise bestseller for Macmillan for eight years. Serious discussions were underway, with various commercial and university presses, about the desirability and feasibility of starting a dedicated periodical, an *English Historical Review*, largely because historians were dissatisfied with what they called the »popular and sketchy articles« available in existing periodicals (Howsam 2009: 59). In 1882, the range of those periodicals was wide as well as deep. The Religious Tract Society had been making a success of publishing its *Boy's Own Paper* since 1879 and the *Girl's Own* since 1880. Both sought to combat the »pernicious« influence of the penny newspapers by providing wholesome literature in an entertaining and attractive format (*DNCJ* 2009: 535-536). And while religious publications of this kind were flourishing, so were quarterly reviews, monthly journals, weekly magazines and daily newspapers, offering news, opinion and literature across a range of genres to readers of all ages, both genders and various levels of social class and educational background.

Two sets of scholars have looked at this moment of historical interest. Students of the periodical press are interested in the dynamics of what is arguably the world's first mass medium, in how the popular discourse available to ordinary readers was produced and consumed (cf. ibid.: v-viii). In the case of mass-market periodicals for adolescents, this has meant close readings of the imagery (of domesticity for girls and masculinity for boys) in the journalistic and fictional prose the papers carried, with an eye to the reinforcement of separate gender spheres. Students of historiography, on the other hand, are concerned with the formation of history as an academic discipline complete with a scholarly journal. This journal, the *English Historical Review*, was founded in 1886, but it had taken twenty years and several reimaginings to get it off the ground (cf. Howsam 2004: 529-535). In what follows, I will combine the two approaches, looking for history in the periodical press, and examining how the past was mediated to young impressionable readers who were regularly exposed to the popular articles of which professional historians complained.

HISTORY FOR YOUNG READERS

The 1882 article on »How to Study History« in the *Girl's Own* ultimately relates historical knowledge to Protestant Christian religious belief. It starts with an etymological discussion of the word *history* which includes the Latin *historia* (a narrative) and the German *Geschichte* from the root *schicht* (a layer or stratum). The hybrid definition casts history as »a picture or narrative of Time's events, arranged into *strata*, or an orderly series of corresponding portions« (»How to Study« 1882: 826). But the reader is also urged to remember three things. First, that real flesh-and-blood men and women experienced the events of the past. Secondly, that those stories demand to be learned in an orderly manner, beginning with »a rational account of the origin of the primitive races and the earliest monarchies, and above all, [tracing] intelligently the growth of that enlightened religion which has brought with it all the blessings of civilization and freedom« (ibid.). The article's third point, about learning dates, reinforces and actualizes that orderly arrangement and sets the stage for a further line of argument. The young woman who reads the *Girl's Own* and wishes to learn historical facts with the object of studying history for its own sake, is advised to teach them to »some tiny pupils – some little brothers or sisters, nephews or nieces« (ibid.). Then domestic pedagogy becomes the departure point for a hierarchy of historiographical priority: Girls are advised to study England's history first, then France's, after which the article sets them free to explore a special interest. This program of »systematic readings« is soon overtaken, however, by the admonition that »History is the chronicle of God's world and His dealings with it« (ibid.).

The article was unsigned, and it appeared amidst the customary heterogeneity of the *Girl's Own Paper* which, like many periodicals, jumbled together fiction and fact, instruction and entertainment, the latest fashion and the efficacy of prayer. Scholars of the periodical press have stressed the hybridity of the medium, and also insisted upon the significance of its periodic character (cf. Beetham 1990). Readers received their copies week by week, or month by month. This pattern created powerful, recurrently-reinforced relationships with the editorial voice of the paper. If such voices resonated strongly for adults, it is worth asking what sort of impact they had on child readers.

The category of the ›nursery history‹ has been explored in studies of the authorship, publishing and reading of books. Before they encountered school books, middle-class children were exposed to stories from English history at their mother's knee, and mother was guided in her narrative by the works of people like Elizabeth Penrose (pseud. ›Mrs Markham‹), Lady Callcott (the author of *Little Arthur's History of England*) and by Charlotte Yonge, who wrote English history »for the little ones«, and later French and German histories for the same readers.[2] Working from mid-century to her death in 1901, Yonge was a historical novelist who occasionally switched over to writing accounts of the past that purported to be true (cf. Mitchell 2000: 56-83, 248-260).

All these writers, and others, knew how to select appropriate accounts from the past – simple, straightforward and morally unambiguous stories – and how to frame them with such devices as the family circle where mother

---

2   *Aunt Charlotte's Stories of English History for the Little Ones* (1873), *Aunt Charlotte's Stories of German History for the Little Ones* (1878) and *Aunt Charlotte's Stories of French History for the Little Ones* (1893).

tells the tale and children ask the questions. Research in the archives of publishers shows that people in the book trade were aware of the power of nursery histories. The surviving correspondence of the newly profession-alized, almost entirely male, proto-academic historians reveals how scorn-ful these writers could be of the works they were seeking to supplant. Children who learned a purely narrative and anecdotal approach to the past would have to un-learn it and replace it with a scientific one. So believed E.A. Freeman, who prepared an *Old English History for Children* for publi-cation, at about the same time he was bringing out his very learned *Norman Conquest of England* with the Oxford University Press (cf. Howsam 2004: 539-540).

A remarkable amount of history appeared in periodical form. Freeman's historical essays and reviews were published in the *Contemporary Review*, the *Fortnightly*, the *North British Review* and several others. His London publisher Macmillan was proprietor and founder of *Macmillan's Magazine*, which included important essays by a number of major historians. Narra-tives or reviews of history can be found in every one of the forty-five dom-inant and widely-read periodicals indexed in the *Wellesley Index of Victor-ian Periodicals* (cf. Houghton 1965-1988), but scholarship on those and other periodicals has been focused much more on literary and (to some extent) scientific material than on historical narratives. Research in these publications is being transformed in the present decade, however, as digitized editions of periodicals become available from commercial firms like ProQuest and Gale Cengage, and academic projects like the Nine-teenth-Century Serials Edition. Many of the titles involved are more ephemeral than those captured in the *Wellesley Index*, though no less wide-ly-read. Scholars are finding that the discourse of history – England's past, Britain's, Europe's and the world's – was a commonplace subject in maga-zines, reviews and journals.

One such obscure title is *The Little Wide-Awake: An Illustrated Maga-zine for Children*. The editor was Lucy Sale-Barker, who wrote stories for her own family and later put them into publishable form. She edited the magazine for 17 years, from 1875 until her death in 1892.[3] A series of art-

---

3   Much of Sale-Barker's creative work was in fiction and poetry; her name is often associated with that of Kate Greenaway, whose illustrations appeared in the periodical (cf. North 2003: »Little Wide-Awake«).

icles on »Scraps of English History« ran in the *Little Wide-Awake* in fifteen parts beginning in January 1877. The first item was the arrival of Julius Caesar, followed by King Alfred, the Norman Conquest and Richard the Lion-Heart. The fifth, on Edward I, begins:

»After Richard Coeur-de-Lion, the next king, whose reign would interest you, is Edward I. You see, my dear children, I wish to tell you just those parts of English history which, I think, would amuse or strike you – such parts, in fact, as would alone be likely to remain in your memory, if you were to read the history all through. In that way you will be saved from plodding through a good deal that might appear rather dry and dull to you, while you are so young. Of course, my little ones, when you grow older you must study history thoroughly.« (»Scraps« 29: 148)[4]

These words typify the tone of the series and indeed of much of the discourse of history for children in the periodical press: the apparently obvious assumption that little children will remember only certain kinds of events; the equally self-evident »truth« that history must eventually be studied »thoroughly« rather than in scraps. The first anecdote of Edward's career is an explanation of how the eldest son of the English monarch came to be called the Prince of Wales. The author refers to the king's subterfuge as »a trick« (he assured the Welsh chieftains their new prince had been born in Wales and spoke no English, and then presented them with his infant son) but makes no further overt value-judgment (ibid.: 149-150). The author then turns to Edward's attempt to conquer Scotland, which leads directly to an account of William Wallace – »a famous hero of Scottish history. He was gigantic in stature, and as brave and hardy as he was tall« (ibid.: 150) – and then of Robert Bruce. The series continued through the ages, hitting the usual high-spots and finishing up with the last of the Stuarts. Many histories, for children and for adults, treated the eighteenth century rather vaguely and cursorily, and left the nineteenth untouched. An episode entitled »The Reformation« (»Scraps« 36: 366-370) presented a strongly Protestant message. While entirely typical of the English historiography of the period – to the despair of Roman Catholic scholars then and now – it is

---

4   All references to periodical articles cite first the volume/issue number then the page number.

worth noting nevertheless that the strong ›anti-Popery‹ sentiments of the period were being instilled, and reinforced, through historical narratives.

Scholars can only speculate about the effect on the very young reader of having the *Little Wide-Awake* (or something similar) read aloud to them; we cannot know with certainty about the reading experience of any particular child – unless they happened to leave a written record which has survived. Children might not remember very much about Edward I, or have the chronology very straight; but they might well remember a king's ›trickery‹ or the height and bravery of a Scot.

After the nursery came the schoolroom. Here the history lessons offered to young children were presented largely in book form, though not necessarily in long stretches of continuous prose. Some of those books were dedicated histories, such as Henry Ince's *Outlines of English History* (first published in 1834 and still in print in the 1860s). However the great majority were compilations created by combining literary excerpts from well-known writers of the past, anecdotes about dramatic episodes from history, poems and verse, and so forth. The purpose of these »school readers« was primarily to impart the skills of basic literacy, but they also provided »a lexicon for the development of personal and collective identity« (Heathorn 2000: 9). Publishers and school authorities were adamant that admirable and heroic figures should be featured, and the more discreditable or arcane episodes in the nation's past ought to be downplayed. And they were impatient with the convention of terminating historical accounts somewhere around 1688 or 1714. Comparatively recent history was important to educators for reasons of citizenship, so it was felt that the later periods should not be delayed until the point in the curriculum when working-class children would have left school and missed the benefit of learning about such an upstanding figure as Prince Albert, for example (cf. Howsam 2009: 54-59).

Middle-class children who developed a taste for reading were not, however, limited to books. Commercial publishers had taken advantage of the cheaper paper, new printing technologies and removal of newspaper taxes to market periodicals for adolescents. In the 1850s it was Samuel O. Beeton, editor of the *Boy's Own Magazine*, who first focused on the market of male middle-class adolescents. Although Beeton did include some ›true‹ history, his monthly magazine was more oriented to fiction, some of it historical, to competitions and to a discourse of adventure and manliness. Later periodicals took the production of sensational narratives much further, creating anxiety on the part of evangelicals who set about providing an alternative to the secular and even violent messages embedded in the ›penny dreadfuls‹. The most successful of these was the *Boy's Own Paper* (edited by George Andrew Hutchison) published by the Religious Tract Society beginning in 1879; they followed up in 1880 with the *Girl's Own* (edited by Charles Peters). Such penny weekly magazines had very high production values and put a strong emphasis on entertainment, while still communicating the moral values of their backers.

The characteristics of these two papers are readily visible when their treatments of certain subjects are compared and contrasted along gender lines. The *Boy's Own*, for example, published a 12-part series in 1879 called »Boys of English History«. Anonymous from the perspective of readers, the author has been identified as Talbot Baines Reed, a frequent contributor who later wrote a book under the same title. Reed's subjects included Richard II, described as »the boy who quelled a tumult« ([Reed] 13: 205), the princes in the tower, and other standards. In a similar vein of celebrating masculine leadership, Albert E. Hooper's 1891 series on »Chivalry« might be expected as a model of gentlemanly conduct for boys. The *Girl's Own* could be equally stereotypical with respect to gender roles, as in Sarah Tytler's lengthy series on various Tudor women (Tytler 1890-92). Still, it is important not to oversimplify an analysis of gender stereotypes. For a couple of weeks in 1885 the *Boy's Own* had featured a two-part article by S.F.A. Caulfield on »stitchery«, which raised the question of whether it was a man or a woman who made the Bayeux tapestry (Caulfield 351: 6; 352: 31). A *Girl's Own* series published in 1887 on »The History of Home; or Domestic Ways since the Time of Henry VIII«, by Nanette Mason is not about domesticity in the household management sense. It is about what we would now call social or cultural history. Mason's article on the eighteenth century alone (Mason 403: 805) covered a broad range of cultural issues: marriage customs and child custody; costume; disease, medicine and prevention; tea-drinking, alcohol and abstention; astrology and fortune-telling; the lottery; provincial versus metropolitan customs; the music of Handel; swearing and scolding. The series is antiquarian in tone, very detailed, and presented without any moral or religious lesson.

The *Girl's Own* writers were quite capable of making deprecating remarks about the capacities of women as opposed to men. For example, the article on »How to Study History« was prefaced by a few comments about the intellectual weaknesses of the female sex:

»And these luminous conceptions of that which we are thinking or speaking of are very often just that which we least possess; will it sound a cruel cynicism to add ›we women especially‹? Nay, we mean no unkind reflection on our own sex, girls; there is no reason why the feminine intellect should not be whetted to a mental weapon as keen, as bright, and of as fine an edge and temper as that of the lords of creation; but it is a painful fact for all that, that logical clearness and systematic perspicacity are not *always* the characteristics of ladies' thinking and reasoning.« (»How to Study« 1882: 826)

Similarly, »The History of Home« included an observation about the damage done to women by Georgian wedding customs (»One of the great scandals of the time was the readiness with which unlicensed and clandestine marriages could be contracted.«) (Mason 403: 805). Such messages were hardly unambiguously feminist, but in their very ambiguity they demonstrate that, in historical narratives, the periodical press offered mixed messages about the gender roles to which their girl readers should aspire. Indeed it is possible that especially in history, the narratives of queens and their power – the Tudor queens in particular, with their power exercised for both ›evil papist‹ ends and the goodness of Queen Bess (who was also the martial Elizabeth) – might have been a place where girls found an opportunity to think about questions of gender and power. Although a great deal more content analysis of the texts of these children's periodicals would be necessary to investigate this possibility, preliminary research suggests that the teenaged girls and young women who read the *Girl's Own* were getting to know a lot about the past of their own country, and quite a bit about the lives of women and girls in their own history.

HISTORY FOR ADULT READERS

When the child reader of *Little Wide-Awake* and the *Girl's* or *Boy's Own* graduated to adult periodicals, which ones did they read? Beyond personal choice, the answer depends upon the titles most popular among their class and gender peers. A handful of popular and widely-distributed titles illustrates the range of articles about the past, about history, that appeared in their pages. *Chambers's Journal of Popular Literature, Science and Arts* was one of the first cheap general-interest weekly magazines published in Britain, beginning in 1832. From that early date, *Chambers's* aimed »to take advantage of the universal appetite for instruction which at present exists [and] to supply to that appetite food of the best kind« (qtd. in *DNCJ* 2009: 106). In the 1860s and 70s, for example, a succession of articles appeared, detailing the histories of wood-engraving, music, advertising and the Pitcairn Islanders. And the 1879 title »History Repeats Itself« was repeated – though with different text under it – in 1892. The history articles in *Chambers's Journal*, like those on other subjects, can be characterized as moralistic and fragmentary, and often focused on disjointed bits of antiquarian knowledge, mostly about objects or places. A magazine like *Chambers's* – or its rival the *Penny Magazine* – was aimed at the respectable members of the working class, though many readers were comfortably established in the middle-class ranks. Its readers were not, however, expected to have had the benefit of a great deal of education.

The great quarterly reviews were different. At a cost of 4 to 6 shillings, they were aimed at educated readers with broad intellectual interests and the leisure in which to exercise them. The quarterlies were »the prestigious, influential, mandarin periodical form of the early to mid-century« (Shattock 1989: vii). They rejoiced in 40-page essays rather than *Chambers's* brief paragraphs. It was in the Whig-affiliated *Edinburgh Review* that Thomas Babington Macaulay's essays on history first appeared, along with other serious journalism. The *Edinburgh*'s rivals, the *Quarterly Review* (Tory) and the *Westminster* (Benthamite-Radical) also published many discussions of history books, reviews which often became essays in their own right.[5] Another review publication, appearing monthly rather than quarterly, was the *Dublin Review,* aimed at a primary readership of English Roman Catholics. Published in London (not Dublin) from 1836, it cost 6 shillings. In 1863 a New Series of the *Dublin* began under the editorship of William George Ward. A scan of Proquest's *British Periodicals* online database reveals a remarkably large number of articles on history, almost all of them

---

5   Walter Bagehot spoke in 1855 of »the review-like essay and the essay-like review« and his characterization has recently been probed in terms of the generic quality of periodical journalism (Liddle 2009: 37).

reviews of histories. The range of works covered by the *Dublin*'s reviewers is also remarkable – everything from Ranke and Froude to school histories and an 1874 *Children's Bible History*. The readers of the *Dublin* could find in its pages relief from the relentlessly Protestant historiography to which they had been introduced in school, and which still circulated in books and periodicals throughout English culture. The *Dublin* reviewed all the Catholic historiography it could lay its hands on – for example every volume of John Lingard's *History of England* as it emerged from the press, and many reissues and epitomes as well.

An influential monthly periodical, the *Nineteenth Century*, sought to establish »an open forum for serious discussion« (*DNCJ* 2009: 456). Founded in 1877 by James Knowles, it has been characterized in terms of »engaged, energetic, dialogic, symposium-style discourse [which] allowed contributors to exchange opinions, and to disagree« in signed articles covering a wide range of topics (ibid.). From the perspective of its coverage of history, the *Nineteenth Century* is notable for the celebrity of its contributors. J.A. Froude's *Life and Times of Thomas Becket* appeared there in six parts in 1877 before being republished in book form. W.E.H. Lecky weighed in with remarks on William Gladstone's *History of the Evangelical Movement* in 1879, while Gladstone returned the compliment with respect to Lecky's *History of England in the Nineteenth Century* in 1887.

A weekly journal that found its way to the tables of the educated upper middle classes, both Protestant and Catholic, was *The Athenaeum*, which aimed to be »the resort of the distinguished philosophers, historians, orators and poets of our day« (qtd. in *DNCJ* 2009: 26). The *Athenaeum* had a number of eminent editors. In the 1870s, 80s and 90s, the editor was Norman MacColl. In addition to opening the pages of the journal to such progressive movements as Darwinism and Pre-Raphaelitism, and recruiting a number of women reviewers, MacColl also made room in his pages for reviews of accounts of the past (cf. ibid.: 26-28). The reviews are relatively laconic, but their collective and recurring presence in the pages of the influential *Athenaeum* demonstrates that some of the readers who had grown up with history continued to find it at their disposal in the periodical press.

This small sampling of the vast range of Victorian reviews, magazines and journals for adults reinforces what scholars have identified about the hybrid and heterogenous nature of periodicals. History was everywhere, and part of everything, cheek by jowl with fiction and journalism, opinion and prejudice. The seven periodicals discussed above, three for children and four others aimed at adult general readers of various class, religious and educational backgrounds, were part of the background to the journalistic world in which the young and ambitious professional historians of the 1870s and 1880s lived. When Mandell Creighton (bishop and professor) complained to his Cambridge colleague Oscar Browning that »existing reviews [would] only publish popular and sketchy articles« (qtd. in Howsam 2009: 59) on historical subjects, this is what he was objecting to. What Creighton yearned for was something like the *Historische Zeitschrift* coming out of Munich edited by Heinrich von Sybel from 1859, or the *Revue Historique* founded by Gabrielle Monod in France in 1876. Like those, but an *English* historical review.

The project was promoted by a circle of historian-friends made up of men like E.A. Freeman, his young protégé J.R. Green, Creighton himself, Frederick York Powell from Oxford and A.W. Ward from Manchester, with a few others. These men had been initiated by nursery and school histories, but later learned to scorn the habits of writers who glossed over the documented factual truth in search of a charming anecdote, or who engaged in blatant religious partiality. Nor did they want to linger too long over the role of history in training the minds of citizens and future leaders, even though they probably took that responsibility for granted. What they wanted was something rock-solid and razor-sharp, a scientific history that could take its place beside the new natural sciences that were reshaping Britain's university curricula. They knew that history, at Oxford for example, was regarded as »an easy school for rich men« (Freeman, qtd. in Southern 2004: 93) and they wanted to remake it as a rigorous discipline for serious professional academics. What they needed, they believed, was a journal, something like the reviews out of continental Europe whose contents they devoured every quarter. They had a potential ally in Alexander Macmillan, a publisher who loved history and who had nurtured many of these men's works in book form. Macmillan was doing well with *Nature*, a periodical dedicated to scientific knowledge. The historians envisioned one dedicated similarly, only to historical knowledge, but Macmillan explained patiently that there was not much of a market for it. For a few years J.R. Green discussed with Macmillan plans for a review that would have appealed to a broad general readership by dwelling on comparisons between past and contemporary events, offering a rich biographical component, and embracing a broad definition of history that incorporated both literature and science on an equal footing with politics and diplomacy. Those plans did not bear fruit.

Two contemporary periodicals, in particular, stood in the way of the *English Historical Review* imagined as a popular journal in the 1860s, and eventually brought to fruition as an academic one in 1886. Although history continued to flourish across the range of review journalism, the weekly *Saturday Review* and monthly *Academy* are worth examining more closely. Freeman, Green and other historians were themselves frequent contributors to the *Saturday Review of Politics, Literature, Science, and Art*, which had been founded in 1855. Although it was weekly like the *Athenaeum*, the *Saturday* was in some ways reinventing at mid-century the traditions of the older quarterlies, providing a forum for debate about the critical issues of the day. The articles were unsigned, so that the paper seemed to present a unified voice. That voice was robust and opinionated: hence the paper's nickname, »The Saturday Reviler« (cf. *DNCJ* 2009: 558). Not only did it despise Robert Browning and Algernon Swinburne, it turned thumbs down on James Anthony Froude, the historian of Tudor England who had found a wide audience with his deeply-researched yet highly readable works. The research happened not to match the historiographical culture that E.A. Freeman revered, and his mocking anonymous reviews of Froude in the *Saturday* were unkind as well as clever. If you could enjoy Freeman excoriating Froude in the *Saturday,* a reader or publisher might reasonably have thought, why should you need a dedicated historical review?

The *Saturday* is quite well-known among scholars of the Victorian periodical press, while few have looked at *The Academy: A Monthly Record of Literature, Learning, Science and Art*. It was founded in 1869 as direct competition to the *Athenaeum*. Articles were signed, and the tone was more scholarly. In fact the model was another German periodical, *Literarisches Centralblatt für Deutschland* (founded by philologist Friedrich K.T. Zarncke in Leipzig in 1850). The *Academy*'s first editor-proprietor was Charles Appleton, an Oxford don who had an eye for semi-scholarly publishing opportunities. He commissioned hundreds of reviews of history books, from a pool of contributors which included many familiar names from late-Victorian historiography. That pool was not limited, however, to the names of writers of whom Creighton, Freeman and Green would have approved. Readers of the *Academy* had access to a good supply of historical knowledge in the form of reviews by journalists who did not necessarily subscribe to the tenets of the new scientific history. Alexander Macmillan pointed out firmly to the history-as-a-science faction that any new periodical they thought of launching would have to compete with *The Academy* for readers (cf. Howsam 2009: 37).

CONCLUSION

Readers grew up with history, and so did writers. Portraits and photographs of historians like Freeman, Creighton and Froude present the viewer with stereotypical Victorian images, virtually always male and often bearded, usually mature if not elderly. It is difficult to imagine these men in their childhood and youth, and even harder to conjure up the girls and young women who were their sisters and schoolmates. But the nascent historians were, like every other boy and girl of their respective generations, encountering the past through the mediation of print. When they grew up to be professional historians, their counterparts did not. For most readers, history remained a part of ›general knowledge‹– a set of narratives they had encountered repeatedly in books and periodicals, half-remembered-half-forgotten, tangled up with Biblical lore and fictional tales, sometimes a matter of burning importance and other times of numbing boredom. When history turned up in their leisure-time reading, they could seize upon it, or turn the page and focus on something else. It was part of the background, part of the culture.

In the twenty-first century we speak of the mass media, more often than not referring to broadcast and digital media, rather than print. And we speak of ›public history‹ referring to either the ancient sites which are open to the public, or certain popular films and television broadcasts, characterized by high production values, whereby the narratives of the past are brought into competition with present-day ones. Contemporary values were, and are, embedded in historical narratives: Now we find them in TV productions like *The Tudors*, offering a sexualized narrative with anachronistically feisty women and a robustly post-confessional world-view; then readers found, in articles and reviews of history books, a reinforcement of their contemporary gender codes, religious beliefs and spiritual values. Conventional expressions of patriotism and national identity were reinforced just as strongly. The public history of Victorian Britain was to a large extent the periodical press. Its production standards were often high, as evidenced in the elaborate woodcuts favoured by the *Boy's Own* and *Girl's Own* magazines. Print culture was the medium for public history in the nineteenth century, and it began in the nursery, developed in adolescence and into adulthood. A perspective based on a reader's life cycle offers a useful way of thinking about the way in which ordinary people came to know about the past, through the medium of print in the periodical press.

WORKS CITED

Beetham, Margaret (1990): »Towards a Theory of the Periodical as a Publishing Genre«. In: Laurel Brake/Aled Jones/Lionel Madden (eds.), *Investigating Victorian Journalism*, London: Macmillan, 19-32.

Caulfield, S.F.A. (1885): »A Boy's Chapter on Stitchery«. *Boy's Own Paper* 351: 6; 352: 31.

DNCJ: Laurel Brake/Marysa DeMoor (eds.) (2009): *Dictionary of Nineteenth-Century Journalism*, London: British Library. Available online through ProQuest's *Nineteenth-Century Index* (http://c19index.chadwyck.com). Accessed 4 April 2011.

Heathorn, Stephen (2000): *For Home, Country, and Race: Constructing Gender, Class, and Englishness in the Elementary School, 1880-1914*, Toronto: University of Toronto Press.

»›History Repeats Itself‹« (1879): *Chambers's Journal* 794: 173-176.

»History Repeats Itself« (1892): *Chambers's Journal* 9.432: 225-226.

Hooper, Albert E. (1891): »Chivalry«. *Boy's Own Paper* 647: 570; 648: 586-587; 649: 605-606; 650: 622-623.

Houghton, Walter et al. (eds.) (1965-1988): *The Wellesley Index to Victorian Periodicals, 1824-1900*, 5 vols., Toronto: University of Toronto Press. Available online through ProQuest's *Nineteenth-Century Index* (http://c19index.chadwyck.com). Accessed 4 April 2011.

Howsam, Leslie (2004): »Academic Discipline or Literary Genre?: The Establishment of Boundaries in Historical Writing«. *Victorian Literature and Culture*, 525-545.

Howsam, Leslie (2009): *Past into Print: The Publishing of History in Britain 1850-1950*, London: British Library.

»How to Study History« (1882): *Girl's Own Paper* 143: 826.

Liddle, Dallas (2009): *The Dynamics of Genre: Journalism and the Practice of Literature in Mid-Victorian Britain*, Charlottesville/VA: University of Virginia Press.

Mason, Nanette (1887): »The History of Home or Domestic Ways since the Time of Henry VIII«. *Girl's Own Paper* 367: 228-230; 380: 442-444; 395: 678-680; 399: 738-740; 403: 805-807.

Mitchell, Rosemary (2000): *Picturing the Past: English History in Text and Image, 1830-1870*, Oxford: Clarendon Press.

North, John (ed.) (2003): *Waterloo Directory of English Newspapers & Periodicals*, 20 vols., Waterloo: North Waterloo Academic Press. Published online at (www.victorianperiodicals.com). Accessed 4 April 2011.

[Reed, Talbot Baines] (1879): »Boys of English History«. *Boy's Own Paper* 2: 30; 5: 67-68; 7: 99-100; 13: 205-206; 15: 238-239; 20: 309-310; 22: 347-348; 23: 355; 26: 405-406; 29: 463-464; 36: 570-571; 40: 43.

»Scraps of English History« (1877): *Little Wide-Awake* 25: 22-26; 26: 55-58; 27: 88-92; 28: 116-121; 29: 148-152; 30: 184-187; 31: 210-214; [32]; 33: 282-235; 34: 310-313; 35: 345-347; 36: 366-370; 37: 24-27. Note: Number 32 is missing in the Nineteenth Century Periodicals (Gale Cengage) database. Numbers 25-36 run monthly January-December 1877; Number 37 is dated January 1878.

Shattock, Joanne (1989): *Politics and Reviewers: The Edinburgh and the Quarterly in the Early Victorian Age*, Leicester: Leicester University Press.

Soffer, Reba (1994): *Discipline and Power: The University, History and the Making of an English Elite, 1870-1930*, Stanford: Stanford University Press.

Southern, R. W. (2004): *History and Historians: Selected Papers of R.W. Southern*, ed. by R.J. Bartlett, Malden/MA: Blackwell Publishing.

Tytler, Sarah (1890): »Tudor Queens and Princesses«. *Girl's Own Paper* 526: 270-271; 529: 308-309; 531: 340-342; 539: 467-470; 544: 552-557; 548: 612-616; 553: 694-695; 556: 746-750; 558: 776-780; 560: 808-815; 577: 250-251.

Tytler, Sarah (1891): »Mary Tudor«. *Girl's Own Paper* 583: 340-342; 585: 376-379; 590: 457-459; 591: 475-476.

Tytler, Sarah (1891-2): »Elizabeth Tudor«. *Girl's Own Paper* 595: 542-543; 597: 562-565; 604: 684-686; 605: 701-702; 640: 420-422; 643: 467-471; 645: 499-501.
Tytler, Sarah (1892): »Queen Elizabeth«. *Girl's Own Paper* 654: 641-645; 659: 721-724; 663: 794-796.

Nineteenth-Century Magazines and Historical Cultures in Britain and Germany

Exploratory Notes on a Comparative Approach

BARBARA KORTE AND SYLVIA PALETSCHEK

THE MAGAZINE IN NINETEENTH-CENTURY HISTORICAL CULTURE(S) – BRITAIN AND GERMANY

The rise of periodical literature is a hallmark of mid-nineteenth-century media culture. As has been shown before, the period's revolution on the print market was the result of advanced technologies coupled with increased literacy throughout the population. Since around 1850, the number of newspapers and magazines increased continually, and magazines soon came to serve all major and many minor societal interests, groups and institutions – from parties to confessions, and from landmark reforms to such special concerns as temperance or spiritualism. Britain was in the van of this development, with a proliferation and diversification of publications at first unmatched by countries on the Continent.[1] However, with a slight delay, the output in Germany was also significant as the number of German mass-market periodicals grew continually and reached a high point in the years between 1850 and 1880 (cf. Stöber 2005: 266-269).

---

1 Cf. Altick's pioneering study (1998 [1957]) and later ones such as Vann/VanArsdel (1994).

It is unsurprising that the booming magazine market converged with an-other hallmark of nineteenth-century culture: its unprecedented, widespread interest in history and the orientation it could provide for societies challenged by accelerated industrialisation and urbanisation, revolutions in transport and communication, or the advance of secularisation.[2] While other factors of nineteenth-century historical culture(s) have already been looked into, the presentation of history in magazines for a general audience is still widely unconsidered.[3] Such magazines had a strong interest in present-day topics because they were of immediate concern for the intended readerships and were an incentive for subscribers and buyers. But they also regularly included articles with historical content and were thus an important means for creating and disseminating knowledge and opinions about the past. Furthermore, they observed and advertised other facets of historical culture: Even popular magazines reviewed (popular) history books and biographies, directed their readers to exhibitions, panoramic shows and lectures about past worlds, pointed out historical sights in cities, the country and abroad, and depicted for their readers the opening of monuments and historical festivals. Magazines are thus a rich source for the study of nineteenth-century historical consciousness, and they suggest themselves as objects for a comparison of national historical cultures.[4]

---

2   Cf. such influential studies as Bann (1984), Mitchell (2000) and Melman (2006). Billie Melman defines (English) historical culture as »the productions of segments of the past, or rather pasts, the multiplicity of their representations, and the myriad ways in which the English – as individuals and in groups – looked at this past (sometimes in the most literal sense of ›looking‹) and made use of it, or did not, both in a social and material world and in their imaginary« (Melman 2006: 4).

3   The research group from which this book developed has therefore embarked on a study of history in German and British family magazines. The respective projects are conducted by the authors of the present contribution as well as Nina Reusch and Doris Lechner, whom we would like to thank for their support and helpful comments. Thanks are also due to Christiane Hadamitzky for assembling material from the British periodicals.

4   For a discussion of comparative approaches to history cf., among others, Haupt/ Kocka (1996) and Kaelble/Schriewer (2003). The development of history as an academic discipline has been discussed in national comparison by Conrad

Rewarding as they may potentially be for this purpose, however, their comparison also raises a number of practical and conceptual problems.

It is the aim of this contribution to sketch some of the opportunities and difficulties which a comparative look at magazines from different national contexts and cultures entails. An initial and substantial problem is caused by the enormous diversity of publications even within a single context and especially between nations. In both Britain and Germany magazines were published by institutions and editors with different ideological outlooks and interests, who tailored their publications to the needs and interests of various sectors of their countries' readerships, that is, people of different genders, age groups, classes, regional and religious backgrounds and, again, ideological sympathies. Not only was there an overwhelming proliferation of magazines, but each publication had its specific agenda. One also has to consider that the British and German print markets were embedded in different national historical cultures with specific traditions and lines of development. This diversity, between nations and also within nations, is an asset for the study of historical cultures in so far as it indicates precisely how multi-faceted such cultures were and still are. But it also makes it practically impossible to study *the* relationship between magazines and history even for a single national culture. The only feasible approach to this question seems to be through case studies – also where a comparison across national cultures is attempted.

Our exploratory discussion therefore studies two such cases in comparison: a German magazine, *Die Gartenlaube* (1853-1944), and the British *Household Words* (1850-59), which was continued in *All the Year Round*.[5] Both English magazines were edited by Charles Dickens, the latter until Dickens's death in 1870.[6] Our examination will refer to the years from

---

(2002); there are also comparative investigations of certain aspects of commemorative culture, such as monuments (cf. Tacke 1995). Studies with a comparative approach to popular history are scarce to date, but cf. Berger/Lorenz/Melman (2012).

5   We have conducted preliminary explorations of these magazines elsewhere (cf. Paletschek 2011, which also includes comments on issues of the *Gartenlaube* after 1870, and Korte 2012).

6   It was continued by Dickens's son and others, but the most notable years of the magazine were those of Dickens's editorship.

1853 to 1870, during which the appearance of the *Gartenlaube* and *Household Words/All the Year Round* overlapped. The magazines in question were among the most popular reading matter of their day. They were addressed at a family audience, and regularly featured pieces with a historical focus.[7] For the purpose of our discussion we count as ›historical‹ only factual pieces (of at least a page length) dealing *centrally* with periods, events and historical characters of the past, from classical antiquity[8] onwards. There is a floating gap between what is called contemporary history and the present, and it is impossible to draw a sharp borderline. We therefore decided to adopt the judgement of the magazines' contemporary readers and counted what they labelled as ›historical‹ in the near past, or what they commemorated as ›history‹ on the return of anniversaries – even where the respective events had only happened five years previously. Our criteria exclude historically themed fiction[9] and poetry,[10] as well as the great number

---

7 Depending on what pieces are counted as related to ›history‹, the percentage for the three magazines considered here ranges between roughly 10 and 20 per cent per issue.

8 We do not consider articles concerned with archaeology and prehistory, which also, of course, shaped contemporary readers' images of the past. They feature regularly in the two English magazines, since Britain was a culture in which amateur archaeology (or antiquarianism) and fossil-hunting were popular pursuits and in which the results of professional archaeology (at home, in Egypt and Mesopotamia) as well as scholarly discussions about the age of the world and issues of human evolution were widely disseminated. *Household Words*, for instance, included an article on »Old Bones« (24 September 1853), and *All the Year Round* featured articles such as »England, Long and Long Ago« (7 April 1860), »Opening a Barrow« (21 July 1860), »How Old Are We?« (7 March 1863), »Latest News from the Dead« (11 July 1863, on ancient buried cities) and »Before the Deluge« (13 January 1866). In the *Gartenlaube*, by contrast, archaeology and prehistory play no role during the 1850s and 60s; it appears that the topic was only taken up with Heinrich Schliemann's great excavations since 1870. On the reception of Schliemann in the German press also cf. Samida (2009).

9 *All the Year Round* serialised Dickens's *A Tale of Two Cities*, a novel set in London and Paris during the time of the French Revolution. The *Gartenlaube* featured many historical novellas, such as »Leyer und Schwert: Historische

of factual articles that refer to history in passing but which also, of course, react and contribute to the period's historical consciousness.[11] In the pages to come, we will first profile the respective magazines' take on history, and then attempt to draw some preliminary conclusions as to the possibility of comparing them.

DIE GARTENLAUBE

Founded in 1853 by the former 1848 revolutionary Ernst Keil in Leipzig, the *Gartenlaube* was both the most successful and most popular German family magazine in the second half of the nineteenth century. It has been identified as the first periodical mass publication in Germany (cf. Belgum 1998: 187). As one of its outstanding hallmarks, the weekly featured numerous elaborate illustrations. Based on a liberal political programme and endowed with the impetus of enlightened ideas and education, the magazine strove for the implementation of the nation state and the individual's civil rights. The *Gartenlaube* popularised the German nation and thus contributed to the so-called *innere Nationsbildung* (internal nation-building) as well as to the emergence of a nation-based communicative space (cf. Koch 2003; Zaumseil 2007). Its primary goal was »to entertain and to teach in an entertaining way«, and this included the realm of history. The address to readers (»An unsere Freunde und Leser«) in the *Gartenlaube*'s first issue in 1853 promised that, »through genuine, well-written narratives, we want to introduce you to the history of the human heart and of peoples, to the strug-

---

Novelle« (Lyre and Sword: Historical Novella) by Max Ring (1858) and »Die Locke der Charlotte Corday« (The Lock of Charlotte Corday, 1865).

10 On poetry as a medium of popular history also cf. Stefanie Lethbridge's contribution to this book.

11 Travelogues and travel guides, for instance, often include a significant amount of information on the history of the countries or places they depict. A good example is *All the Year Round*'s series »As the Crow Flies« (beginning in the issue of 12 December 1868), whose ›flight‹ across England mentions many historical sites and monuments.

gles of human passions and of past times« (1853: 1).[12] About half of the contributions in the *Gartenlaube* were fiction, while the other half covered what we now call factual issues: natural history and the natural sciences, medicine, economic issues, travel, mixed news – and history. Indeed, history provided the largest category among the factual topics (between 10 to 20 per cent). It was most frequently presented through the biographies of historical figures, while more general political and cultural contributions and articles on cultural history came second.

Recent historical work on the *Gartenlaube* stresses its significant contribution to nation building, its liberal potential (which has been undervalued in previous research) and its significance in negotiating a modern identity by coping with insecurity and conflicts experienced in the process of modernisation (cf. Belgum 1998: 188). It was particularly the *Gartenlaube*'s historical contributions that served the shaping of a national and modern identity and provided suspenseful entertainment and instructive enlightenment. What, then, were the historical issues and periods covered by this periodical, and how were they depicted? The presentation of history in the *Gartenlaube* has not been systematically analysed to date, and the following observations only result from a first cursory analysis and thus need to be substantiated by further investigations.

Most strikingly, the majority of the *Gartenlaube*'s historically orientated contributions were devoted to the history of the preceding century, i.e. to recent and contemporary history.[13] Accordingly, one column in the annual index of contents is identified as »Beschreibende und geschichtliche Aufsätze/Zeitgeschichtliches« (descriptive and historical articles/matters of contemporary history). Articles under this rubric related predominantly to

---

12 Since the *Gartenlaube*, in contrast to *Household Words* and *All the Year Round*, has not been digitised to date, all page references for this magazine refer to the published volumes rather than issues. Citations from the *Gartenlaube* in English were translated by Sylvia Paletschek. The Dickens magazines are cited from the issues available in the *British Periodicals* online database (http://british periodicals.chadwyck.co.uk/home.do).

13 This assessment is based on the evaluation of the *Gartenlaube*'s »Inhaltsanalytische Bibliographie« for the years 1853 to 1880 (based on Estermann 1995) and of the *Vollständiges Generalregister der Gartenlaube 1853-1902* (1903, reprinted 1978).

historical facts and events pertaining to what Jan Assmann has termed »communicative memory« (J. Assmann 1995: 125-133). It comprises the last three generations and a time span of about 80 to 100 years, is marked by informal structures and oral communication, and overlaps significantly with familial memory. As part of the culture of remembrance, communicative memory is of major importance for identity formation, with regard to both individuals and social groups. This also implies its significance in the formation of nations and political movements.

The *Gartenlaube*'s presentation of history during our period of investigation, the 1850s and 1860s, had a clear focus on the Napoleonic Wars, especially the so-called *Befreiungskriege* (Wars of Liberation against Napoleon) in 1813-14, and the Revolution of 1848-49.[14] These historical events had an important function for internal nation-building, not least because they were warlike occurrences in which family history, the history of the nation and world history converged. Moreover, the war events were excellently suited to personalising, dramatising and emotionalising the historical depictions, i.e. aesthetic elements that have been associated with popular representation up until today. Readers' individual access to these historical events was facilitated both through family members' involvement in them and via identification with well-known heroes and heroines such as the stubborn officer Schill and his *franctireurs*, or the young Eleonore Prochaska,[15] who were model achievers in »Germany's most arduous years«[16] between 1809 and 1814, and/or had an unusual, adventurous life story. By recollecting these events and characters, the *Gartenlaube* also established a dialogue with its readership, which it actively strove to involve.

Despite the *Gartenlaube*'s clear focus on national contemporary history, we must not overlook its policy of depicting national events in their concrete regional specificity. The individual German states and regions provided another self-evident issue which the *Gartenlaube* frequently ad-

---

14 From the 1870s and 1880s onwards, the Franco-Prussian War of 1870-71 was a central topic.

15 Cf., for example, the article »Ein deutsches Heldenmädchen« (A German Girl-Heroine, 1863: 596-600).

16 Cf. also the article series »Aus den Zeiten der schweren Noth« (From the Times of Arduous Adversity, 1863: nos. 3, 8, 9).

dressed. What recent research now refers to as the »federal nation«[17] also crops up in the *Gartenlaube*'s historical contributions: The concept of the nation was made acceptable and comprehensible by giving it a regional slant, and by synthesising a broader and a narrower sense of the nation, an *engeres und weiteres Vaterland*, as it was termed in contemporary parlance. The striking number of articles detailing various aspects of the lives of the poet-heroes Schiller and Goethe, often supported by illustrations, played an important role in the creation of a national sense of identity. Such articles contributed to the manifestation of a kind of national pride regarding the achievements of the German cultural nation.[18]

Simultaneously, it should be noted that the *Gartenlaube* also directed the attention of its readers to historical events outside the German territories, particularly to the national histories of other European states (with an emphasis on France, Austria, Britain and Russia, but also in historical articles about Belgium, Spain, Italy, Serbia or Greece). However, while contemporary history was clearly disposed towards national interests, it was by no means narrowly constricted to national events. The *Gartenlaube* practiced a surprisingly broad, European and almost international access to history. Non-European history was preferably presented as cultural history, and engagement with US-American, Chinese, Arabic or African history was often related to overseas German minorities. Depictions of non-German and extra-European territories, especially in the context of cultural-historical contributions, nurtured the contemporary longing for the exotic and the fabulous, even though, from the 1880s onwards, they also revealed the transnational entwinements of the late *Kaiserreich*.

---

17 Cf. Langewiesche (2000: 55-79) and Langewiesche/Schmidt (2000).

18 Cf. »Goethe, den Schädel Schillers suchend« (Goethe Searching for Schiller's Skull, 1859: 197); »Goethe, beide Humboldt und Schiller in Jena« (Goethe, the Humboldts and Schiller in Jena, 1860: 229); »Goethe im Giebelzimmer des Elternhauses« (Goethe in His Parents' Attic, 1867: 85); »Schiller liest seinen Kameraden die Räuber vor« (Schiller Reading *the Robbers* to His Comrades, 1864: 629); »Schiller's Triumph in Leipzig« (1859: 665); »Schiller's Eltern« (Schiller's Parents, 1855: 511; 1859: 672); »Schiller und Goethe im Leng[e]feld'schen Garten in Rudolstadt« (Schiller and Goethe in the Lengefelds' Garden in Rudolstadt, 1865: 181).

It is striking that there is a scarcity of articles on ancient and medieval history in the *Gartenlaube*. This is, arguably, owed to the fact that ancient history was less suited to supporting the formation of a national identity in the second half of the nineteenth century. Another reason may have been that the significant portion of petit bourgeois readers among the magazine's clientele did not possess any prior knowledge of ancient history – in contrast to the bourgeois contingent of readers who had enjoyed a higher education and were acquainted with the classics. An exception, however, would have been such events and personalities of antiquity which could be related to Germanic history (cf. Belgum 1998: 172-176). Contributions dedicated to Hermann/Arminius, chief of the Cherusci who defeated the Romans in the Teutoburg Forest in 9 AD, are a case in point. The mythification and monumentalisation of such figures, however, was usually not accomplished through the written text, but through large and lavishly designed illustrations that were only marginally commented. The most striking characteristic of this »mythic monumentalism« (ibid.: 174) was its decontextualised nature: The illustrations picked up national stereotypes and popularised a mythical national past.

Topics of medieval history had a somewhat stronger presence in the *Gartenlaube*, even though it was again the scarcely contextualised, monumental illustrations of ›great individuals‹ that caught the eye.[19] Furthermore, the magazine also featured more unspecific scenes taken from cultural history which can be conceived as a tribute to an apparently ›simpler‹, romantic era of national life (cf. ibid.: 172). Concerning the history of early-modern times, great attention was devoted to the reformation and singular heroic figures such as Luther or Frederick the Great.[20]

19　Cf. »Otto von Wittelsbach und die päpstlichen Legaten« (Otto von Wittelsbach and the Papal Legates, 1860: 421); »Konradin's Abschied von seinen Lieben in Hohenschwangau« (Konradin Farewells His Loved Ones in Hohenschwangau, 1868: 37).

20　Cf. »Luther's Ankunft auf der Wartburg« (Luther's Arrival at Wartburg Castle, 1875: 221); »Luther am Sarge seines Töchterleins» (Luther by his Daughter's Coffin, 1860: 12); »Friedrich der Große auf dem Manöver bei Spandau« (Frederick the Great at Maneuvers near Spandau, 1861: 389); »Friedrich's des Großen Versöhnung mit seinem Vater« (Frederick the Great's Reconciliation with His Father, 1855: 567).

In accordance with an enlightened tradition, the usefulness of the historical contributions was very much in the foreground in the *Gartenlaube*. ›Usefulness‹ included the promotion of national identity and the shaping of a modern, bourgeois mentality, but also a critical assessment of politics and society and – last but not least – entertainment value. History was a means for criticising the existing political and social status quo and for assessing one's own position in the present. This is particularly apparent in the contributions on cultural history, for which unresolved contemporary problems and orientation needs often provided the point of departure. Thus, the first episode of the eight-part series »Culturgeschichtliche Bilder« (Images of Cultural History) by Karl Biedermann, which started in 1854,[21] states that the observation of cultural history is unlikely to produce the kind of immediate usefulness provided by the natural sciences. Yet, the author argues, even though it does not provide direct instruction for action, the observation of cultural history is equally instructive in many respects. According to Biedermann, the engagement with historical progress in commerce, science, art and technology reveals »the potential of the human mind [...] and, thus, incites us to a suitable use, to the diligent development of our manifold mental dispositions and abilities« (1854: 377). At the same time, cultural history is said to teach »modesty by pointing out how earlier generations also conceived of themselves as having arrived at a high level of perfection which, in part, was actually true, although they were outdistanced by far by their offspring« (ibid.). Thus, the author tells his readers that they must assume their collective fate to be a similar one in the future. Cultural history is characterised as a preserver from despair when, in the present, much does not appear as one would like to have it, since it teaches the lesson that in former, even in not too distant times, circumstances were far more unsatisfying and that much has improved since. This legitimates the hope that circumstances will become even better and more satisfactory in the future. However, cultural history is also seen to correct erroneous assessments by historical comparison. The engagement with history indirectly

---

21 The series started with an article on »Theure Zeiten« (Expensive Times, 1854: 377-380). A footnote referred to Biedermann's recently published book *Deutschlands politische, materielle und sociale Zustände im 18. Jahrhundert* (Germany's Political, Material and Social Situation in the 18th Century, 1854, reprinted in 1969 as *Deutschland im 18. Jahrhundert*).

stimulates new ideas and constitutes faith in progress, while at the same time it teaches humility and qualifies current problems or puts them into perspective.

For the most part, the contributions on cultural history in the *Gartenlaube* take their start from contemporary problems, as in the article on »Theure Zeiten« in Biedermann's series, which addresses the »now dominant issue of price increase« and introduces the notion that in the past, bread used to be cheaper and the middle classes used to be better off (ibid.: 378).[22] However, the article then proceeds to criticise false generalisations and idealisations of the past and, instead, stresses the accomplished progress; it thus demonstrates how historical reflection can produce a qualified view of the past. This example illustrates the function of popular historical depictions to provide orientation with regard to everyday problems and current social issues, looking at them from a different perspective.

It is the cultural- and social-historical contributions in particular which take up issues of everyday history – a history frequently coded as female even in our time and emphasising household, beauty, consumption, fashion, lifestyle and related issues.[23] All in all, the *Gartenlaube* covers a spectrum of issues of everyday life that is both broad and colourful. Topics such as the history of beer, male hair or beard styles and practices of shaving[24] indicate that the magazine also nurtured the cultural-historical interests of a male readership and that the politics of gendering issues – e.g. political

---

22 A similar approach is chosen for the next article in Biedermann's series, which was devoted to the supposedly increasing phenomenon of begging and a greater altruism in the past. It concludes: »And yet in general nothing is more inaccurate than degrading the present and praising a former, supposedly better time.« (1854: 446)

23 On cultural history in the *Gartenlaube* also cf. the titles listed in Estermann (1995: 277-288), such as »Damentoilette sonst und jetzt« (Ladies' Toilet Then and Now, 1855: 590) and »Urbilder unserer Frauenmode« (Origins of Our Ladies' Fashion, 1867: 726-727).

24 Cf., among other examples: »Alles hat seine Wissenschaft: Alte und neue Art das Rasiermesser abzuziehen« (Everything Has Its Science: Old and New Ways of Handling the Shaving Knife, 1864: 686-687); »Die Geschichte des Bieres« (The History of Beer, 1855: 604-605); »Leute bei der Spritze: Alte und neue Feuerwehr« (People at the Hose: Old and New Fire Brigades«, 1864: 732-734).

history as ›male‹ and cultural history as ›female‹ – made its input felt but was also in part disrupted. This also applies to incidents in which political and national history are depicted with a focus on female protagonists – women rulers, freedom fighters, and, of course, the mother who sacrifices herself for the nation. This ensured the appeal to, and therefore the inclusion of, a female readership.[25]

Anniversaries and jubilees functioned as major points of reference for the *Gartenlaube*'s popular depictions of history. Similar to present-day practice, articles dedicated to such events tended to be published some time in advance of the actual jubilee. Thus media coverage was designed to draw the national audience's attention to the coming event and to provide an informed interpretive framework for its reception. This kind of celebratory practice of anniversaries ensured their periodic recurrence, their consolidation and their transmission through established social practice.

Recent research considers anniversaries or jubilees as »memorials in time« (A. Assmann 2005: 313). As representatives of periodic time, anniversaries are situated between linear historical time and the kind of cyclical time attached to myth and nature which symbolises the eternal return of the same. According to Aleida Assmann, the increasing acceleration of linear time is inextricably related to a growing significance of periodic time with its firmly recurring points of reference. Anniversaries allow for periodic remembrance, they are »memory activists« (Gluck 2007), i.e. authorities for activating collective memory. Depending on temporal circumstances, such activations either facilitate new interpretations of the actual historical event or make for its further consolidation as myth. Anniversaries stabilise recollection through repetition, offer a formation of meaning and a future-directed promise of action.

---

25 There are many articles on famous women, including rulers, noblewomen, female poets and artists, or freedom fighters. Cf. »Louise Dorothee, Herzogin von Gotha und Franziska Buchwald: Eine seltene Frauenfreundschaft«, by Ludwig Storch (A Rare Friendship Among Women, 1858: 585); »›Seine Ehre gebrochen!‹ Eine Erinnerung an Johanna Kinkel« (›His Honour Broken!‹ A Memory of Johanna Kinkel, 1860: 313); »Angelika Kaufmann [sic]: Die Malerin der Grazien«, by Max Ring (Angelika Kaufmann: The Painter of the Graces, 1865: 238).

Returning to the *Gartenlaube*, anniversaries, regardless of their particular rhythm or periodisation, were consistently and almost excessively used for presenting historical issues. For example, the volume for the year 1863 offered a broad retrospection to the *Befreiungskrieg* (1813-14), which had taken place fifty years earlier, but also featured several articles on the occasion of the fifteenth anniversary of the 1848 Revolution.[26] Anniversaries were covered by comprehensive and short articles as well as full-page, elaborate illustrations. Equally popular were historical articles composed as multipart series which covered a jubilee topic. A good example is the series »Aus den Zeiten der schweren Noth« (»From the Times of Arduous Adversity«) which was published over several years, depicting the heroic deeds of well-known as well as unknown figures of the Napoleonic Wars. The series featured the storming of the *Crimmaische Thor* in Leipzig, but also the fates of a shepherd, a second lieutenant, a book-seller and a peasant of that time.[27]

Also en vogue was the connection of an anniversary with a topical current event via historical analogy. Thus, an article published in 1864 criticised the contemporary political situation by comparing the lack of rights found in an assembly of delegates who convened in Frankfurt on 21 December with the far-reaching authorisation of the Parliament which had met in the Frankfurt Paulskirche fifteen years earlier (1864: 93-96). The recourse to contemporary history was, thus, used to critically hold up a mirror to the present political situation. However, such recourse could also celebrate past successes in an affirmative way and, by doing so, consolidate the status quo. The *Gartenlaube* reported on public commemorations occasioned by such anniversaries, such as the construction of a memorial or the

---

26 Cf. the series »Aus den Zeiten schwerer Not« (From the Times of Arduous Adversity, 1863: nos. 3, 8, 9), articles dedicated to the recollection of the Battle of Leipzig (1863: 672; 688) or the articles on Eleonore Prochaska (1863: 596-600). The revolutionary period of 1848-49 was the subject of articles on »Kinkels Befreiung« (Kinkel's Liberation, 1863: 194) and Gustav Struve (1863: 208) and a relatively long article by Moritz Hartmann entitled »Die letzten Tage des deutschen Parlaments« (The Last Days of the German Parliament, 1863: 40-44).

27 On the storming cf. the *Gartenlaube* (1862: 649-654); on the fates of the various characters cf. the volume for 1861 (500-504).

inauguration of a monument, a wreath-laying ceremony or a commemorative speech.[28] The meaning of the event in question was, thus, consolidated via the interconnection of different media, also when popular historical bestsellers (such as the works of Wilhelm Zimmermann or Johannes Scherr) were reviewed in the *Gartenlaube*.[29]

HOUSEHOLD WORDS AND ALL THE YEAR ROUND

Household Words was a weekly publication sold at two pennies per issue; an issue normally had 24 pages printed in double columns, without illustrations, and featured six to seven full-length pieces, whose writers were normally anonymous.[30] Its price made the individual issue affordable to families with a lower income, since Dickens had a cross-class audience in mind which, apart from the middle classes, also included a working-class readership. *Household Words* sold well with roughly 40,000 copies per week (cf. Lohrli 1973: 23), and its profit certainly benefited from Dickens's insistence that pieces of a predominantly informative nature should never be boring and dry: »Dickens's policy in the handling of non-fiction prose was that such material be treated in some distinctive manner – not in literal, matter-of-fact, ›encyclopaedical‹ fashion. Factual, informative, instructional, didactic material was to be presented in a ›fanciful‹, ›imaginative‹, ›picturesque‹, ›quaint‹ way.« (Lohrli 1973: 9) *Household Words'* miscellany of instruction and entertainment was, quite typically of Dickens, strongly committed to social reform and often addressed urgent social issues of the time, especially the plight of the urban poor and the situation of labourers. The Preliminary Word to the first issue (30 March 1850) expressed Dickens's hope that the social evils exposed in the magazine's

---

28 Cf. the reference to the commemorations on the occasion of the fiftieth anniversary of the Battle of Leipzig which took place from 16 to 20 October 1863 (1863: 596).

29 Cf. several enthusiastic reviews and articles on Zimmermann's *Allgemeine Geschichte des großen Bauernkrieges* (1841-1843, General History of the Great Peasant War), such as »Ein Geschichtsschreiber der Wahrheit« (A Historian of the Truth, 1869: 292-294).

30 For a description and the history of *Household Words* cf. Lohrli (1973).

pages should not »render any of us [...] less faithful in the progress of mankind, less thankful for the privilege of living in this summer-dawn of time«. While *Household Words'* focus was thus strongly on the present and the future to which it might lead, Dickens's instinct for popular interests explains why history was also explicitly announced as part of the magazine's programme: »Our Household Words will not be echoes of the present time alone, but of the past too.«

Dickens conducted *All the Year Round* with a different publisher but on the same principles and as successfully as *Household Words.* Both magazines' take on history was generously eclectic; they did not have an overall historical programme or even politics apart from the fact that their editor believed that the present, its obvious social flaws notwithstanding, was preferable to the past. Despite this belief, however, both magazines offered their readers not only articles on diverse historical events and personages; they also frequently alerted them to the various means and media through which they might explore history themselves. They offered accounts of historical city walks, especially of London,[31] and descriptions of what one could see in museums, exhibitions and national monuments.[32] In some instances, topography and biography were combined, for instance when articles on London sights provided readers with precise directions as to where historical people once lived.[33] They also repeatedly mentioned that histor-

---

31 Cf., among others, »Left Behind« (*HW*, 22 July 1854), »My London Ghosts« (*HW*, 11 April 1857), »The Sign of Five Centuries« (*AYR*, 26 August 1865).

32 Apart from the British Museum and the Paris Louvre, wax museums are repeatedly mentioned: »History in Wax« (*HW*, 18 February 1854), »Our Eye-Witness in Great Company« (*AYR*, 7 January 1860, referring to Mme Tussaud's); the sights of »Westminster Abbey« were depicted in *AYR* (25 April 1868).

33 Cf. a series of articles on Kensington in *Household Words* – »Kensington« (3 September 1853), »Kensington Church« (19 November 1853) and »Kensington Worthies« (3 December 1853). Such connections of biography and topography are also found in the *Gartenlaube*. Cf., among others, an article on »Turnvater Jahn's Haus in Freiburg« (Turnvater Jahn's House in Freiburg, i.e. today's Freyburg on Unstrut in Saxony, 1860: 251-252); »Die Luisenburg bei Wunsiedel: Erinnerungen an die Königin Luise von Preußen« by Ludwig Storch (Luisenburg near Wunsiedel: Memories of Queen Louise of Prussia, 1860: 442); »Die Judengasse in Frankfurt und die Familie Rothschild« (Jew's Alley in

ical knowledge and entertainment might be derived from old books,[34] news-papers[35] – and magazines, which are, in the following extract, explicitly noted for the vivid insights they permit into the everyday lifeworlds of past times and the connection they therefore provide between history and the present:

»There is something, we think, strangely interesting in those old records which bring us into *close and vital connexion* with our predecessors *in their daily life*. To be informed of the great events of any era, however distant, seems to be a matter of course: but to be able to rescue the *trivialities* of an hour from utter extinction; to live with our ancestors whom we never knew, and to see them, not on the public stage of history, but *in their private and familiar ways*; to be able to fix and perpetuate what might have seemed as evanescent as a breath, as quickly-fading as the hues of sunset; – this is the *true association of our own humanities with those of perished generations*. We see the sparkle of eyes, and hear the sound of voices, that had faded into the great Eternity before ourselves were born. Surely these things have their interest. They are the electric telegraphs of Time, which *link the living and the dead in a common brotherhood*.« [emphases added][36]

Frankfurt and the Rothschild Family, 1865: 564). Verbal and visual depictions of famous people's graves were a favourite subject matter, such as »Die Asche Napoleons und deren Grabmal in Paris« (Napoleon's Ashes and Tomb in Paris, 1855: 519) or »Humboldt's Ruhestätte« (Humboldt's Final Resting Place, 1859: 364-365).

34 Cf. »A Marvellous Journey with the Old Geographer« (*HW*, 22 April 1854), which praises a work by Peter Heylyn, »clerk, of the reigns of Charles the First and Second«; »London in Books« (*AYR*, 14 October 1865); or a description of »Ancient Guides to Service« found in a publication of the Early English Text Society, which is identified as »a busy printing-club which is laying down, with good metal, a broad and easy highway of communication between us and our forefathers« (*AYR*, 29 February 1868).

35 »Old Domestic Intelligence« (*HW*, 9 September 1854).

36 »Ghostly Pantomimes« (*HW*, 24 December 1853). The value of magazines for later generations is also acknowledged in an article about the pleasure of perusing a magazine from the year 1798: »So I lay by my Mag. for the present. Years hence perhaps our grandchildren may take up some exploded magazine for this present year; and, as they turn it cursorily over, wonder how such things, therein

Some of the historical pieces in Dickens's magazines constitute historiography in a more narrow sense. For the years investigated one can name the final instalments of Dickens's own *Child's History of England* in *Household Words*, which stands in the tradition of earlier nineteenth-century history books for young readers[37] and narrates the history of the nation from ancient times to the present. Dickens used his overview specifically »to provide a variety of antidotes to nostalgic idealization of the past« (Jann 1978: 200), frequently exposing the cruelty of English monarchs in the past, such as Henry VIII in the issues of 8 January and 12 February 1853. Surveys are also sometimes given for aspects of history from other parts of the world, and often they held a special interest for the Victorian English. Accounts of the persecution of the Huguenots in France, for instance, related the history of a migrant group with significant impact on the English economy;[38] Haiti bore a relation to Britain's own history of slavery (and its abolition) and was a neighbour to English possessions in the Caribbean;[39] the history of the Aztecs was relevant as an aspect of the wider European project of colonisation.[40] As in the *Gartenlaube*, however, a far greater amount of historical pieces in Dickens's magazines consists of biographies, more informal anecdotes and information on cultural history – material which was likely to engage the reader's interest through personalisation, emotionalisation and links to his or her own, present-day lifeworld. Not rarely, the history presented was curious and imaginative – and thus particularly entertaining – in accordance with Dickens's general agenda for factual pieces. A case in point is a history of famous storms and their consequences.[41] Another is *All the Year Round*'s series »Old Stories Retold«, which focused on elements of a sensational and scandalous history that

---

recorded, could ever have been« (»An Exploded Magazine«. *HW*, 3 September 1853). *AYR* also demonstrated its awareness of media history with a portrait of Daniel Defoe as a major agent in the development of the English press (»A Gentleman of the Press«, 10 July 1869 and 17 July 1869).

37 Cf. Leslie Howsam's contribution to this book.

38 »Traits and Stories of the Huguenots« (*HW*, 10 December 1853) and »Convicts for Their Faith« (*AYR*, 12 January 1867).

39 »Curly-Headed France« (*AYR*, 3 March 1860).

40 »The Land of Montezuma« (*AYR*, 17 September 1864).

41 »Glass Points to Stormy« (*AYR*, 10 December 1859).

people might be vaguely familiar with but would like to hear more about. Its purpose was explained at the beginning of the first piece:

»There are many events of the past and present century – murders, wrecks, riots, trials, famines, insurrections – familiar by name, but the details of which are unknown to the younger men of this generation. Every one has heard something of the Luddites and their outrages; of Thurtell the gambler, and the cruel murder he committed; of that agonising event the burning of the Kent East Indiaman; of the savage execution of the Cato-street conspirators; of the trickeries of old Patch; of the tragedy of Spafields; but there are few who have had either time or opportunity to collect, compare, and read at full length, the newspapers, pamphlets, and street ballads which refer to them. [...] It is only by reading interesting or vivifying details, that the real nature of the social catastrophes and remarkable occurrences of the past century can be ascertained. Some of these pages of old Time's chronicle we would present for reperusal.«[42]

With its focus on the history of the »past century«, the series of »Old Stories« overlaps with the large group of articles that evoke a past within living or at least communicative memory. With this emphasis, they were especially suited for recording an impression of change, that is, an impression many readers would have had in the second half of the nineteenth century. Articles on city history were a particularly suitable vehicle for this kind of historical observation since they pointed out alterations in the material culture and their social effects by which readers were surrounded in their everyday lives. A piece on »Birmingham a Century Ago«, for instance, observed explicitly that

»Local history, carefully done, is as interesting in its own way as individual biography. On looking back into the condition of past times we can trace *how the*

---

42 »The Two Great Murders in Ratcliff-Highway (1811)« (*AYR*, 20 October 1866); many articles in the series refer to events of earlier decades of the nineteenth century (including Trafalgar and the so-called Peterloo massacre in 1819, when a demonstration in Manchester demanding parliamentary reform was violently dispersed by troops), but characters and events of the eighteenth century are also evoked (such as the famous highwayman Dick Turpin, or the Battle of Culloden in 1746, in which the supporters of the last Stuart rebellion were defeated).

changes in modes of life and thought have been brought about by the discoveries characteristic of the last two or three generations. We can see how gas has diminished the number of street robberies; how railroads have all but put an end to highwaymen, how free trade has altered the course of industrial discontent [...].« [emphasis added][43]

All the Year Round on 22 June 1861 featured an article entitled »My Young Remembrance« that begins with a remark in the same spirit:

»I am barely a middle-aged man; yet I have a distinct recollection of Thirty Years Ago. Looking back to that period – say to the years 1830-31 – I find so many and such strange alterations in this native London of mine, that I am tempted to recal [sic] a few of the old characteristics of those old times, for the edification of young ladies and gentlemen who, having been born ten or fifteen years later than the era I speak of, know little else than the London of the present moment.«

Outside of local history one also repeatedly comes across articles that reflect on the immense changes of English society within a Victorian contemporary's personal memory.[44] Even the colonials in India had an opportunity to observe the march of progress since the transgression to direct rule by the Crown in 1858.[45] »Links in the Chain« (*AYR*, 17 January 1863) touches on a related issue – how sometimes one comes into contact with ›anachronous‹ survivors from the past.[46] As the article states initially:

---

43 »Birmingham a Century Ago« (*AYR*, 17 April 1869). A similar piece is »When London Was Little« (*HW*, 27 January 1855), which states initially that »Londoners of to-day, and more than Londoners, are easily amused by recollections of the Town as it was once«. Also cf. »Forty Years in London« (*AYR*, 8 April 1865), »Exeter Sixty Years Ago« (*AYR*, 28 October 1865), »Salisbury Forty-Five Years Ago« (*AYR*, 24 March 1866)«, »Old Salisbury« (*AYR*, 13 October 1866).

44 Also cf. »Since this Old Cap Was New« (*AYR*, 19 November 1859).

45 »Yesterday and Today in India« (*AYR*, 17 October 1863).

46 Another of the ›quaint‹ history pieces in *HW*, »Stepping Stones« (24 October 1857), presents its narrator as jumping backwards from one period (›step‹) to another, until he reaches 1542. Here, too, the leaps always cover the scope of communicative memory, varying between twenty and sixty years.

»There is something in the progress of successive ages, very analogous to the links of a chain. Occasionally we come in contact with an individual still living, and are startled to find ourselves in the presence of an extinct age. When Thomas Moore met old Mrs. Piozzi, two years before her death in 1821, he appeared to be brought eye to eye with the great spirits of the eighteenth century.«

Later, the article ruminates about the last survivors of Napoleon's Imperial Guard:

»It is sad to think of the days (now not far distant) when that impressive troop will sink to six – to three – to one. What will that one man do when he represents the redoubtable Guard? [...] The Bonaparte period, however, is still sufficiently near, to leave us several remaining links with it.«

One of these links to which *All the Year Round* introduced its readers on 18 August 1866 was a participant of the Battle of Waterloo who found himself in poor circumstances as an old man. The authenticity of »Waterloo and the Workhouse« as a witness report[47] is affirmed at the beginning of the article:

»The following memoir was not actually written down on paper with pen and ink by the narrator himself, but it is a transcript of notes made during the old man's narration, and is in truth what it professes to be: – the real uninterpolated history of a genuine soldier of the 18th of June, '15, given as nearly as possible in the veteran's own vernacular.«

Among the many biographies and biographical anecdotes of the great and famous in Dickens's magazines, a clear majority refers to men.[48] Like in

---

47 Witness reports were also very popular in the *Gartenlaube*. Cf. Emma Niendorf: »Aus meinen Memoiren: Plaudereien mit Napoleoniden« (From My Memoirs: Chats with Napoleonides, 1860: 446); »Erinnerungen eines schleswig-holsteinischen Freiwilligen: 1. Die Schlacht bei Idstedt« (Memories of a Volunteer from Schleswig-Holstein: 1. The Battle of Idstedt, 1860: 616); »Aus den Erinnerungen eines Gefängnißinspektors« (From the Memories of a Prison Inspector, 1865: 150, 717).

48 They include articles on prominent musicians, actors, writers and painters such as »Handel«, whose portrait ends with an announcement of the upcoming cele-

the *Gartenlaube*, however, some women were also portrayed, such as Hester Lynch Thrale Piozzi (prominent in the mid-eighteenth century's Blue-stocking circle),[49] the painter Angelika Kauffmann,[50] Queen Christina of Sweden,[51] Hannah Woolley, a seventeenth-century philanthropist who wrote a book on the education of gentlewomen,[52] and the fossil collector Mary Anning of the early nineteenth century. Like the biographies of the soldiers of the Napoleonic period, Anning's portrait indicates that attention to the history of simple people and their contribution to society was also granted in Dickens's magazines. Not only does Anning induce the writer of her biography to reflect about the (marginalised) status of women in the natural sciences, but she also brings him to comment on the contribution of her *class* to that area of study: »Her history shows what humble people may do, if they have just purpose and courage enough, towards promoting the cause of science.«[53] Stories of female life in a family magazine may have

---

brations of the centenary of his death in 1859 (*HW*, 20 June 1857), David Garrick (»Doctor Garrick«. *HW*, 15 August 1857), Laurence Sterne (*AYR*, 2 July 1864) and Sir Joshua Reynolds (*AYR*, April 29 1865).

49 »The Queen of the Blue Stockings« (*AYR*, 20 April 1861).

50 »Poor Angelica« (*HW*, 25 August 1855); Kauffmann was also portrayed in the *Gartenlaube*; cf. note 25 above.

51 »A Queen's Revenge« (*HW*, 15 August 1857).

52 »Mistress Hannah Woolley« (*HW*, 4 August 1855). She is introduced as »a lady who in the turbulent days of the parliament, kept a ladies' school, and then became waiting-gentlewoman to a person of quality; and who, during the Protectorate, kept, with her husband, a large school at Hackney, and initiated young ladies into all the mysteries of the still and stewpan, together with the more pleasant arts of making rock-work, wax-work, cabinet-work, bugle-work, upon wires or otherwise, together with marvellous flowers of various colours, made of wire and isinglass.«

53 »Mary Anning, the Fossil Finder« (*AYR*, 11 February 1865). Other women-related articles include a piece on »Historic Doubt« in connection with Joan of Arc (*HW*, 25 September 1858), and »The Light of Other Days« (*HW*, 29 September 1855), on the history of the belief in witches.

been of specific interest to female readers, as were articles on certain areas of cultural history, such as the diet of former periods.[54]

However, social and cultural history was a staple of the Dickens magazines in general, and a series in *All the Year Round*, »Small-Beer Chronicles«, seems to programmatically assert this fact. »Where is the historian of our social life?«, it asked at the beginning of its first article and continued:

>»While the great events of the History of Europe are duly recorded; while the diplomatic struggles, the commercial transactions, the political progress, of the civilised world, are discussed, reviewed, and commemorated; does any one note down the social changes which follow the progress of those greater developments, which are in some sort brought about by them, which may perhaps help to elucidate them, and which, even if they do not, are in themselves sufficiently interesting to have an historian of their own? Where is the Registrar-General who shall from time to time furnish a report how the great nation whose public doings are so adequately recorded, behave in the seclusion of private life? Where, in a word, is the Chronicler of the Country's Small-Beer?
>Here he is, at the reader's service.«[55]

In a society obsessed with material things (cf. Briggs 1988), a major group of cultural-historical articles introduced readers to the history of objects and consumer goods in their everyday lives. They observed changes in food (as already mentioned), fashion[56] or means of transport.[57] Other articles pointed

---

54 »Meat and Drink in Shakespeare's Time« (*HW*, 13 March 1858), »The Growth of Our Gardens« (*HW*, 19 June 1858, with notes on the importation to England of such vegetables as potatoes and tomatoes), »Obsolete Cookery« (*HW*, 3 February 1855), »Metamorphoses of Food« (*AYR*, 30 March 1861).

55 »Small-Beer Chronicles« (*AYR*, 30 August 1862). A later part of the series deals, for instance, with the history of such a small but important subject of everyday life as the doorknocker (27 September 1862).

56 »Old Clothes and New Clothes« (*HW*, 28 October 1854).

57 »Flying Coaches« (*HW*, 2 August 1854, about coaches in the seventeenth century), and »An Excursion Train, Before Steam« (*HW*, 30 September 1850, about travel in the age »of our great-grandfathers«). The fascination with the materiality and concrete lifeworld of earlier periods is also expressed in an article im-

out changes in manners and beliefs,[58] and in social institutions from clubs[59] to the law.[60]

In terms of period, emphases are also quite apparent. The attention given to communicative memory explains in part why the long eighteenth century, including the period of the French Revolution and the succeeding wars, features prominently both in *Household Words* and *All the Year Round*. But the eighteenth century was also an age to which Victorian Britons could look back with pride, as a period in which parliamentary monarchy was consolidated and confessional troubles came under control, and an age in which the arts and sciences flourished. However, the seventeenth century is almost of equal interest – as a time in which the country experienced the trauma of a civil war, the succeeding restoration of the Stuart monarchy and its final deposition in the Glorious Revolution of 1688, which re-defined the powers of Crown and Parliament. In our sample years, pieces that can be assigned to the seventeenth century, the long eighteenth century and the short phase between the end of the Napoleonic Wars and the present far outweigh the number of articles on classical antiquity, the middle ages and even the sixteenth century. For the latter, Queen Elizabeth (whose gender and power invited comparison to Queen Victoria), her courtiers (including Sir Walter Raleigh as an early coloniser) and Shakespeare (the 300th anniversary of whose birth sparked numerous articles in 1864) are at the centre of interest. Classical antiquity and the middle ages are presented with a focus on literary history[61] and cultural history,[62] that is,

---

agining photographs of Bourbon Paris (»Bourbon Paris, Photographed«. *HW*, 26 September 1857).

58 »Shadows of Dark Days« (*HW*, 18 March 1854, about the history of superstition); »Duelling in England« and »Duelling in France« (*HW*, 20 June 1857 and 27 June 1857 respectively).

59 »Clubs and Club-Men« (*AYR*, 29 September 1866).

60 »An Old Picture of Justice« (*HW*, 12 May 1855), »Time's Sponge« (*HW*, 17 May 1856), »Court-Martial History« (*AYR*, 30 January 1864).

61 Cf. articles on Apuleius's »A Golden Ass« (*HW*, 5 April 1856), »A Primitive Old Epic« (*HW*, 1 May 1858, about *Beowulf*), »Celtic Bards« (*HW*, 3 April 1858), »Havelok the Dane« (*HW*, 22 May 1858). The publication of a volume of Ibn Battuta's travels gave rise to the article »The Black Sea Five Centuries Ago« (*HW*, 17 February 1855). *AYR* included a biography of the late-medieval scholar

aspects with which Victorian middle-class readers might still feel some connection.

In terms of geographical region, the history presented in the Dickens magazines is most frequently a national one.[63] However, other countries are also presented with facets of their past, most notably France (not only in connection with Napoleon).[64] As might be expected, there is some interest in the past of colonial areas[65] and other destinations of contemporary emigration, including the United States.[66] The histories of Russia and Italy gained interest with contemporary political events that concerned and interested the British: the frictions with Russia leading to the Crimean War (1854-56), and the Italian movement for unification and independence.[67]

Roger Bacon (»Friar Bacon«, 29 June 1861) and a description of the Bayeux Tapestry (»A Chronicle in Worsted«, 28 December 1867).

62 Cf. »Latin London« (*AYR*, 5 May 1860), »Dining with an Ancient Roman« (*AYR*, 11 July 1868), »Very Old News« (*AYR*, 29 June 1867, about Julius Caesar's *Acta Diurna* as a predecessor of the modern newspaper); »Five Hundred Years Ago« (*AYR*, 6 October 1860, with a focus on London in the fourteenth century).

63 And here primarily an English one; the so-called Celtic fringe of the British Isles is given only minimal attention, at least in historical perspective.

64 Apart from topics already mentioned, articles were devoted to the Mongolfiers and their famous balloon (»A Royal Pilot-Balloon«. *HW*, 30 January 1858), the philosopher Ramus (»A Forgotten Notability«. *HW*, 11 April 1857) and the French piano maker »Pierre Erard« (*HW*, 6 October 1855).

65 »The First Sack of Delhi« (*HW*, 19 September 1857); »Unfortunate James Daley« (*HW*, 21 July 1855, about a convict sent to Australia).

66 »Old Settlers of Tennessee« (*HW*, 22 October 1853).

67 Czar Peter the First of Russia received attention not least because he had visited England (»Peter the Great in England«. *HW*, 6 October 1855); Italian history of the sixteenth century was told in a nine-part series about »Vittoria Accoramboni« (*AYR*, 21 January to 11 February 1860); it ended with an explicit reference to the contemporary situation: »And so ends the history of the marvellously beautiful Vittoria Accoramboni and her two husbands; a striking, but by no means unique or abnormal sample of a state of society produced and fashioned, according to the certain and invariable operation of God's moral laws, by the same evil influences, lay and spiritual – absolutely the same in kind, if some-

German history appears to have been less of an interest; in the period investigated, only Frederick the Great received an article,[68] and this was due in the first place to the publication of the first half of Thomas Macaulay's biography of the Prussian king, which was widely talked about. The turmoil of Germany's recent experience of a revolution and its aftermath was hardly noted, although an earlier number of *Household Words* at least introduced its readers to one of the leading figures of the revolution, Gottfried Kinkel, for whose liberation from prison it pleaded in 1850.[69]

All in all, *Household Words* and *All the Year Round* presented their readers with many facets of and possible attitudes towards the past. Their main emphasis was on aspects of history to which their readers might easily relate and by which they might also be entertained. Dickens's magazines, due to the prominence of their editor, had strongly idiosyncratic features – a focus on the fanciful and quaint – that set them apart in tone from other contemporary family magazines in Britain (for instance *The Leisure Hour*, which was published by the Religious Tract Society). Nevertheless, they also exemplify general features of the Victorian (family) magazine's approach to history. Most notable was an effort to make history interesting and significant to readers of a modern world: by focusing on cultural history, by personalising history through biography and anecdote, by pointing out connections between the present and the past (and laying a special emphasis on communicative memory), by casting history in the light of contemporary ideologies and values and, last but not least, by pointing out how readers might actively engage themselves with history.

STEPS TOWARDS A COMPARATIVE APPROACH

A comparative look at the contents of the *Gartenlaube* and *Household Words/All the Year Round* yields some obvious similarities and differences which shed a spotlight on the popular historical cultures in Germany and Britain. Regarding the similarities, our case studies display a parallel narra-

---

what mitigated in intensity – from which Italy is now straining every nerve to escape.«

68 »Apprenticeship of Frederick the Great« (*HW*, 9 October 1858).

69 »Gottfried Kinkel: A Life in Three Pictures« (*HW*, 2 November 1850).

tive of historical progress. Also, the German and British cases both show a marked preference for presenting history through biography and cultural history, through the everyday life of the past, and they tend to relate history to the lifeworlds of their readers. Contemporary history and events, developments or persons within communicative memory are at centre stage. The French Revolution and the Napoleonic Wars received significant attention in Germany and Britain since they were historical events of a cataclysmic nature for Europe and the world beyond; furthermore, they still reverberated in the communicative memory of both cultures. Also, like the *Gartenlaube*, the British publications pay least attention to classical antiquity and the middle ages; where they do, they tend to emphasise a cultural history to which one could relate without the benefit of an education in the classics or knowledge about the complexities of medieval dynastic and clerical history.

Differences in content, the preference for certain spaces and historical events or developments are partly explained by the different political contexts of the two countries. Victorian Britain was not in the process of building a nation state as fragmented Germany still was until 1871, and it was therefore less pertinent in Britain to functionalise history for the purpose of political reform. Arguably, this explains why the revolution of 1848-49 does not play a very significant role in either *Household Words* or *All the Year Round*, while it is an important topic in the *Gartenlaube*. Although 1848 was not ignored in Britain (and some German 48ers were granted political exile in Britain), it was most of all a Continental affair that Britain witnessed from across the Channel, especially after it had become history. In Germany, by contrast, the revolution of 1848 was firmly inscribed in the ongoing process of nation-building and the formation of national and oppositional liberal-democratic movements. Mid-century Britain was more involved in a colonial project that would expand into an imperialist one later in the century. In the two Dickens magazines, a certain interest in colonial history and the history of colonisation is to be noted, if much less strongly than it would be in British magazines of the late nineteenth century. When the *Gartenlaube* was concerned with non-European history, it normally took as its departure point German minorities abroad. It devoted far more attention to state and regional history, which can be accounted for by the federal nature of German nationalism.

Rather than promoting nationalism, *Household Words* and *All the Year Round* seem to employ history in order to support a *patriotic* spirit that is proud, for instance, of British achievements since the late seventeenth century and especially in the arts and sciences of the eighteenth century. The significant attention given to the late seventeenth century in the British magazines (as compared to the *Gartenlaube*) is explained by the formative importance of that period for the modern English/British nation: From the trauma of the English Civil War and the danger of re-strengthening Roman Catholicism during the Restoration, it emerged as a consolidated nation after 1688, when the Glorious Revolution placed the crown firmly in Protestant hands and secured for parliament the power granted in a constitutional monarchy. In the *Gartenlaube* early-modern history is not absent – the Reformation, Luther, the Peasants' War, Frederick the Great and the uprising of Prussia are important subjects – but the time span from the sixteenth to the mid-eighteenth century seems less prominent than in the British case.

That Britain had its Anglican state religion[70] arguably also explains why confessional history appears to be less of an issue in *Household Words/All the Year Round*. Articles with an explicit interest in religion in the Dickens magazines are relatively rare, although an anti-Popish attitude can occasionally be identified.[71] A secular and anti-Popish impregnation also characterised the historical articles in the *Gartenlaube* in the 1850s and 1860s, while other magazines, such as *Daheim*, chose a Protestant perspective on history. In a country which was still strongly divided along confessional lines between Roman Catholicism and Protestantism, this divide was deeply imprinted in historical culture (and also in print and reading culture). To study the religious impetus on historical pieces, not only the historical presentations of Christian but also of Dissident, Jewish, or other world religions, would be an interesting topic for further comparisons.

---

70 In the nineteenth century, this religion could afford to tolerate Roman Catholicism. The Emancipation Act of 1829 removed most forms of discrimination against Roman Catholics.

71 This is the case for instance in Dickens's *Child's History of England*, the Vittoria Accoramboni series, or such articles as »Roman Sheep-Shearing« and »Phases of Papal Faith«, both in *AYR* (11 August 1860 and 25 February 1860 respectively).

While many differences and similarities in historical content can be explained by variations in political and societal backgrounds and were to be expected, the magazines we have investigated compare less conveniently in other respects. Outwardly, their make-up appears to be similar: Both the *Gartenlaube* and *Household Words/All the Year Round* were family magazines and offered miscellaneous contents that were meant to appeal to a cross-age and cross-gender readership which was largely comprised of members of the middle classes. They were also not too remote from each other in terms of political and ideological sympathies, both being predominantly secular in outlook and propagating liberalism or social reform. But the *Gartenlaube* was illustrated and complemented its texts with images, while the Dickens magazines did not have any pictures. This picture-text relation should be taken much more into account in the case of the *Gartenlaube* and it would be useful to ask whether this made a difference in the historical statements when compared to articles without illustrations. Furthermore, there is a marked difference in tone between the *Gartenlaube* and the Dickens magazines: The presentation of history in *Household Words* and *All the Year Round* is often humorous and fanciful, looking for original ways of presenting history and dragging the readers with all their senses into history, linking »the living and the dead« through »the electric telegraphs of Time«, as Dickens phrased it masterfully. Because of Dickens's editorship, his magazines may be extreme in this respect, but they are not entirely untypical within the British context. Although the *Gartenlaube* too professed an intention to entertain as well as instruct, its tone is more sober and didactic (it also seems to focus less on scandal and crime in history than its British counterparts), and one might speculate as to whether this is due to a difference in national taste and mentality.

Differences in style and tone can only be discovered in an analysis that is not only focused on content and theme (as was our exploratory probe), but also takes modes of writing and style into account, i.e. qualities of a *literary* nature. Comparisons of magazines should therefore be conducted not only in terms of historical content, but also in terms of presentation and literary quality, and this calls for an interdisciplinary approach and exchange of methods between History and Literary Studies.

To achieve more reliable results in all the areas addressed in this contribution, one requires a much broader basis for comparison than just two national cases. What also calls for a broader basis is the great number and variety of magazines that makes it difficult to find perfect matches for comparison. We will need *many* case studies which can then be combined into a composite picture that will be more reliable in its tendencies than our preliminary exploration here. One also has to take into account processes of transfer and entanglement. Nineteenth-century magazines did not exist in isolation but observed and reacted to each other within national markets.[72] The extent to which they also did this cross-nationally (for instance through translations or the reports of correspondents in other countries) is still to be explored. It would also be interesting, in a comparative and transnational perspective, to compare how magazines deal with the national history of their counterparts from other countries. German history seems to be less important in British magazines of the mid-nineteenth century than British history in the German ones (though less interesting than French history, which was an important point of historical reference in both national contexts). The interrelation of academic historiography and popular historical representations in the magazines could be another important question in further comparative and transnational studies. What we need in light of all these objectives for further research, and to advance the cross-national study of the role of magazines in historical culture(s), is a concerted, interdisciplinary and collaborative effort, and we would like to finish our discussion here with an invitation to other scholars to join us in that effort.[73]

WORKS CITED

Altick, Richard D. (1998 [1957]): *The English Common Reader: A Social History of the Mass Reading Public, 1800-1900,* 2nd ed., Columbus/OH: Ohio State University Press.

Assmann, Aleida (2005): »Jahrestage: Denkmäler in der Zeit«. In: Paul Münch (ed.), *Jubiläum, Jubiläum: Zur Geschichte öffentlicher und privater Erinnerung,* Essen: Klartext, 305-314.

---

72 This is apparent, for instance, where magazines quote or review each other.

73 The newly founded European Society for Periodical Research (ESPRit) might provide an ideal forum for such efforts. Cf. http://www.ru.nl/esprit/.

Assmann, Jan (1995): »Collective Memory and Cultural Identity«. *New German Critique* 65: 125-133.

Bann, Stephen (1984): *The Clothing of Clio: A Study of the Representation of History in Nineteenth-Century Britain and France*, Cambridge: Cambridge University Press.

Belgum, Kirsten (1998): *Popularizing the Nation: Audience, Representation, and the Production of Identity in* Die Gartenlaube, *1853-1900*, Lincoln/NE: University of Nebraska Press.

Berger, Stefan/Chris Lorenz/Billie Melman (eds.) (2012): *Popularizing National Pasts: 1800 to the Present*, London: Routledge (publication forthcoming).

Briggs, Asa (1988): *Victorian Things*, London: Batsford.

British Periodicals (http://britishperiodicals.chadwyck.co.uk/info/about.do).

Conrad, Christoph (ed.) (2002): *Die Nation schreiben: Geschichtswissenschaft im internationalen Vergleich*, Frankfurt am Main: Campus.

Die Gartenlaube: Illustrirtes Familienblatt, vol. 1-48 (1853-1900), Berlin: Scherl.

Estermann, Alfred (1995): *Inhaltsanalytische Bibliographien deutscher Kulturzeitschriften des 19. Jahrhunderts*, vol. 3: *Die Gartenlaube (1853-1880 [-1944])*, München: Saur.

Gluck, Carol (2007): »Operations of Memory: Comfort Women and the World«. In: Sheila Miyoshi Jager/Rana Mitter (eds.), *Ruptured Histories: War, Memory and the Post-Cold War in Asia*, Cambridge/MA: Harvard University Press, 47-77.

Haupt, Heinz-Gerhard/Jürgen Kocka (eds.) (1996): *Geschichte und Vergleich: Ansätze und Ergebnisse international vergleichender Geschichtsschreibung*, Frankfurt am Main: Campus.

Jann, Rosemary (1987): »Fact, Fiction, and Interpretation in *A Child's History of England*«. *Dickens Quarterly* 4, 199-205.

Kaelble, Hartmut/Jürgen Schriewer (eds.) (2003): *Vergleich und Transfer: Komparatistik in den Sozial-, Geistes- und Kulturwissenschaften*, Frankfurt am Main: Campus.

Koch, Marcus (2003): *Nationale Identität im Prozess nationalstaatlicher Orientierung, dargestellt am Beispiel Deutschlands durch die Analyse der Familienzeitschrift ›Die Gartenlaube‹ von 1853-1890*, Frankfurt am Main: Lang.

Korte, Barbara (2012): »History in *Household Words*«. In: Joachim Frenk (ed.), *That's the Way to Do It: British Popular Culture of the Nineteenth Century* (publication forthcoming).

Langewiesche, Dieter (2000): »Föderativer Nationalismus als Erbe der deutschen Reichsnation: Über Föderalismus und Zentralismus in der deutschen Nationalgeschichte«. In: *Nation, Nationalismus und Nationalstaat in Deutschland und Europa*, München: Beck, 55-79.

Langewiesche, Dieter/Georg Schmidt (eds.) (2000): *Föderative Nation: Deutschlandkonzepte von der Reformation bis zum Ersten Weltkrieg*, München: Oldenbourg.

Lohrli, Anne (ed.) (1973): *Household Words: A Weekly Journal 1850-1859*, Toronto: University of Toronto Press.

Melman, Billie (2006): *The Culture of History: English Uses of the Past 1800-1953*, Oxford: Oxford University Press.

Mitchell, Rosemary (2000): *Picturing the Past: English History in Text and Image 1830-1870*, Oxford: Clarendon Press.

Paletschek, Sylvia (2011): »Popular Presentations of History in the Nineteenth Century: The Example of *Die Gartenlaube*«. In: Sylvia Paletschek (ed.), *Popular Historiographies in the 19th and 20th Centuries: Cultural Meanings, Social Practices*, Oxford: Berghahn, 34-53.

Samida, Stefanie (2009): »Heinrich Schliemann, Troia und die deutsche Presse: Medialisierung, Popularisierung, Inszenierung«. In: Petra Boden/Dorit Müller (eds.), *Populäres Wissen im medialen Wandel seit 1850*, Berlin: Kadmos, 135-151.

Stöber, Rudolf (2005): *Deutsche Pressegeschichte*, Konstanz: UTB.

Tacke, Charlotte (1995): *Denkmal im sozialen Raum: Nationale Symbole in Deutschland und Frankreich im 19. Jahrhundert*, Göttingen: Vandenhoeck & Ruprecht.

Vann, Jerry Don/Rosemary T. VanArsdel (eds.) (1994): *Victorian Periodicals and Victorian Society*, Toronto: University of Toronto Press.

Vollständiges Generalregister der Gartenlaube vom 1. bis 50. Jahrgang (1853-1902) (1978 [1903], comp. and ed. by Friedrich Hofmann/J. Schmitt, Hildesheim: Gerstenberg.

Zaumseil, Franka (2007): *Zwischen Nation und Region: Die Zeitschrift ›Gartenlaube‹ in der 2. Hälfte des 19. Jahrhunderts*, Hamburg: Diplomica.

The Opening of the Archives and Its Limits

Contested Interests in »Tÿrol«

PHILIPP MÜLLER

THE OPENING OF THE ARCHIVES

In early April 1824, Dr. Joseph von Fink (1770-1843), Director of the Royal Bavarian Secret State Archive, presented »a couple of ideas concerning a closer connection between the Royal Archives and the Royal Academy of Sciences« in Munich (Heydenreuter 1992: 30-32). As detailed in his report, Fink contemplated a closer cooperation between the two institutions, with the resulting effect that the state archive be opened for historical research. However, Fink's idea of a »general opening of the archive for scientific research« (ibid.: 30) was not to materialise, with King Maximilian I Joseph (1756-1825, ruling 1799-1825) ultimately rejecting his proposal. Interestingly enough, Fink's proposal did not even enjoy the support of his peers at the Academy of Sciences; the main thrust of the arguments levelled against his ideas being that any such ›opening‹ of the Secret State Archive would necessarily conflict with its main purpose, essential to the business of the state government. With regard to Fink's proposal, the privy council Georg Karl von Suttner (1763-1836) stated that

»the first and foremost purpose of archives is [...] the safekeeping of diploma[s], enabling the representation of the legal status quo concerning state and private property; [the archives] are in the possession of the superior governmental authority, and any other merely scientific institution is not to be entrusted with any responsibility concerning these [records and files].« (qtd. in Heydenreuter 1992: 32)[1]

Suttner's objections were rooted in the early-modern political theory and practice of the *arcana imperii* (cf. Kantorowicz 1965; Münkler 1987: 167-168; Stolleis 1990: 37; Stolleis 1996: 82-83). Accordingly, state archives were an integral part of the state administration, and were directly subordinated to the sovereign and the state government respectively. In keeping »highly guarded state secrets« (Münckler 1987: 239) separate from the public, state archives concealed state knowledge, as well as any political actions of the state government (cf. Hölscher 1979; Wegener 2006). In addition, they furnished the state government with the details of fiscal rights and territorial claims, thereby advantaging the current government and its policies. Above all, the state archives preserved the status quo and helped to secure the existence of the state per se. Through the safekeeping of such legal information, the state archives functioned as a central pillar of the country's legal peace, and thus essentially contributed to the welfare of the state's society (cf. Hohkamp 1998: 81). As a result, and in accordance with notions of the *arcana imperii*, the strictly governmental purpose and conception of state archives did not generally cater to, or provide the opportunity for, historical research. Against this backdrop, it is fair to say that historical research was regarded as something of a *contradictio in adjecto*.

Despite our contemporary understanding of these institutions, state archives were not primarily designed as centres of historical research, nor did they function as such. Indeed, as the archivist Joachim Prochno pointed out in 1944, the understanding of state archives, ignorant as it is of »the task of the archive as authority«, simply conceives of these institutions as »auxiliary facilit[ies] for historical research« (Prochno 1944: 288). With this institutional profile informing our notions of state archives, the primary function of these archives is, accordingly, perceived to be that of documenting the past. Importantly, however, this notion serves only to impair our understanding of the history of archives when the idea of the scholarly use of archival material is falsely projected onto the nineteenth-century

---

1   All translations of German sources in this article are mine.

archival institution.[2] As a result, archival politics are either described in terms of the equation of state and history (cf. Vismann 1999: 242, 245), or are tacitly measured against the modern ideal of the »historical archive« and thus subsequently perceived by their relative shortcomings (cf. Schenk 2008: 19, 26). In the first case, the state appears as the central agency of history, with the state, its archives and history ultimately coinciding. In the case of the latter, the modernisation of state archives is narrated along the lines of the modern *telos*, i.e. the »historical archive«: The negative ramifications for historical research are conceived as institutional deficiencies, and accounted for by the »pre-archival« institutional state of state archives (ibid.). In regard to the first, however, it must be said that there was no initial connection between state archives and historical research; in regard to the second, it must be stated that neither in conceptual nor in institutional terms were records and files strictly separated into those serving governmental purposes only and those that did not, the latter being left for scholarly use. To put it succinctly, all records and files were in the hands and thus also under the control of the state government. Thus the question arises as to how a scholarly use of the archive was rendered feasible if the secret sphere of the state was to remain intact.

This article explores how historical interest in state archives was communicated, and under which circumstances access to such holdings was granted by examining a failed request to use the Bavarian state archives (cf. Zimmermann 1962; Rumschöttel 1997; Jaroschka 1989; Liess 2001; in general: Reininghaus 2008). The failed request belonged to a writer called

---

2   Similar concerns and objections have been raised about the development of academia in the nineteenth century. For quite a while, the idea of »the research imperative« (Turner 1973) – the alleged implementation of a research imperative in the early nineteenth century, the so-called Humboldt reforms being the most apparent manifestation of this – was undoubted. Various studies on single cases (cf. Moraw 1984), the statistical calculation of recruiting patterns (cf. Baumgarten 1997) and the examination of administrative and institutional changes (cf. Paletschek 2001; Lingelbach 2003) have, however, compellingly undermined the idea of a swift transformation radiating out from the epicentre of German academia in the early nineteenth century in Prussia. In actual fact, this idea is revealed as an invented tradition, and one that was fabricated in the early twentieth century (cf. Paletschek 2002; also cf. Müller 2004).

Alessandro Volpi, who, having a special interest in the history of Tyrol, wished to study the holdings of the Bavarian state archives in 1858. Volpi had just contributed to a popular topic of the history of Tyrol by editing a book on historical memories concerning the Tyrol uprising in 1809, not lacking in its overall anti-napoleonic tone.[3] Obviously, he wished to further his historical knowledge of this small stretch in the north-eastern Alps. However, Volpi was thwarted in his desire to learn more about the past in the Bavarian state archives. Volpi's unsuccessful attempt provides a useful insight into the administrative examination process of such requests, the notions behind it and also its sensitivities – thereby revealing a political communication process concerning the boundary between the state's sphere of secrecy and historical research by members of the public.[4]

ASKING FOR ACCESS TO THE BAVARIAN STATE ARCHIVES

In contrast to the ideas of the Director of the Secret State Archive, Dr. Fink, state archives and their holdings were never entirely accessible or available for members of the public throughout the nineteenth century. Although a political development in the early nineteenth century, termed by contemporaries as »the opening of the archives«, provided the possibility of limited access to the records and files of the state archives, the historical

---

3   Alessandro Volpi (1856): *Andrea Hofer, o la sollevazione del tirolo del 1809: Memorie storiche di Girolamo Andreis*, Milano. Interestingly enough, Bavarian officials did not learn of this book.

4   This case study closely examines the files of the Bayerische Hauptstaatsarchiv Munich, BayHStA MA 72203 and BayHStA MInn 41944, comprising the following writs: BayHSta MA 72203 Writ by King Max II, 26.11.1857 (Abbr. Max 26.11.1857); Writ by Pfordten to King Max II, 16.12.1857 (Abbr. Pfordten 16.12.1857); BayHSta MInn 41944 Copy of the King's Writ 26.11.1857; Writ by the Minister of Exterior, Ludwig v.d. Pfordten, 27.11.1857 (Abbr. Pfordten 27.11.1857); Expert Opinion by the Director of the Imperial Archive, Georg Thomas Rudhart, 4.12.1857 (Abbr. Rudhart 4.12.1857); Copy of Article of the *Neueste Nachrichten* 29.11.1857 (Abbr. *Neueste Nachrichten* 29.11.1857). Any emphases originate from the administrative writs themselves.

interest in archival material had to go through the needle eye of the state government in the first place.

First and foremost, researchers had to ask for permission to use the archives of the state. Whereas in Revolutionary France the Law of 7 Messidor Year II, i.e. 25 June 1794, granted, at least in theory, every citizen of the republic the civic right to use archival material, subjects of the monarchies in Central Europe were required to ask their sovereign for the use of the state archives (cf. Müller 2009: 81-82; Wiegand 2009: 12). Thus, those researchers interested in a copy, an excerpt or the concrete use of material *in loco archivi* were obliged to formally petition the state authority for access to the archival material they desired. In autumn 1857, the writer and researcher Dottore Alessandro Volpi performed this requirement during his stay in Munich: Whilst being received in audience with King Maximilian II Joseph (1811-1864, ruling 1848-1864) and other members of the Wittelsbach dynasty, Volpi directly presented his plea to Max II, asking him for the use of the archive.

Volpi was neither the first nor the last to seek entrance to the secret sphere of the Bavarian state. Materialising in 1804, the first request belonged to the priest Hellerberg, who sought to inspect a medieval document. In the following years, some further requests were to materialise: Remarkably, this initial interest in the holdings of state archives was not in response to any initiatives ›from above‹, but expressed the petitioners' desire to participate in the state (cf. Holenstein 2009: 25-28) long before any history society had been founded under the auspices of the Bavarian state government (cf. Kunz 2000: 65-67; Clemens 2004: 309). Unsurprisingly, there were only very few petitioners in the beginning of the nineteenth century, given the most vital resources for this sort of undertaking such as time, literacy and the proficiency in reading old handwritings. However, in the years to come, the number of petitioners rose and many of them were not professional scholars (cf. Stefan Berger's article in this volume), but men like the priest Hellerberg who had enjoyed the privilege of education or were to some degree familiar with administrative business. These early researchers almost literally knocked at the gates of the state archives, and it was only in 1812 that the sovereign of the fledgling Bavarian Kingdom, King Max I, decreed that his archivists were to generally support »the interest in the history of the fatherland and scientific research«

(Reference to the King's instruction of 21.4.1812: BayHStA MInn 41361 Writ 15.5.1826).

As a necessary response to these incoming requests, the government and the state administration developed a vetting procedure for both applications and applicants. For state officials, permitting insight into governmental knowledge was a precarious act that threatened to undermine the *arcana imperii* and its basic principle, i.e. secrecy (cf. Hölscher 1979; Wegener 2006). As the examination procedure was essentially meant to protect the political integrity of the state's secret sphere, the process of examining requests to use the archive was thus developed along the lines of older administrative traditions such as requests to use archives in legal matters (cf. Clanchy 1979; Algazi 1998: 344-348, 349; Hohkamp 1998: 79-81; Potin 2000: 52) and was also cognisant of the more general concerns of the *arcana imperii* regarding fiscal and territorial rights.

Nevertheless, it was precisely this examination procedure that Dottore Alessandro Volpi was to fall foul of. Initially, his plea for archival access showed some promise: According to the *Neueste Nachrichten* (a newspaper published since 1848, lacking any manifest political leanings), the visitor was »graciously encouraged« to continue with his studies whilst being received in audience with the King and his family (*Neueste Nachrichten* 29.11.1857). Ultimately, however, Volpi's request turned out to be a complete failure. In spite of the apparent positive reception of his historical interest, the King, with the support of his state government, eventually disapproved of the writer's plea. There were two immediate problems. Firstly, Volpi's request did not aid state officials in clarifying essential details concerning his character, nor those regarding his chosen research subject. Secondly, Volpi's orally presented plea was not supported with the required written form of a ›request‹, the petition letter, this medium being the *sine qua non* in the political communication process between petitioner and authority in terms of the boundary between the secret state sphere and historical research (the public).

THE DECISION MAKING PROCESS:
THE GOVERNMENT AND ITS ADMINISTRATION

Following the reception of Alessandro Volpi, King Max II informed his government that »Dr Volpi from Milano had asked Me for permission to use the archives in this place [Munich]«, with a view to furthering his studies about »a history of Tÿrol« (Max 26.11.1857). Max II proceeded to demand an »expert opinion« (*gutaechtliche Aeusserung*) on this matter, thereby prompting the examination of Volpi's personally presented »request« (*Gesuch*) (ibid.). Given the authorship of the »autograph letter« (Pfordten 27.11.1857), the brief note was swiftly put into circulation; the simple remark »*Cito*«[5] (Max 26.11.1857), situated on the right-hand margin of the writ, urged Bavarian state officials to quickly answer the demand of their »most superior King and Master« (Pfordten 27.11.1857; Rudhart 4.12.1857). The next day, the State Secretary and head of the Foreign Ministry, Ludwig von der Pfordten (1811-1880), advised the Interior Ministry (cf. Götschmann 1993) which finally relayed the urgent matter to its Royal General Imperial Archive. A few days later, Dr. Georg Thomas Rudhart (1792-1860), the archive's Director, answered his superiors with a detailed report of several pages, examining and evaluating Volpi's request.

THE PETITIONER: PROFILE AND MOTIVES

Rudhart was originally trained in law, but furthered his career through specialisation in historical research. With his studies, based on archival research, Rudhart contributed to contemporary questions regarding the national past of the then very recently forged monarchic state of New Bavaria. The obvious political significance of this historical work, the reputation he gained through it and not least his double expertise in law and history made him an apt candidate for the directorship of the Imperial Archive. Following his appointment to the position in 1848, Rudhart was, amongst other duties, in charge of the assessment of incoming requests to use the archive. When dealing with these requests, the Director was first and fore-

---

5   All original emphases in archival material are italicised.

most concerned with the »personality of the petitioner« (*Petenten*; Rudhart 4.12.1857): Understandably, the state administration wished to know exactly who had asked to learn about the secret knowledge of the state, so that leading archivists and state officials were required to scrutinise the identity and the character of the »*petitioner*« (*Bittsteller*; ibid.) before any such petitions could be approved. It was thus that, in the autumn of 1857, Rudhart sought to ascertain the personal details of the »Dr Volpi from Milan« (Max 26.11.1857). Whilst trying to gauge the genuine interest and possible motives of Volpi's plea, Rudhart was frustrated in his efforts to firmly establish the identity of the petitioner. As a result of a query to the Royal Police Headquarters in Munich, Rudhart learned that the petitioner was named »Alexander Volpi«, and that »he holds a doctorate in medicine, he was born in Trient, is thirty-six years old, is married and a member of the catholic church« (Rudhart 4.12.1857). Searching for more information about him, the Director also considered a »rather overly admiring article« (ibid.) that had been recently published in the *Neueste Nachrichten*. Unsatisfied, the Director finally sought to establish the profile of the allegedly »well known writer« (*Neueste Nachrichten* 29.11.1857) by skimming through catalogues of the nearby Royal Court and State Library, housed in the same premises as the Imperial Archive in Ludwigstrasse. As a result of this, Rudhart was confronted with more than one Dottore Volpi:

»It is true, the Italian literature does know of a *Guiseppe* di Volpi who published a Manuale di Technologia generale, 1854.8$^{\underline{o}}$ in Milano; but there is not anyone with this particular name who busied himself with history and who presented himself as an author in the field of historical studies.« (Rudhart 4.12.1857)

Ultimately, it was judged that the present petitioner had not expressed any serious interest in literary or historical studies, a judgement based on the fact that he had not yet introduced himself to the Court and State Library. Clearly then, the issues surrounding the confirmation of Volpi's identity also cast doubts on his reasons for wanting to use the archive. With his very person being deemed suspect, his original motives for using the archive, those of historical interest, were thus also considered highly questionable.

For archivists and members of the government, there were many sources that could produce the required confidence in the genuine historical motives of a petitioner: The scholarly prominence of a petitioner, previous studies the petitioner had carried out of records and files *in loco archivi*, manifestations of historical interest (e.g. research publications), as well as specific local knowledge concerning the honesty of the petitioner could all aid in proving him trustworthy. Indeed, as has been seen with Rudhart's efforts to prove Volpi's identity, state officials considered almost anything that would help them to establish a petitioner's profile. With an almost complete dearth of any form of information on him, Volpi's request for archival access was naturally placed at a large disadvantage. This problem was greatly compounded by another, even more important factor: Volpi's foreign origin. State officials generally considered foreigners to be »alien« to the archive (Pfordten 16.12.1857), and thus applied even more caution to their supervisory efforts – the dangers of feigned historical interest into state knowledge loomed large. There were some ways around this problem, however: By being equipped with additional references, for instance, foreigners were sometimes in a position to ease the minds of state officials. Foreign researchers could also call on a number of other forms of support to overcome their status as an »alien scholar«, in the form of the diplomatic actions of attachés, or the supplementation of their requests with certificates issued by their governments (cf. Müller 2009: 88-89). Remarkably, Volpi lacked these means of support; his request was neither relayed by the Austrian legation in Munich, nor by any research association.

THE SUBJECT OF HISTORICAL RESEARCH: TIME AND TOPIC

Besides the concern over Volpi's identity, there was another essential problem with his request: the combination of the topic of his proposed research and the unspecified time period over which he wished to examine the documents. Although the unspecified time scale was not necessarily harmful in itself, the few indicators that there were suggested that Volpi had a particular interest in modern history, an interest that focused on far too recent events. When combined with »the *subject* of his work« (Rudhart 4.12.1857), this more modern focus ran the risk of touching upon a less than favourable chapter of New Bavaria's formation at the turn of the century.

According to the autograph letter of Max II, Alessandro Volpi wished to further his studies regarding the »history of Tÿrol« (Max 26.11.1857). Although a seemingly innocuous request, the history of Bavaria's entanglement with this particular stretch in the north-eastern Alps reached back to the early medieval period. Given the lack of specific details in Volpi's case, Rudhart took his cues from the article published in the *Neueste Nachrichten* (cf. Rudhart 4.12.1857), an article that stated that Volpi had studied the »interesting history of Bavaria, France and Austria from 1793 until 1815«, and thus sought to gather »evidence and notices pertaining to the Napoleonic wars« (*Neueste Nachrichten* 29.11.1857). As well as perturbing Rudhart, Volpi's potential interest in the modern period also prompted concerns amongst other members of the state government. Accordingly, the State Secretary Ludwig von der Pfordten advised the Interior Ministry, the authority supervising the Imperial Archive,

»that it would be appropriate to ask the King for the approval of the relevant request as long as the use of the archive remains limited to diplomas, records and files, pertaining to Tÿrol, from the oldest time until the end of the 13th century, i.e. until the first cession to Austria, [and that the use of the archive] excludes modern history, namely from the Peace of Füßen 1745 onwards.« (Pfordten 27.11.1857)

Indeed, for the state government, modern and contemporary history was a sensitive issue. Developments and political occurrences in modern history were still entwined with the present, and this was certainly the case with Volpi's interest in the »modern and contemporary history« of the Bavarian state (Rudhart 4.12.1857). Volpi's special interest in the more recent period of time proved particularly difficult for state officials, as this span of time touched upon the sensitive topic of Tyrol. The dukedom of »Tyrol was, of course, incorporated into the Bavarian Kingdom from 1803 until 1814« (Pfordten 16.12.1857). However, Bavaria had both gained and subsequently lost Tyrol only recently. In addition, »the occurrences in this span of time, namely during the insurrection of Tyrol in the year 1809« (ibid.) were rather a source of embarrassment for the Bavarian state: Not only did they demonstrate the apparently limited reach of the fledgling New Bavaria, but they also had the potential to tarnish its reputation.

About five decades earlier, in the aftermath of the Third Coalition War against France in 1805, Napoleon had adjudged Tyrol to his loyal ally

Bavaria, thus handing her control of the alpine dukedom. Traditionally a heartland of the Habsburg monarchy, Tyrol proved to be unruly whilst under control of her new masters. Reforms instigated by the state government antagonised the local population and also undermined what authority Munich had in the region, the disquiet ultimately turning into a popular uprising. With Bavarian forces struggling to maintain control, it was not until the French army joined in the efforts to quell the rebellion that popular discontent within Tyrol was finally suppressed. By then, however, the damage had already been done: As a result of its proven incompetence, Bavaria was deprived of South Tyrol in 1810 and, in 1815, the whole duchy was once again back under Austrian control. Besides the loss of territory, the political and military defeat associated with the Tyrol uprising epitomised the very limits of the reforms designed and instigated by the Bavarian state at the turn of the century: The belief of the newly reformed monarchic state that it could successfully implement a rationalised type of governance in its new acquisition – a system of governance that was almost designed on a drawing board – had been sharply exposed as little more than a fantasy. Even fifty years later, when Volpi lodged his petition, the state officials were still aware of the Tyrol uprising and the effective rejection of Bavarian rule and thus their notion of history informed their administrative reasoning concerning the use of the archive. In contrast to the theoretical assumptions of Wolfgang Ernst, history did not prove to be merely an epiphenomenon of the archive with the archive being the apriori of historical knowledge (Ernst 2003: 35, 44, 45). Rather, notions of history played a pivotal role in the administration of the use of the archive for historical purposes and thus were instrumental in the transformation of governmental records and files into sources for historical research. Due to the compromising potential of this period of the New Bavaria, any potential revelations concerning this matter were, unsurprisingly, not welcome at all (cf. Pfordten 16.12.1857).

THE REJECTION

As mentioned above, Volpi's plea to use the archive was ultimately rejected. Given the uncertainty surrounding both the petitioner and his motives, as well as the political sensitivity of his chosen topic, neither of the offices involved in the decision-making process supported Volpi's plea. Rudhart argued that Volpi should not be granted insight into any records and files of the Imperial Archive, »for, if other things that inspire more confidence in his personality do not come to the fore, it seems that [the petitioner] hardly deserves this trust *for now*« (Rudhart 4.12.1857). Similarly, Ludwig von der Pfordten voiced serious concerns in regard to the potential use of the Secret State Archive, which was supervised by the Foreign Ministry. Largely borrowing from Rudhart's expert opinion, the State Secretary concluded in his request to the King (*Ministerial-Antrag*) that, »due to political reasons«, the records and files of the Secret State Archive should not be rendered accessible:

»whatever is available in the form of documents in the archives, or records and files [*Archive und Registraturen*; of the Foreign Ministry], is of such a recent date that historical research by a foreign scholar, particularly an Austrian one, must not take place.« (Pfordten 16.12.1857)

Two days later, by signing the proposal from his government, King Max II expressed his concurrence with the request prepared by his state administration.

THE ADMINISTRATIVE PROCEDURE: THE MISSING PETITION LETTER

The lack of information concerning Volpi's plea was rooted mainly in the absence of an administrative means, as well as an administrative requirement: the formalised »*request* for the use of the archive« (*Eingabe*; Rudhart 4.12.1857). Generally speaking, requests to use the archive were conveyed in a petition letter that produced the essential details of both the researcher's personality and the chosen topic of his research. With regard to Volpi's somewhat abnormal petition, Director Rudhart pointed out:

»The best indication for the production of an expert opinion concerning Volpi would possibly be the submission of his request [*Eingabe*] for the use of the archive, because [...] any kind of motive as to why he has chosen just this historical subject in

particular could be gathered from it; yet, this request is, unfortunately, not at hand.«
(Ibid.)

Whereas Rudhart was very explicit about the lack of a written application in this particular case, State Secretary Pfordten disregarded this irregularity: In his request to the King, Ludwig von der Pfordten simply posited that any interest in the recent history of Tyrol was to be deemed a political risk to the Bavarian state and its interests (Pfordten 16.12.1857). However, Rudhart could not help but take the lack of the request into consideration. Despite his suggestion that Volpi's request be rejected, his observations and reflections nevertheless provided Volpi with some leeway: He argued that, although Volpi »hardly deserve[d] this trust *for now*«, »other things«, which might clarify and establish the genuine motives of the petitioner could still surface (Rudhart 4.12.1857). To be slightly more specific, the submission of a formal, written petition by Volpi might well have helped to provide the details required to gain the official's confidence.

Rudhart's consideration reflected the pivotal role of requests in the vetting procedure of the state administration. These written requests were an essential administrative medium, a medium that furnished state officials with the details required to try to ascertain »the *truth*« (ibid.) regarding a petitioner's motivation to work with archival material. Whether the details related to a researcher's chosen historical topic, the period of time he wished to study, or even the individual documents he wished to view, it was all used by state officials to put the researcher's demands into perspective, and, concomitantly, allowed for the effective monitoring of any historical interest in the sphere of secrecy.

CONCLUSION

Gaining access to state archives and their holdings depended essentially on successful communication between petitioners, the sovereign and the state government respectively. As the case of Volpi's request and particularly its failure shows, the petition letter was a *conditio sine qua non* in an established communication pattern that had its origins in the early-modern tradition of supplications. The requests to use the archive borrowed from the old custom of alerting the authorities to a particular matter, for example a rule, and usually involved asking them to consider a deviation or exemption from official protocol (cf. Holenstein 2003: 282-304; Schwerhoff 2000: 479, 489). By the same token, in petitioning for the use of the archive, the researchers asked the sovereign to discard the strict principles of secrecy, at least momentarily and only in a limited manner. Provided with the specifics of a researcher's historical interest, the different agencies of the state assessed – in secrecy of course – the potential risks to the state, and concluded as to whether and to what extent the request was to be approved; in the end, using archival material was a favour granted by the sovereign, and only under specific conditions.

It is also important to note that Volpi's lack of success is, in itself, not representative of mid-nineteenth-century Bavarian archival politics. By this time, history had become an established political means of fostering the Kingdom's political cohesion (cf. Kunz 2000: 58, 65-66; Clemens 2004: 307-309; Körner 1982: 197, 202); the scientific use of state archives was both a governmentally recognised and a politically endorsed activity. More importantly, political reflection upon the historical use of state archives had left its imprint on the architectural design of the new premises of the Imperial Archive: The complex in Ludwigstrasse provided two reading rooms for those visitors who wished to inspect the archive's various holdings (cf. Volkert 1977: 133). To put it succinctly, in 1857, Volpi's plea had simply failed to meet an essential criterion of the inspection process, and thus also failed to pass the administrative threshold established by the state government. This failure notwithstanding, historical research was, by this time, an established characteristic of the institutional culture of the Bavarian state archives. Volpi's failure to gain access rather provides an example of the processes surrounding the use of these archives, illustrating the manifest and less implicit notions of the governmental vetting procedure – a persistent feature of historical research in state archives. In view of the missing petition letter, the Bavarian authorities were unable to establish a sufficient administrative »*truth*« (Rudhart 4.12.1857). Mindful of the worst-case scenario, caution prevailed whilst examining requests to use the archive; the ultimate reconciliation of historical interests with those of the state was mandatory for the approval of any request. In this way, from case to case, the boundary between the secret sphere of the state and the public was (re-) defined, modified and enhanced. With this, and as a result, the idea of the opened archives emerged, but this opening comprised limitations and, in

Volpi's case, even a lack of access. Yet Bavaria's archival politics could not prevent popular imagination from taking an interest in the history of this uprising (cf. Berger 2012). The romantic depiction of the Tyrol uprising and its main hero, Andreas Hofer (1767-1810), was just about to start.

WORKS CITED

Algazi, Gadi (1998): »Ein gelehrter Blick ins lebendige Archiv: Umgangsweisen mit der Vergangenheit im fünfzehnten Jahrhundert«. *Historische Zeitschrift* 266, 317-357.

Baumgarten, Marita (1997): *Professoren und Universitäten im 19. Jahrhundert: Zur Sozialgeschichte deutscher Geistes- und Naturwissenschaftler*, Göttingen: Vandenhoeck & Ruprecht.

Berger, Stefan (2012): »The Role of National Archives in Constructing National Master Narratives«, Ms. (publication forthcoming).

Clanchy, Michael T. (1993 [1973]): *From Memory to Written Record: England 1066-1307*, Malden/MA: Blackwell Publishers.

Clemens, Gabriele (2004): *Sanctus Amor Patriae: Eine vergleichende Studie zu deutschen und italienischen Geschichtsvereinen im 19. Jahrhundert*, Tübingen: Niemeyer.

Ernst, Wolfgang (2003): *Im Namen von Geschichte: Sammeln – Speichern – Er/zählen*, München: Fink.

Götschmann, Dirk (1993): *Das bayerische Innenministerium 1825-1864*, Göttingen: Vandenhoeck & Ruprecht.

Heydenreuter, Reinhard (1992): »Archive zwischen Staatsräson und Geschichtswissenschaft: Zur bayerischen Archivgeschichte zwischen 1799 und 1824«. *Mitteilungen für die Archivpflege in Bayern*, Sonderheft 9, 20-54.

Hohkamp, Michaela (1998): *Herrschaft in der Herrschaft: Die vorderösterreichische Obervogtei Triberg von 1736 bis 1780*, Göttingen: Vandenhoeck & Ruprecht.

Holenstein, André (2003): *›Gute Policey‹ und lokale Gesellschaft im Staat des Ancien Régime: Das Fallbeispiel der Markgrafschaft Baden (-Durlach)*, Epfendorf: Bibliotheca Academica.

Holenstein, André (2009): »Introduction: Empowering Interactions: Looking at Statebuilding from Below«. In: André Holenstein/Wim Blockmans/Jon Mathieu (eds.), *Empowering Interactions: Political Cultures and the Emergence of the State in Europe 1300-1900*, Burlington/VT: Ashgate, 1-31.

Hölscher, Lucian (1979): *Öffentlichkeit und Geheimnis: Eine begriffsgeschichtliche Untersuchung zur Entstehung der Öffentlichkeit in der frühen Neuzeit*, Stuttgart: Klett Cotta.

Jaroschka, Walter (1989): »Von Montgelas' Archivreform zum modernen Zentralarchiv«. *Mitteilungen für die Archivpflege in Bayern* 31, 5-8.

Kantorowicz, Ernst H. (1965): »Mysteries of the State: An Absolutist Concept and Its Late Mediaeval Origins«. In: *Selected Studies*, Locust Valley/NY: J.J. Augustin, 381-399.

Körner, Hans-Michael (1982): *Staat und Geschichte im Königreich Bayern, 1806-1918*, München: Beck.

Kunz, Georg (2000): *Verortete Geschichte: Regionales Geschichtsbewußtsein in den deutschen Historischen Vereinen des 19. Jahrhunderts*, Göttingen: Vandehoeck & Ruprecht.

Liess, Albrecht (2001): »History of Reorganisation and Rearrangement of the Holdings of the State Archives in Bavaria«. *Archivalische Zeitschrift* 84, 123-153.

Lingelbach, Gabriele (2003): »*Klio macht Karriere: Die Institutionalisierung der Geschichtswissenschaft in Frankreich und den USA in der zweiten Hälfte des 19. Jahrhunderts*, Göttingen: Vandenhoeck & Ruprecht.

Moraw, Peter (1984): »Humboldt in Gießen: Zur Professorenberufung an einer deutschen Universität des 19. Jahrhunderts«. *Geschichte und Gesellschaft* 10, 47-91.

Müller, Philipp (2004): »Geschichte machen: Überlegungen zu lokal-spezifischen Praktiken in der Geschichtswissenschaft und ihrer epistemischen Bedeutung im 19. Jahrhundert. Ein Literaturbericht«. *Historische Anthropologie* 12, 415-433.

Müller, Philipp (2009): »Doing Historical Research in the Early Nineteenth Century: Leopold Ranke, the Archive Policy, and the *Relazioni* of the Venetian Republic«. *Storia della Storiografia* 56, 80-103.

Münkler, Herfried (1987): *Im Namen des Staates: Die Begründung der Staatsraison in der frühen Neuzeit*, Frankfurt am Main: Fischer.

Paletschek, Sylvia (2001): *Die permanente Erfindung einer Tradition: Die Universität Tübingen im Kaiserreich und in der Weimarer Republik*, Stuttgart: Steiner.

Paletschek, Sylvia (2002): »Die Erfindung der Humboldtschen Universität: Die Konstruktion der deutschen Universitätsidee in der ersten Hälfte des 20. Jahrhunderts«. *Historische Anthropologie* 10, 183-205.

Potin, Yann (2000): »L'État et son Trésor: La science des archives à la fin du Moyen Âge«. *Actes de la recherche en sciences sociales* 133, 48-52.

Prochno, Joachim (1944): »Zur Archivgeschichtsschreibung«. *Archiv für Kulturgeschichte* 32, 288-293.

Reininghaus, Wilfried (2008): »Archivgeschichte: Umrisse einer untergründigen Subdisziplin«. *Der Archivar* 61, 352-360.

Rumschöttel, Hermann (1997): »Die Generaldirektion der Staatlichen Archive Bayerns«. *Archivalische Zeitschrift* 80, 1-36.

Schenk, Dietmar (2008): *Kleine Theorie des Archivs*, Stuttgart: Franz Steiner.

Schwerhoff, Gerd (2000): »Das Kölner Supplikenwesen in der frühen Neuzeit: Annäherungen an ein Kommunikationsmedium zwischen Untertanen und Obrigkeit«. In: Georg Mölich/Gerd Schwerhoff (eds.), *Köln als Kommunikationszentrum*, Köln: DuMont, 473-496.

Turner, Roy Steven (1973): *The Prussian Universities and the Research Imperative (1806 to 1848)*. PhD thesis: Princeton University.

Stolleis, Michael (1990): *Staat und Staatsräson in der frühen Neuzeit: Studien zur Geschichte des öffentlichen Rechts*, Frankfurt am Main: Suhrkamp.

Stolleis, Michael (1996): »Die Idee des souveränen Staates in Entstehung und Wandel verfassungsrechtlichen Denkens«. *Der Staat*, Special Issue 11, 63-85.

Vismann, Cornelia (2000): *Akten: Medientechnik und Recht*, Frankfurt am Main: Fischer.

Volkert, Wilhelm (1977): »Zur Geschichte des Bayerischen Hauptstaatsarchivs 1843-1944«. *Archivalische Zeitschrift* 73, 131- 148.

Volpi, Alessandro (1856): *Andrea Hofer, o la sollevazione del tirolo del 1809: Memorie storiche di Girolamo Andreis*, Milano: Giacomo Gnocchi.

Wegener, Bernhard (2006): *Der geheime Staat: Arkantradition und Informationsfreiheitsrecht*, Stuttgart: Morango.

Wiegand, Peter (2009): »Etappen, Motive und Rechtsgrundlagen der Nutzbarmachung staatlicher Archive: Das Beispiel des sächsischen Hauptstaatsarchivs 1834-1945«. *Archivalische Zeitschrift* 91, 9-56.

Zimmermann, Fritz (1962): »Die strukturellen Grundlagen der bayerischen Zentralarchive bis zum Ausgang des 18. Jahrhunderts«. *Archivalische Zeitschrift* 58, 44-94.

Wars and ›Little‹ Heroes

Historical Topics in Popular Poetry Anthologies

from the Nineteenth Century to the Present

STEFANIE LETHBRIDGE

INTRODUCTION

»Most of us, I suppose, can remember with what delight we first listened to such flowing buoyant verse as *Lochinvar* or *The Battle of the Baltic*. [...] The easy cadence of the rhythm, the beat of the rhyme, pleased and soothed our ears, and through that easy channel stole with soft and gradual step upon our young unconscious minds.« (Morris 1907: xi)

In his 1898 preface to the school anthology *Poet's Walk*, the critic and editor Mowbray Morris thus described his youthful encounter with poetry. More precisely, he described the impact of poetry with a *historical* topic on his youthful mind: »The Battle of the Baltic« by Thomas Campbell deals with Nelson's victory in the Battle of Copenhagen (1801) and »Lochinvar« is an excerpt from Sir Walter Scott's *Marmion*, a poem which centres around the battle of Flodden Field (1513), fought between England and Scotland, with disastrous results for the invading Scots. The young readers described in Morris's reminiscence do not focus on the historical event but on the aesthetic experience of cadence, rhyme and rhythm. Nonetheless, through this »easy channel« as he calls it, a rendering of a historical event entered their minds and memories.

School anthologies, until well into the twentieth century, were usually designed to serve the double purpose of furthering the moral education of pupils as well as acquaint them with the literary tradition of their country. The double focus becomes evident in typical titles for school anthologies, such as *Poems on Various Subjects: Selected to Enforce the Practice of Virtue and to Comprise in one Volume the Beauties of English Poetry* (ed. E. Tomkins 1778) or *Elegant Extracts, or Useful and Entertaining Pieces of Poetry: Selected for the Improvement of Youth, in Speaking, Reading, Thinking, Composing; and in the Conduct of Life* (ed. V. Knox 1785). As this last title suggests, the boundaries between school anthologies and poetry collections of more general use were blurred. In fact, many collections designed for a general audience were taken over by institutions of education for instructional use, notably Francis Turner Palgrave's *Golden Treasury* (1861) and Arthur Quiller-Couch's *Oxford Book of English Verse* (1900), which were used in schools and institutions of higher education not only in Britain but all over the Empire and Commonwealth. All these anthologies offer their selections invested with national significance, frequently bearing the epithet ›British‹ or ›English‹ in their title. They present a historical survey of poetic heritage, usually starting with either Chaucer or Milton, and thus they claim to represent the nation's history in the art of poetry. Such survey anthologies started to emerge after the removal of copyright restrictions in 1774 and their number increased rapidly from the late 1790s onwards.

Typically, poetry collections since the early nineteenth century offer lyrical poetry and thus not a form of poetry that one necessarily expects to have a historical subject – as one might expect from the epic. Nonetheless, a considerable number of popular lyrical poems do in fact deal with topics that are connected with national history. As Stefan Berger points out elsewhere in this volume, the literary rendering of history was, from the point of view of the professional historian, considered a popular approach by definition, singularly lacking in that scientific seriousness that was deemed necessary for professional history. E.A. Freeman, Regius Professor of History in Oxford, and himself an author of popular history, in the 1880s still described the study of English literature as »mere chatter about Shelley« and sneered at any aspirations that English literature might have to become a serious academic subject (cf. Palmer 1965: 96).

In place of ›serious‹ history, lyrical poems offer moments of emotional engagement with specific moments in national history. The more popular the poem, that is, the more widespread its reception, the more likely this poem is to contribute to a nation's perception of certain historical events. These poems offer, in other words, personal or personalised moments in history which each reader of the poem shares (at least potentially) with other readers and members of the cultural group. Where such poems were made available in anthologies, their cultural significance was even increased by the authoritative character of the selection, especially when this collection was edited by an acknowledged expert in poetry and it was offered as a national survey. National anthologies posit the private as a personal instantiation of the national and in this sense invite buyers and readers, as Sara Lodge has put it, »to construct their ›private memories‹ upon the foundational ›public memories‹ (literal or figurative)« which the collection purveys (Lodge 2004: 28). Popular poems with historical topics thus inscribe specific emotional experiences onto nationally relevant historical events. In this sense, moments of national history are turned into »a pattern / Of timeless moments«, as T.S. Eliot expresses it in »Little Gidding« (Eliot 1943: 58). The concept of historical awareness as the shared experience of »timeless moments« will serve as starting point and as conclusion for this investigation of historical topics in popular British poetry anthologies since 1800. The result of this exploration suggests three main conclusions: First, there was a boom of interest in historical subjects in anthologies in the second half of each century. Second, the national history that is presented in popular poetry anthologies is what could be described as ›incidental‹, largely because the poems are chosen for reasons other than historical. And third, while there is a slight shift in the *kinds* of emotional experiences that are offered in the nineteenth compared to the twentieth century, there is no dramatic change in the assessment of historical achievement which usually centres on the validation of a personalised version of the heroic and in this sense a timeless moment of and in history. This personalised dimension of the heroic is, in my assessment, the most significant aspect of poetry's contribution to the popular awareness of historical events.

First, a word on procedure: The following figures are based on an examination of 56 survey anthologies published between 1785 and 2007.[1] The exploration focuses on poems that were considered popular enough to be reprinted in at least three different anthologies and that deal with British history. Thus, what follows is not a survey of *all* poems that have historical topics reproduced in any one of these survey anthologies, but is restricted to those texts that have a reasonable chance of being inscribed in collective memory because they are repeated in different survey anthologies.[2] Through their use in schools, these anthologies achieved a high degree of circulation. Even though not all poems of an anthology were usually read in the classroom or at home, nineteenth-century teaching relied to a considerable extent on the memorisation of text passages, including poems. Many of these poems thus became entrenched in cultural memory through the education system. The most successful of these anthologies, however, like the *Golden Treasury* or the *Oxford Book of English Verse*, achieved cultural status beyond the education system. Invested with the cultural capital of their publishers (Macmillan and Oxford University Press) and exported to the colonies, they represented a reservoir of approved national heritage that was actively used abroad to represent Britain. Survey anthologies might be considered popular in a double sense. On the one hand, on account of a wide distribution (though not necessarily liked), on the other, as a genre that, per definition, aims to be representative – and that means both what had been judged ›good‹ by acknowledged experts, but also (and this often against the preferences of the anthologist) what had been well liked in the past by a large number of people.

---

1   A list of these anthologies can be found in the appendix. Data based on Lethbridge (2007).

2   *Marmion* and the »Lochinvar« excerpt mentioned above can be considered widely popular in the nineteenth century. Not only did the poem itself achieve bestselling status, but various excerpts were included in poetry anthologies: The »Lochinvar« excerpt can be found in ten of the survey anthologies under examination in this paper.

NATIONAL SURVEY ANTHOLOGIES AND POPULAR HISTORY

In its origin, the lyric is frequently an occasional poem and thus historical in the sense that it refers to a specific occasion in history. In theory, there is a difference between poetry that refers to events current at the time of writing – poems about contemporary history in that sense – and poems that refer to an event already in the distant past at the time of writing. Thus, for instance, Milton's »On the Late Massacre in Piedmont«, written in 1655 and referring to the massacre of Waldensians in Piedmont in the same year, is a poem about contemporary history that has little distance to the event described and as such, falls into a different category than, for instance, Scott's *Marmion*, which describes and appropriates events that lie about 300 years in its past. In the context of national survey anthologies, however, it is possible to ignore this difference. National survey anthologies are by definition backward-looking collections and largely include poetry written by poets that wrote some time ago and are considered canonical writers rather than current bestsellers (this is also done for copyright reasons, of course, as current writers are usually more expensive to reprint). In this sense, even the poems that deal with current events at the time of composition have become poems that deal with a past historical event by the time of the poem's inclusion in the poetry anthology. Thus, both the poems about contemporary history and those about the distant past deal with past events at the time of reception. The canonical status of poet and poem also confers canonical status on the historical event. The following exploration treats as ›historical poems‹ those that make a clear reference to a dateable historical event, time period or person of national history. Poems that deal with events of exclusively personal relevance, which is, of course, also a form of history, are not included. It might be worth noting, however, that poems about contemporary history at the time of composition are more frequent than those about events long past. The conversion of a poem with contemporary, often political, relevance into a text of largely aesthetic values which, on the surface, weakens its political impact, gives a first indication as to how anthologies turn history into an aesthetic experience.

The date 1785 serves as a convenient starting point for this exploration, as this was the first publication of Vicesimus Knox's long-lived poetry collection *Elegant Extracts*, which went through several editions and was used, particularly in schools, until well into the nineteenth century. Between 1796 and 1824 the *Elegant Extracts* reached publication figures of 23,000 (cf. St Clair 2004: 540). At the other end of the time span under examination in this paper, 2007 saw the publication of George Courtauld's anthology *England's Best Loved Poems*, which targets a general audience that responds to the revival of English (as opposed to British) patriotism. All the anthologies included in this survey were designed to reach a wider market – unlike editions of individual poets which were frequently not expected to sell more than a few hundred copies (cf. Erickson 1996: 36-38). Many publishers of such survey anthologies used marketing strategies to make these collections affordable, also for smaller budgets. Thus John Sharpe published the *British Anthology* in individual numbers between 1824 and 1825. *Beeton's Great Book of Poetry* was sold in shilling numbers in 1869 and in sixpenny numbers in 1881. Influential anthologies like Francis Turner Palgrave's *Golden Treasury* (1861) and Arthur Quiller-Couch's *Oxford Book of English Verse* were deliberately marketed at a moderate price – 3s6d for the *Golden Treasury* and 7s6d for the edition of the *Oxford Book of English Verse* on regular paper.[3] Both the *Golden Treasury* and the *Oxford Book of English Verse* achieved remarkable sales figures. The *Golden Treasury* was reprinted 27 times before the turn of the century. By the mid-twentieth century, the anthology's original publisher Macmillan alone had printed more than 650,000 copies and other publishers, like John Dent for the Everyman series or Oxford University Press for the Oxford Classics series, had started to publish reprints (cf. Ricks 1991: 444). The *Oxford Book of English Verse* had sold over half a million copies

---

3   The edition on thin India paper was more expensive at 10s6d (cf. Sutcliffe 1978: 124). The prices both for the *Golden Treasury* and the *Oxford Book of English Verse* place it in a medium price range (cf. Eliot 1994: 70, 74). While many reprint novels sold at significantly lower prices in one shilling or even sixpence editions, new poetry like Tennyson's *Idylls of the King* (1859) or Kipling's *The Seven Seas* sold for five to seven shillings (cf. Eliot/Nash 2009: 435, 439). Cheap poetry series, like the English Classics Series or the Shilling Garland Series, also offered poetry for prices between 6d and 1s (ibid. 437-438). However, while the Garland Series, for instance, offered 32 pages with paper wrappers, the *Oxford Book of English Verse* with over 1000 pages in hard cover cloth binding represented very good value for money.

by the mid-twentieth century (cf. Waller 2006: 63). Like Palgrave's *Golden Treasury*, it also spawned follow-up expanded versions with Helen Gardner's *New Oxford Book of English Verse* (1972) and Christopher Ricks's *Oxford Book of English Verse* (1999). But perhaps more important still than sales figures is the immense status and cultural presence that both Palgrave and the Oxford Books achieved: »[N]o civilized person in Great Britain, the Dominions or the United States is married or given in marriage without an Oxford Book«, the Oxford Magazine quipped in 1912 (qtd. in Brittain 1947: 39). And Frank Kermode described the general perception of Quiller-Couch's collection as »a body of verse which won cultural acceptance as in some way canonical« and »an index of the owner's participation in the culture« (Kermode 1990: 301). Even given that few people read anthologies from cover to cover, national poetry achieved much of its circulation and cultural presence – not only in reading but also in public recitations, like school recitations – through the medium of such poetry anthologies that were read both in the schools and the general market. Even though poetry sales were, with a few exceptions, easily outstripped by fiction, poetry continued to have a leading cultural function until well into the twentieth century (cf. Fussell 2000: 158 and passim).

In fact, schools deliberately encouraged the use of historical poetry to develop patriotic sentiment. »History fosters patriotism«, David Salmon remarked in his teaching manual, *The Art of Teaching* (1898) (qtd. in Heathorn 2002: 105). In the endeavour to encourage civic and patriotic pride, poetry frequently proved useful, as it evoked an emotional response in the children and thus empathy for people and events in their national past, as remarked by Mowbray Morris in the epitaph to this article.

»Death in battle in these accounts is depicted as glorious and worthy of poetry. Indeed, Tennyson's ›war‹ poetry figured frequently in both English and history readers. Perhaps the most popular was his 1878 poetic rendering of the tale of Richard Grenville's ship *The Revenge*. [...] School inspectors found that this story and Tennyson's poem were favourites in the elementary school classroom.« (Heathorn 2002: 107)[4]

---

4   Unlike in school histories, however, Tennyson's »Revenge« did not prove popular in survey anthologies. It can be found in Ward, *English Poets* (1880) and in Herbert, *Everyman's Book of Evergreen Verse* (1981).

Official educational policy as well as teaching practice towards the end of the nineteenth century thus encouraged an emotional engagement with the past as part of a child's cultural identity formation, and it considered poetry a valid vehicle with which to create such an emotional engagement with the national past.[5] This policy is in fact still pursued in a modern teaching environment which, as Jerome de Groot has pointed out, frequently »figures history as a school subject as something to encourage active citizenship through empathy with [...] historically othered people« (de Groot 2009: 41), though a modern teaching environment tends to prefer media other than poetry. Nonetheless, at the end of both the twentieth as well as the nineteenth centuries an increased interest in historical subjects manifests itself, among other things, in a higher density of poems with historical subjects in national survey anthologies.

HISTORY BOOM AT THE END OF CENTURIES

Poems with historical subjects occur more frequently in survey anthologies produced in the second half of the century. This is the case both for the nineteenth and the twentieth centuries.[6] In the nineteenth century, Palgrave's *Golden Treasury* (1861) seems to have started a trend for lyrical presentations of the historical. In the twentieth century, Helen Gardner explicitly announces her intention to include a larger number of poems with

---

5   This is developed in detail in Howsam (2009: ch. 1).

6   It is less the case for the end of the eighteenth century. In many ways the history boom at the turn of the eighteenth to the nineteenth century took a different form. Rather than in individual poems, it manifested itself in the appearance of survey collections which included poems from earlier periods in the first place, collections like Bishop Percy's *Reliques of Ancient English Poetry* (1765) or George Ellis's *Specimens of the Early English Poets* (first ed. 1790). Under the influence of such collections many Romantic poets became interested both in the lyric and in vernacular history. Given this interest in history in the Romantic period (cf., for example, Rigney 2001; Mitchell 2000), it is not surprising that many of the frequently appearing historical poems in nineteenth- and twentieth-century anthologies are those written by Romantic poets (i.e. Campbell, Southey, Gray, Shelley).

historical focus: »This anthology balances against poems of the private life poems that deal with public events and historical occasions [...]« (Gardner 1972: vii). Both Palgrave and Gardner are imitated on this score by other anthologists in the decades that follow. Overall, I identified 41 poems by 29 different poets that deal with British historical events and occur in at least three of the 56 anthologies under review here. Of these Palgrave includes 14 and Gardner 16 in their respective collections, Thomas Humphry Ward's *English Poets* (1880) has 20 and Ricks's *Oxford Book of English Verse* offers 16, like Gardner, though not all the same ones. By comparison, anthologies published earlier in their respective centuries tend to include a notably smaller number of popular poems with historical subjects: Thomas Campbell's *Specimens of the British Poets* (1819) offers three, Thomas Hazlitt's *Select British Poets* (1825) has eight and Gerald Bullet's *English Galaxy of Shorter Poems* (1933) includes only one. While there are some marked exceptions to this trend – the BBC's popular vote anthology *The Nation's Favourite Poems* (1996), for instance, includes only five popular historical poems and Anthony Thwaite's *Six Centuries of Verse* (1984) has a meagre three, most survey anthologies published at the end of each century included more poems with historical subjects than anthologies published earlier in each century. This might be taken as a response to a general upsurge in historical interest towards the end of each century, though on the whole, this correlation is likely to be accidental rather than a deliberate attempt to include historical poems.[7]

INCIDENTAL HISTORY

Poems with an historical topic are not likely to be chosen for national survey anthologies on account of this topic. The editor of a survey poetry anthology tends to bear three considerations in mind when making his or her selection: Does the poem fulfill certain aesthetic standards? Is the poem

---

7   For the history boom at the end of the twentieth century cf. Korte/Paletschek (2009: 9). Leslie Howsam connects the origin of an increased interest in history at the end of the nineteenth century with the parallel development of history as a professional discipline and the expansion of publishing activity on the history market (cf. Howsam 2009: xi).

particularly representative of the time or the work of an author? And, not to be overlooked, is this likely to sell copy? This last consideration will also take the accessibility of the poem for the non-expert reader into account, particularly on the textbook market. The history that is thus presented in these anthologies is not chosen on the grounds of its historical importance, but on largely aesthetic or commercial grounds. This results in a form of ›incidental history‹ and the historical events we find represented in popular historical poems are not necessarily the events one would expect to be the focus, or the exclusive focus, of a ›regular‹ history. The following historical events or persons are represented in frequently repeated poems with historical topics. The list is in the order of frequency of appearance, not in chronological order. Topics covered by more than one poem are marked in italics. If not italicized, this historical event or person maintains a presence in survey anthologies as the result of the popularity of one particular poem, as in the case of Robert Southey's »After Blenheim« or Alfred Lord Tennyson's »Charge of the Light Brigade«:

Napoleonic Wars (turn of 18th/19th century, 81 occurrences)
English Civil War and Interregnum (17th century, 50 occurrences)
First and Second World Wars (38 occurrences)
Battle of Agincourt (1485, English victory against France,
    22 occurrences)[8]
Battle of Flodden (1513, English victory against Scotland, 22 occurrences)
Monmouth Rebellion (1685, against King James II, 21 occurrences)
Elizabeth of Bohemia (17th century, daughter of James I, Queen of Bohemia,
    21 occurrences)
Invasion of Wales (under Edward I, 13th century, 21 occurrences)
Condition of England (early 19th century, 17 occurrences)
Queen Victoria's Jubilee/British Empire (1897, 10 occurrences)
Robert Bruce's March on Bannockburn (1314, Scottish Wars of Independence,
    10 occurrences)

---

8   In one case this is a mistaken connection: Laura Valentine's *Gems of National Poetry* (1880) titles the speech before Harfleur in Shakespeare's *Henry V* as »Agincourt«. Henry's campaign in France was here obviously conflated into one event associated with the victory at Agincourt.

Loss of the Royal George (1782, sinking of famous warship during repairs at Spithead, 10 occurrences)

Charge of the Light Brigade (1854, Battle of Balaclava, Crimean War, 9 occurrences)

Boadicea (68 AD, uprising against Roman occupation of Britain under Boadicea, 8 occurrences)

Defeat of the Spanish Armada (1588, 8 occurrences)

Battle of Blenheim (1704, Marlborough victory in the War of Spanish Succession, 8 occurrences)

Restoration of the Monarchy after the Civil War (1660, 7 occurrences)

Battle of Culloden (1745, defeat of Jacobite rising, 4 occurrences)

Newton (4 occurrences)

Slavery debate/Abolition movement (early 19th century, 4 occurrences)

Immediately noticeable is the dominance of war events in various forms. By far the most popular topic of representation are the Napoleonic Wars with 81 representations in five different poems.[9] This is followed, in terms of frequency of representation, by the English Civil War and Interregnum with 50 representations in four poems.[10] Remarkable is also the *absence* of British historical events that historians usually consider important, such as William the Conqueror in 1066, the reign of Elizabeth I or the Glorious Revolution of 1688.

This is not because no poems have been written on these topics – as collections like Kenneth Baker's *The Faber Book of English History in Verse* (1988) and M.E. Windsor and J. Turral's *Lyra Historica: Poems of British History* (1911) amply demonstrate. Frank Kermode points out that countless poems have been written to commemorate occasions that are perceived as historically important. In fact, it is the explicit duty of the British

---

9   Including Thomas Campbell's »Ye Mariners of England« into the count which alludes to Nelson and appears in 16 anthologies. The other poems are Byron's »Waterloo« (an excerpt from *Childe Harold*) with 14 occurrences, Campbell's »Hohenlinden« (18), Campbell's »Battle of the Baltic« (10) and Charles Wolfe's »Burial of Sir John Moore« (23).

10 The poems are Richard Lovelace, »To Lucasta, Going to the Wars« (24 occurrences), Andrew Marvell, »Horatian Ode upon Cromwell's Return from Ireland« (17), Thomas Babington Macaulay, »The Battle of Naseby« (5) and John Milton, »To the Lord General Cromwell« (4).

poet laureate to commemorate such occasions. Though, as Kermode also notes, these poems do not necessarily enter a national canon of poetry:

»A vast number of poems have been written in celebration of historical events, from great victories to royal birthays [sic], and on the whole we pay them little attention. One reason may be that many such poems simply comply with their occasions, and pass into oblivion with those occasions.« (Kermode 1990: 50)

Historical poems in national survey anthologies attempting to represent a national poetic canon thus are in no sense a record of historical events, neither in terms of comprehensiveness of events represented, nor in terms of accurate historical representation of those events that are depicted. They are, however, as Kermode puts it, »a variety of history with obvious mnemonic attractions; [...] in celebration of the great events given historical centrality by communal acts of historical imagination« (Kermode 1990: 50).

Despite such more or less incidental compilations of historical material, there are a few general trends that can be identified: The nineteenth-century poetic preoccupation with the wars against France and Napoleon at the turn of the eighteenth to the nineteenth century is replaced in the twentieth century with a focus on the two *World Wars*. The 61 poetic depictions of the wars against France in the nineteenth century drop to 20 in the twentieth century. Instead, the two World Wars are represented by 38 occurrences of 6 different poems.[11] The Battle of Blenheim (with Southey's poem) disappears almost completely in the twentieth century (one occurrence),[12] which instead represents the Battle of Balaclava with Tennyson's »Charge of the Light Brigade« (with seven occurrences).[13] On the whole, the anthologies

---

11 It needs to be stressed here again that this count only includes those poems that are repeated in at least three of the anthologies under consideration. The absolute number of representations of the two world wars is much higher.

12 In Wain, *The Oxford Anthology of English Poetry* (1990).

13 In the supplementary volume to Ward, *The English Poets* (1919), Herbert, *Everyman's Book of Evergreen Verse* (1981), Wain, *The Oxford Anthology of English Poetry* (1990), *The Nation's Favourite Poems* (1996), Ricks, *The Oxford Book of English Verse* (1999), Ferguson et al., *The Norton Anthology of Poetry* (2005) and in Courtauld, *England's Best Loved Poems*.

of the twentieth century are slightly more interested in socio-historical conditions than those of the nineteenth century – even though socio-historical poems in twentieth-century anthologies frequently deal with nineteenth-century conditions (such as P.B. Shelley's »England in 1819«, John Davidson's »Thirty Bob a Week« or Thomas Hood's »Song of the Shirt«). Susan Bassnett has explicitly pointed to the twentieth-century preference for a political Shelley for instance, who partly replaced the lyrical and highly emotional Shelley of earlier selections.

»Ricks' selection [in *The Oxford Book of English Verse*, 1999] reflects the late twentieth-century view of Shelley as a committed poet, a writer critical of his own society and more concerned with the rights of man than with extolling the splendours of the English countryside.« (Bassnett 2001: 260-261)

Another general trend is that the nineteenth-century disregard for eighteenth-century poetry and satire relegated historical events of the eighteenth century to a backseat of poetic cultural memory from which there is no noticeable recovery in the twentieth century. In the nineteenth century, Marlborough makes an appearance through Robert Southey's poem »After Blenheim«. The only historical figure from the long eighteenth century to emerge in the twentieth century is Newton. He gains a footing in the historical poetic memory with Pope's epitaph: »Nature and nature's law lay hid in night / God said, Let Newton be! and there was light« which appears in Knox's collection and again in three twentieth-century anthologies.[14] Such changes in representation can be taken to reflect a shift in the events that resonate with the readership beyond aesthetic considerations. While the wars with France and the heroes they created on both sides engage the nineteenth-century imagination, they no longer figure very significantly in the twentieth century. With the topics that no longer resonate, either publicly or in critical circles, some of the poets who are the foremost celebrators of these topics, like Thomas Campbell who contributed three popular poems about the Napoleonic Wars, also lose their canonical status.

---

14 Hayward, *The Penguin Book of English Verse* (1978), Ricks, *The Oxford Book of English Verse* (1999) and Keegan, *The New Penguin Book of English Verse* (2001).

PERSONALIZED HEROISM

Perhaps the most important result of this analysis is the marked personalisation of historical events presented in survey anthologies. This is partly a consequence of the generic preoccupation with the lyric in survey anthologies which lends itself to the presentation of moments of personal experience more than other poetic genres. While certain war engagements seem to dominate poetical renderings of history in survey anthologies, the celebration of famous war heroes is, to a surprising extent, subordinated to the celebration of ›little‹ heroes, of more or less ordinary people who become involved in heroic moments of history. In this sense, history in survey anthologies offers moments of empathy with persons on the same social level as the readers are likely to be.

According to Stephen Heathorn, the favourite public heroes in school readers of the late nineteenth and early twentieth centuries were General Gordon (who was killed at Karthoum in 1885) and Admiral Nelson. These figures were cast as heroic models for school boys to imitate (cf. Heathorn 2002: 108-109). In historical poems written throughout the nineteenth century, Nelson also figures repeatedly,[15] but more frequently it is the common man or the poet-speaker rather than the publicly known hero who function as the centre of perception. With a few exceptions, and even in poems where public heroes appear, the speakers of historical poems adopt the perspective of what one might call the ›ordinary person‹, that is, the perspective of the follower, the one in the crowd, or perhaps the spectator, who is nonetheless aligned with the heroic and thus becomes a ›little‹ hero. This personalised view of history from the perspective of the common man (rarely common woman) can be aptly illustrated with two of the most frequently reprinted historical poems that demonstrate slightly different aspects of this personalisation of history and the heroic. The first example is Charles Wolfe's poem »The Burial of Sir John Moore after Corunna«, a poem which occurs 17 times in nineteenth-century survey anthologies and six more times in the twentieth century.

---

15 For instance in Campbell's »Battle of the Baltic« and »Ye Mariners of England«, in an excerpt from Scott's *Marmion* entitled »Pitt – Nelson – Fox« and in the anonymous poem »On Lord Nelson, at Merton« (the last two examples have only one occurrence each).

The Battle of Corunna took place in January 1809 during the British retreat from Spain after the Spanish had been defeated by Napoleon. Moore was trying to ship his troops back to England, but was forced to fight at Corunna when the French caught up with the retreating British. Moore was hit during the battle and lived only long enough to see the British victory (cf. Hilton 2006: 216). In Wolfe's poem the death of the general is presented from the perspective of the soldiers who buried him.

The Burial of Sir John Moore after Corunna

Not a drum was heard, not a funeral note,
  As his corse to the rampart we hurried;
Not a soldier discharged his farewell shot
  O'er the grave where our hero we buried.

We buried him darkly at dead of night,
  The sods with our bayonets turning,
By the struggling moonbeam's misty light
  And the lanthorn dimly burning.

No useless coffin enclosed his breast,
  Not in sheet or in shroud we wound him;
But he lay like a warrior taking his rest
  With his martial cloak around him.

Few and short were the prayers we said,
  And we spoke not a word of sorrow;
But we steadfastly gazed on the face that was dead,
  And we bitterly thought of the morrow.

We thought, as we hollow'd his narrow bed
  And smooth'd down his lonely pillow,
That the foe and the stranger would tread o'er his head,
  And we far away on the billow!

Lightly they'll talk of the spirit that's gone,
  And o'er his cold ashes upbraid him –
But little he'll reck, if they let him sleep on
  In the grave where a Briton has laid him.

But half of our heavy task was done
  When the clock struck the hour for retiring;
And we heard the distant and random gun
  That the foe was sullenly firing.

Slowly and sadly we laid him down,
  From the field of his fame fresh and gory;
We carved not a line, and we raised not a stone,
  But we left him alone with his glory.[16]

The poem captures a moment of defeat (the death of the general as well as the retreat) which is presented as a moment of resistance. It expresses this in a series of events that ought to happen at the funeral of a military hero but that do in fact *not* happen at this burial: »*Not* a drum was heard, *not* a funeral note / *Not* a soldier discharged his farewell shot« (first stanza, my emphasis) and »We carved *not* a line, and we raised *not* a stone« (last stanza, my emphasis). Present in the poem, though absent in the historical world, these funeral rites are contrasted by a series of replacement actions, all introduced by the conjunction ›but‹ and all actions that denote the genuine hero – rather than the one merely surrounded by pomp and circumstance: »But he lay like a warrior taking his rest« (line 11), »But we steadfastly gazed on the face that was dead« (line 15), »But little he'll reck« (line 23), »But we left him alone with his glory« (last line).

The tone of the poem is sombre, there is a sense of mystery and a sense of emergency: It is the »dead of night«, the light is dim and misty (»By the struggling moonbeam's misty light« and »the lanthorn dimly burning«, stanza 2), there is the sound of distant guns (»we heard the distant and random gun«, line 27). These sense impressions communicate a sensation of immediacy. The reader sees and hears what is happening at the burial. Notably, while the text gives an internal view of people's thought, this remains

---

16 Quoted from Quiller-Couch (1900: 695-696).

a communal experience, it is »*we* bitterly thought of the morrow« (line 16, my emphasis). The speaker remains one of the group. The persistent use of the first-person plural, rather than the first-person singular, draws the reader into this experience. Reading this poem, he or she becomes part of this group that raises a textual monument in place of an actual gravestone. Through the shared sense experiences and the use of the first-person plural, the reader is given the opportunity to re-live this moment in history, knowing that this is of national historic relevance and also knowing that other members of the cultural group are likely to share this experience because it is in a national survey anthology. The specific historical moment becomes a timeless moment in shared, explicitly communal, national history and it also becomes incident to – in the sense of ›attaching to‹ – the reader's life. This poem thus expresses the combination of concrete experience or incident, shared memory and national history that characterises historical poems in survey anthologies.

The second example illustrates a slightly different category of personalised history: »To Lucasta, Going to the Wars« by the seventeenth-century poet Richard Lovelace.

To Lucasta, Going to the Wars

Tell me not, Sweet, I am unkind,
  That from the nunnery
Of thy chaste breast and quiet mind
  To war and arms I fly.

True, a new mistress now I chase,
  The first foe in the field;
And with a stronger faith embrace
  A sword, a horse, a shield.

Yet this inconstancy is such
  As thou too shalt adore;
I could not love thee, Dear, so much,
  Loved I not Honour more.[17]

---

17 Quoted from Quiller-Couch (1900: 370-371).

Like Wolfe's »Burial«, this poem is also among the most frequently represented historical poems in survey anthologies. 23 of the 56 anthologies
under examination include it. Unlike Wolfe's poem, which was clearly a
nineteenth-century favourite, Lovelace's »Lucasta« maintains an equal
popularity in both centuries, with 12 representations in the nineteenth and
11 in the twentieth.

The poem makes a reference to a specific war, the English Civil War,
easily identifiable for anyone who knows that Lovelace fought on the Ca-
valier side, the side of the king. Within this setting of a public occasion, the
poem offers a private side of the historical moment, the lover's apology and
explanation as he leaves the arms of his mistress to take up the arms of
battle. Again, heroic virtue – honour in this case – is praised and the needs
of the community are placed above, in fact made the condition of, individual needs: »I could not love thee, Dear, so much / Loved I not Honour
more« (lines 11-12). Despite the reference to a specific historical moment,
the poem maintains its popularity over time, possibly because it offers a
paradigm of emotional response to the opposing demands of group and
individual that is in fact historically non-specific, that is transferable to *any*
historical situation involving armed conflict and the parting of lovers (even
when the accoutrements of the knightly hero, »A sword, a horse, a shield«
(line 8) are replaced by different weapons). The poem thus offers a type of
emotional response and meaning potential to moments that are likely to
repeat in a nation's history. Frank Kermode regards the conversion of the
public into the private as the particular potency of historical poetry: These
poems »make history strange and they are very private in their handling of
the public themes. They can protect us from the familiar, they stand apart
from opinion; they are a form of knowledge.« (Kermode 1990: 67) Once
again, the shared paradigm of emotional response through the shared poetic
heritage turns the individual reader of this poem into an instantiation of the
group and the emotional response becomes incident to the life of the individual within the paradigm of the national.

ENTRENCHED HISTORIES

The last question that is worth addressing is whether there are any significant changes in the attitude to historical moments over time. Does the

twentieth century offer the same paradigms of shared emotional response to historical events as the nineteenth century? Perhaps somewhat surprisingly, the answer to this question seems to be in the affirmative, albeit with some qualifications. One might expect the twentieth century to take a much more critical stance to celebrations of heroic values. On the whole, this is not the case. Lovelace's elevation of honour above the love for his mistress maintains its popularity in the twentieth century. While the poems on the Napoleonic Wars in anthologies of the nineteenth century are largely replaced by poems on the two World Wars in the twentieth century, one of the two most popular war poems in survey anthologies of the twentieth century is Rupert Brooke's »The Soldier« (10 occurrences), which precisely does *not* question the ideals of heroic self-sacrifice for the community: »If I should die, think only this of me: / That there's some corner of a foreign field / That is forever England«.[18] On the other hand, the second most frequently reprinted war poem is Wilfred Owen's »Anthem for Doomed Youth« (also 10 occurrences) which does introduce a clearly critical stance to traditional heroism and describes the young soldiers as »these who die as cattle«.[19] In terms of sheer numbers, about one third of the poems with historical topics in twentieth-century anthologies take a more or less critical stance to traditional heroic values, while only about one eighth of the poems in nineteenth-century anthologies question the celebration of the heroic. Henry Reed's poem »Today we have naming of parts«, part I of Reed's *Lessons of the War* (1942), might serve as an example for the twentieth-century distance to heroics. The poem refers to the Second World War and derives its force from the stark contrast between the deadly parts of a gun and the life-producing parts of nature.

And this you can see is the bolt. The purpose of this
Is to open the breech, as you see. We can slide it
Rapidly backwards and forwards: we call this
Easing the spring. And rapidly backwards and forwards
The early bees are assaulting and fumbling the flowers:
  They call it easing the Spring (lines 19-24)[20]

---

18 Quoted from Courtauld (2007: 187).

19 Quoted from Ricks (1999: 578).

20 Quoted from Ricks (1999: 619).

As the language merges from the description of the gun into the process of renewal in nature, with clear sexual undertones, warfare is exposed as a perversion. Told from the perspective of the young and awkwardly fumbling recruit, the poem dissociates the war experience from any heroic sentiment. Reed's poem is represented in seven post-war survey anthologies and can thus be described as a popular anthology poem. In contrast to Reed's quiet irony, Tennyson's »Charge of the Light Brigade«, which is also represented in seven twentieth-century anthologies, clearly celebrates heroic sacrifice.[21] Even though Tennyson praises the achievements of a select group, he continues the notable focus on group achievement, rather than the heroics of an individual. At the end of the poem, the reader is explicitly addressed and given a task in the commemoration of group achievement:

Cannon to right of them,
Cannon to left of them,
Cannon behind them
　Volley'd and thunder'd;
Storm'd at with shot and shell,
While horse and hero fell,
They that had fought so well
Came thro' the jaws of Death,
Back from the mouth of Hell,
All that was left of them,
　Left of six hundred.

21　The poem is only in two of the nineteenth-century anthologies under consideration here. This is more likely on account of difficulties to obtain the copyright than a lack of popularity. Tennyson died in October 1892, so the poem entered the public domain in 1899 under the then current copyright law. Tennyson, who was a close friend of Palgrave's, refused to be included in the *Golden Treasury*. During the nineteenth century the poem was printed in Thomas Humphry Ward's anthology *The English Poets* (1880 and 1919), published by Macmillan, who held the Tennyson copyrights.

When can their glory fade?
O the wild charge they made!
  All the world wonder'd.
Honour the charge they made!
Honour the Light Brigade,
  Noble six hundred![22]

While there is a notable increase of doubt in the twentieth century or, at any rate, an absence of heroic sentiment in several poems, the majority of poems with historical topics in both the nineteenth and the twentieth centuries, like Tennyson's »Charge of the Light Brigade«, celebrate the heroic and its value for the cultural group as well as the individual. In this sense national survey anthologies of poetry present what might be called a conservative view of history and the nation; it does not follow the critical trends of the novel in the late twentieth century for instance. Instead, it affirms group values and group membership in ways that have become entrenched during the nineteenth century.

Historical topics in British national poetry anthologies proliferate towards the end of the nineteenth and twentieth centuries. Such historical poetry is not history in a factual sense, it does not cover history systematically, nor does it try to render events objectively. »You are not here to verify, / Instruct yourself, or inform curiosity / Or carry report« as T.S. Eliot says (Eliot 1943: 50-51). Historical poems in national survey anthologies offer moments in national history as shared emotional experience which turns the history that is presented ›incidentally‹, into an ›incident‹ for the reader and ›incidental‹ to his or her memory of a historical moment, a timeless moment of shared cultural significance. There, »the intersection of the timeless moment / Is England and nowhere. Never and always« (Eliot 1943: 51).

WORKS CITED

Bassnett, Susan (2001): »A Century of Editing: *The Oxford Book of English Verse*, 1900-1999«. *European Studies* 16, 251-264.

---

22 Quoted from Ricks (1999: 430, lines 49-55).

Brittain, Frederick (1947): *Arthur Quiller-Couch: A Study of Q*, Cambridge: Cambridge University Press.

Courtauld, George (ed.) (2007): *England's Best Loved Poems: The Enchantment of England*, London: Ebury Press.

De Groot, Jerome (2009): *Consuming History: Historians and Heritage in Contemporary Popular Culture*, Abingdon: Routledge.

Eliot, Simon (1994): *Some Patterns and Trends in British Publishing 1800-1919*, London: The Bibliographical Society.

Eliot, Simon/Andrew Nash (2009): »Mass Markets: Literature«. In: David McKitterick (ed.), *The Cambridge History of the Book in Britain*, vol. VI: *1830-1914*, Cambridge: Cambridge University Press, 416-442.

Eliot, T.S. (1943): *The Four Quartets*, New York/NY: Harcourt Brace Jovanovich.

Erickson, Lee (1996): *The Economy of Literary Form: English Literature and the Industrialization of Publishing 1800-1850*, Baltimore/MD: Johns Hopkins University Press.

Fussell, Paul (2000 [1975]): *The Great War and Modern Memory*, Oxford: Oxford University Press.

Gardner, Helen (1972): »Preface«. In: *The New Oxford Book of English Verse*, Oxford: Oxford University Press, v-viii.

Heathorn, Stephen (2002): »Representations of War and Martial Heroes in English Elementary School Reading and Rituals, 1885-1914«. In: James Marten (ed.), *Children and War: A Historical Anthology*, New York/NY: New York University Press, 103-115.

Hilton, Boyd (2006): *A Mad, Bad, and Dangerous People? England 1783-1846*, Oxford: Clarendon Press.

Howsam, Leslie (2009): *Past into Print: The Publishing of History in Britain 1850-1950*, London: The British Library.

Kermode, Frank (1990 [1973]): »Poetry à la Mode«. In: *The Uses of Error*, London: Collins, 300-307.

Kermode, Frank (1990): *Poetry, Narrative, History: The Bucknell Lectures in Literary Theory*, Oxford: Basil Blackwell.

Korte, Barbara/Sylvia Paletschek (2009): »Geschichte in populären Medien und Genres: Vom Historischen Roman zum Computerspiel«. In: Barbara Korte/Sylvia Paletschek (eds.), *History Goes Pop: Zur Repräsentation von Geschichte in populären Medien und Genres*, Bielefeld: transcript, 9-60.

Lethbridge, Stefanie (2007): *Index Britischer Lyrikanthologien* (http://ibl. ub.uni-freiburg.de). Accessed 29 December 2010.

Lodge, Sara (2004): »Romantic Reliquaries: Memory and Irony in The Literary Annuals«. *Romanticism* 10.1, 23-40.

Mitchell, Rosemary (2000): *Picturing the Past: English History in Text and Image 1830-1870*, Oxford: Clarendon Press.

Morris, Mowbray (1907): »Preface«. In: *Poet's Walk*, new and rev. ed., London: Macmillan, vii-xxi.

Palmer, David John (1965): *The Rise of English Studies: An Account of the Study of English Literature from its Origins to the Making of the Oxford English School*, Oxford: Oxford University Press.

Quiller-Couch, Arthur (ed.) (1900): *The Oxford Book of English Verse*, Oxford: Oxford University Press.

Ricks, Christopher (1991): »The Making of the *Golden Treasury*«. In: Christopher Ricks (ed.), *The Golden Treasury* by Francis Turner Palgrave, London: Penguin, 437-450.

Ricks, Christopher (ed.) (1999): *The Oxford Book of English Verse*, Oxford: Oxford University Press.

Rigney, Ann (2001): *Imperfect Histories: The Elusive Past and the Legacy of Romantic Historicism*, Ithaca/NY: Cornell University Press.

St Clair, William (2004): *The Reading Nation in the Romantic Period*, Cambridge: Cambridge University Press.

Sutcliffe, Peter (1978): *The Oxford University Press: An Informal History*, Oxford: Clardendon Press.

Waller, Philip (2006): *Writers, Readers, and Reputations: Literary Life in Britain 1870-1914*, Oxford: Oxford University Press.

APPENDIX: LIST OF ANTHOLOGIES

Aikin, John (ed.) (1820): *Select Works of the British Poets*, London: Longman, Rees, Orme, Brown, Green & Longman.

Beeching, H.C. (ed.) (1899): *A Paradise of English Poetry*, new ed., London: Rivingtons.

Beeton, Samuel (ed.) (1881): *Beeton's Great Book of Poetry*, London: Ward, Lock and Tyler.

Benson, Gerard/Judith Chernaik/Cecily Herbert (eds.) (2003): *Poems on the Underground*, London: Cassell.

Bullet, Gerald (ed.) (1933): *The English Galaxy of Shorter Poems*, London: J. Dent.

Campbell, Thomas (ed.) (1819): *Specimens of the British Poets: With Biographical and Critical Notes, and An Essay on English Poetry*, 7 vols., London: John Murray.

Chambers, William/Robert Chambers (eds.) (1865): *Chambers's Readings in English Poetry*, London: William and Robert Chambers.

Collins, A.S. (ed.) (1931): *Treasury of English Verse: New and Old*, London: W.B. Clive.

Courtauld, George (ed.) (2007): *England's Best Loved Poems: The Enchantment of England*, London: Ebury Press.

Croly, George (ed.) (1828): *The Beauties of the British Poets with a Few Introductory Observations*, London: Seeley/Burnside.

Davis, William (ed.) (1881): *The Book of Poetry for Schools and Families*, rev. ed., London: Simpkin, Marshall and Co.

Dulcken, H.W. (ed.) (1860): *Pearls from the Poets: Specimens of the Works of Celebrated Writers*, London: Ward, Lock and Tyler.

Ellis, George (ed.) (1811): *Specimens of the Early English Poets: To Which is Prefixed an Historical Sketch of the Rise and Progress of the English Poetry and Language*, 3 vols., 4th ed. corr., London: Longman.

Favourite English Poems of the Two Last Centuries (1859), London: Sampson Low.

Ferguson, Margaret/Mary Jo Salter/Jon Stallworthy (eds.) (2005): *The Norton Anthology of Poetry*, 5th ed., New York/NY: Norton & Company.

Gardner, Helen (ed.) (1972): *The New Oxford Book of English Verse, 1250-1950*, Oxford: Oxford University Press.

Gilfillan, George (ed.) (1851): *Book of British Poesy: Ancient and Modern*, Liverpool: John Walker/London: William Tegg.

Giraldus [William Allingham] (ed.) (1860): *Nightingale Valley: A Collection, Including a Great Number of the Choicest Lyrics and Short Poems in the English Language*, London: Bell & Daldy.

Graham Smith (ed.) (1952): *100 Best Poems in the English Language*, London: Ernest Benn.

Hall, S.C. (ed.) (1836-8): *Book of Gems*, 3 vols., London: Saunders and Otley.

Hayward, John (ed.) (1978): *The Penguin Book of English Verse*, London: Allen Lane.

Hazlitt, William (ed.) (1825): *Select British Poets*, London: Hall.

Herbert, David (ed.) (1981): *Everyman's Book of Evergreen Verse*, London: Dent.

Heritage (1941), London: News Chronicle.

Inglis, Robert (ed.) (1862): *Gleanings from the English Poets, Chaucer to Tennyson, with Biographical Notices of the Authors*, Edinburgh: Gall & Inglis.

Keegan, Paul (ed.) (2001): *The New Penguin Book of English Verse*, London: Penguin.

Knox, Vicesimus (ed.) (1785): *Elegant Extracts, or Useful and Entertaining Pieces of Poetry: Selected for the Improvement of Youth, in Speaking, Reading, Thinking, Composing; and in the Conduct of Life*, London: Charles Dilly.

Leeson, Edward (ed.) (1980): *The New Golden Treasury of English Verse*, London: Pan.

Mackay, Charles (ed.) (1867): *A Thousand and One Gems of English Poetry*, London: George Routledge and Sons.

Mavor, William (ed.) (1823): *Classical English Poetry*, London: Longman, Hurst, Rees, Orme and Brown.

Meynell, Alice (ed.) (1897): *The Flower of the Mind: A Choice Among the Best Poets*, London: Grant Richards.

Motion, Andrew (ed.) (2002): *Here to Eternity: An Anthology of English Poetry*, London: Faber and Faber.

Palgrave, Francis Turner (ed.) (1861): *The Golden Treasury of the Best Songs and Lyrical Poems in the English Language*, London: Macmillan.

Pennie, J.F. (ed.) (1822): *The Harp of Parnassus: A New Selection of Classical English Poetry*, London: Whittaker.

Poetical Selections, Consisting of the Most Approved Pieces of Our Best British Poets [...] (1811), Birmingham: Thomas and Wrightson.

Poetry Please! Popular Poems from the BBC Radio 4 Programme (2003), London: Phoenix.

Pratt, Samuel (ed.) (1809): *The Cabinet of Poetry: Containing the Best Entire Pieces to be Found in The Works of The British Poets*, 6 vols., London: Richard Phillips.

Quiller-Couch, Arthur (1900): *The Oxford Book of English Verse 1250-1900*, Oxford: Clarendon Press.

Read, Herbert/Bonamy Dobrée (eds.) (1949): *The London Book of English Verse*, London: Eyre & Spottiswoode.

Readings in Poetry: A Selection from the Best English Poets, from Spenser to Present Times; and Specimens of Several American Poets (1843), 7th ed. with additions, London: Parker.

Rhys, Ernest (ed.) (1914): *The New Golden Treasury of Songs and Lyrics*, London: J.M. Dent and Sons.

Rhys, Ernest (ed.) (1939): *The Golden Treasury of Longer Poems*, school ed., London: J.M. Dent & Sons.

Ricks, Christopher (ed.) (1999): *The Oxford Book of English Verse*, Oxford: Oxford University Press.

Ritson, Joseph (ed.) (1793-4): *The English Anthology*, 3 vols., London: T. and J. Egerton.

Scott, Elizabeth (ed.) (1823): *Specimens of British Poetry: Chiefly Selected from Authors of High Celebrity, and Interspersed with Original Writings*, Edinburgh: James Ballantyne and Co.

Specimens of the British Poets (1809), 2 vols., London: W. Suttaby.

The Beauties of English Poetry; or, Extracts from the Most Eminent British Poets (1818), new ed., London: n.p.

The British Anthology, or, Poetical Library (1824-25), 8 vols., London: John Sharpe.

The Nation's Favourite Poems (1996), London: BBC Books.

Thwaite, Anthony (ed.) (1984): *Six Centuries of Verse*, London: Thames Methuen.

Trench, Richard (ed.) (1879): *A Household Book of English Poetry: Selected and Arranged with Notes*, London: Macmillan.

Valentine, Laura (ed.) (1880): *Gems of National Poetry*, London: Frederick Warne & Co.

Wain, John (ed.) (1981): *Everyman's Book of English Verse*, London: Dent.

Wain, John (ed.) (1990): *The Oxford Anthology of English Poetry*, 2 vols., Oxford: Oxford University Press.

Ward, Thomas Humphry (ed.) (1880): *The English Poets: Selections with Critical Introductions by Various Writers and a General Introduction by Matthew Arnold*, 4 vols., London: Macmillan.

Wavell, A.P. (ed.) (1944): *Other Men's Flowers*, London: Jonathan Cape.

Popular History, Gender and Nationalism
Female Narratives of a National Myth

BIRTE FÖRSTER

INTRODUCTION

One of my former fellow students once insisted that Queen Louise of
Prussia was the author of Goethe's famous poem »Wer nie sein Brot mit
Tränen aß«.[1] All my arguments against his conviction were fruitless; he
insisted he had learnt this in school. Queen Louise – according to myth –
was indeed supposed to have quoted the poem while dangerously ill and
exhausted during her flight from French troops. In some versions she inscribed the poem on the windowpane of her humble refuge using her dia-
mond ring. Within the story of the myth the poem functions as a narrative
abbreviation for her own and her country's poor state and for her humility
as well as her perseverance. At least in the above-mentioned incident the
poem became so intertwined with the Queen's myth that my acquaintance
firmly believed her to have written the poem. It is a fine example of how
the popularization of history operates: Firstly, historical accuracy is reduced. Here the origin of the poem is taken from its initial context and
fitted into the mythical narrative. Secondly, through this re-contextualiza-

---

1   »He who never ate his bread with tears«. The poem from *Wilhelm Meisters
     Lehr- und Wanderjahre* speaks of personal troubles and grief brought upon by
     heavenly powers.

tion it is both personalized and emotionalized; the poor suffering Queen finds consolation only in a poem that speaks of troubles and grief.

The analysis of popular history has only recently become an evolving field in German historiography (cf. Korte/Paletschek 2009; Paletschek 2010, Hardtwig/Schütz 2005). In light of the richness of the material historians encounter while examining popular versions of history, this is all the more astonishing. There are, I argue, three main reasons why historians should take the analysis of popular history into account. Firstly, the aesthetic dimensions of popular media hint at individual perceptions of the respective media products. Examining popular media provides us with information about how meaning is ascribed and constituted both individually and collectively. Secondly, popular representations of the same past event or historical figure only *seem* to tell the same tale. The historical knowledge they present is not unchanging but constantly negotiated, reshaped and reinvented. Within these processes popular media may well offer a very different version of the past than educational institutions. Thirdly, analyzing popular history allows us to scrutinize women's roles as addressees and – more importantly – as producers of collective memory and national identity. While lacunae in research on nationalism in general and on the gendered structure of nationalisms in particular have lately been addressed (cf. Frevert 1996; Blom/Hagemann/Hall 2000; Hagemann 2002; Streubel 2006; Förster 2011), this does not yet hold true for the topic of gender and memory (cf. Paletschek/Schraut 2008). Analyzing popular media reaches far beyond the recent and justified demand to take into account the respective media product and the particular ways in which reality is constituted (cf. Crivellari/Sandl 2003). It also provides insights into the ways in which women were involved in producing collective memory and national identity. Hence, we may gain knowledge about how women contributed to national discourses and how they negotiated gender roles within this discourse (cf. Frevert 1996: 167-168). Ultimately, investigating popular media, at least to some extent, implies bridging the gap between women as historical actors and the sources originated by women.

These three aspects, however, require a broad definition of popular history or historiography. Sylvia Paletschek has recently suggested that popular historiography should be defined as »representations of history in written, visual, artefactual and personal forms of presentation addressing a broad, non-expert audience« (Paletschek 2010: 4). This definition takes into account that popular historiography manifests itself in a large spectrum of different representations: textually and visually, audio-visually and performatively and through the intersection of different media as well as in social practices. In short, this definition invites the inclusion of material that is not traditionally defined as historiography (cf. Nissen 2009: 22-23). Thus, it widens our perspective both on the material we explore and on the historical actors involved in encoding and decoding meaning. Broadening the category of popular historiography as Paletschek suggests lessens the scarcity of women writers within popular historiography (cf. ibid.: 33) substantially. Though women were apparently very little involved in writing what is traditionally considered popular historiography, they nevertheless participated in disseminating historical knowledge, for example, by writing historical and biographical fiction for both adults and young readers. Within both genres women writers play a prominent role.

Looking at a popular *Geschichtsbild* (image of history) in a long-term study permits a diachronic analysis of narratives of the past. Hence, we may gather insights into the translation of those narratives from one medium to another. Moreover, we come to understand how these media shaped the respective narratives. The accelerating media development in the nineteenth and early twentieth centuries intensified these processes. At the same time this development made different versions of the past accessible to a rising number of readers or recipients, thereby crossing social and religious as well as gender- and age-related boundaries. Long-term studies thus enable us to make statements about the highs and lows of historical knowledge. Furthermore we may draw conclusions about the geographic, confessional, social and temporal dissemination of historical knowledge.

In what follows I shall start with a commentary on the analysis of the aesthetic and social dimension of ›popular‹ media. I will then examine several examples of how women participated in shaping collective memory and national identity with particular reference to the Prussian Queen Louise (1776-1810), wife of Frederick William III and mother of Emperor William I. Looking at different genres such as historical novels, literature for young readers and film I take the liberty of focusing on women in order to stress my argument. I shall conclude with some remarks on the additional value that the analysis of popular history has to offer.

Analyzing Popular History

It is common knowledge that the meaning of the term ›popular‹ is highly contested; there are no sharp-cut definitions. There exists, however, an agreement not to consider ›popular‹ culture only as the less valuable opposite to highbrow culture (cf. Ruchatz 2005; Hügel 2007: 58-61; Korte/Paletschek 2009: 14). Hans-Otto Hügel emphasizes that ›popular‹ refers to the interaction between recipient, artifact and context. He suggests defining the term by the quality of this interaction rather than by fixing what is ›popular‹ and what is not. Popular media, he argues, have both an aesthetic and a social function, which differ over the course of time, and accordingly need to be historicized. Hence, the term ›popular‹ indicates a process in which meaning is constituted (cf. Hügel 2007: 60, 86-87). Whereas Hügel accentuates the aesthetic ambivalence of popular media and the manifold ways in which they constitute meaning (cf. ibid.: 44), Barbara Korte and Sylvia Paletschek consider the »meaningful, coherent narrative« as one of the main characteristics of popular tales of the past (Korte/Paletschek 2009: 15). Even then, popular history in general offers multifaceted versions of past events or historical figures, which allows different interpretations and different appropriations of the past (cf. ibid.: 49). Besides interaction and coherent narratives, a third, and in my opinion prominent, characteristic of popular media needs to be taken into account: Their aesthetic form is generally very distinct; sometimes it is actually hyperbolic. Popular artifacts therefore offer many hints as to how the historical recipient may have interacted with it. They provide information about the intended reception from which we may draw at least some conclusions about the constitution of meaning, both individually and collectively. Here I agree with Hügel who points to the fact that this meaning is not randomly produced. Quite the opposite: Readers react to what the texts and also the contexts of the respective media offer (cf. Hügel 2007: 86). Drawing on Umberto Eco's notion of the ›ideal reader‹, I consider in particular those genres which expressly aim at the dissemination of societal norms, such as biographical narrations or school festivals, as ›closed texts‹. Moreover, this applies to texts that – due to their hyperbolic language – leave the reader in little doubt as to how to interpret his or her reading. ›Closed texts‹ lead the reader along a fixed path, offering patterns of identification by using narrative structures and affective rhetoric. Thus, closed texts create compassion and anxiety, excitement and grief – feelings that are relieved or rewarded during the narration, thereby meeting exactly those expectations that they had raised before (cf. Eco 1995: 198-199; Nusser 1991: 112). Even if popular media offer more than one line of interpretation (cf. Hügel 2007: 44), they nonetheless provide us with information about how meaning is constructed.

Besides these aesthetic and rhetorical means, the ideal reader's response to the texts may be guided by the following parameters:

- paratexts such as introductions or other comments on the respective artifact (cf. Genette 1992: 9-15, 188-189),
- addresses directed to the reader or comments by the author (cf. Iser 1976: 238-239),
- strategies to create authenticity such as references to historical sources: a diary, personal letters or witnesses,
- the comments of an authoritative narrator,
- other measures in favour of identification such as direct speech or introducing a subjective perspective by adding a fictional character with whom the historical one forms a friendship.

These parameters mainly offer insights into how the popular media were supposed to be perceived. But the fictitious ›ideal‹ reader and the factual historical reader are not the same. Moreover, the reception of popular media is a creative act and can be influenced only to a certain degree (cf. Chartier 1989: 156-157). Since sources for the reception of popular media, except for movies, are scarce between 1860 and 1960, we have only very little material on the individual response to popular media. In spite of this, I suggest that we may still draw conclusions about the appropriation of popular media by considering the following factors:

- taking into account the success or failure of the respective media, e.g. print runs, presence in libraries, cinema audiences,
- looking at potential differences between institutional and popular versions of the same topic or figure,
- regarding contexts of the reception such as reading magazines like the *Gartenlaube* aloud within the family circle, taking part in a school play,

avid rather than reflective reading, watching a movie in a backyard cinema or a movie palace,

- looking at book or ticket prices that narrow down (or broaden) the social strata that had access to the respective media,
- considering which social strata, gender or age groups or events (jubilees for instance) are targeted by the respective popular media,
- including public reactions to the respective media, such as reviews.

Analyzing popular media nevertheless remains just one side of the coin when it comes to examining popular history. In order to understand how historical subjects adopt a historical myth, for instance, we have to pay close attention to the practices of appropriations both within state institutions, such as schools, and within private initiatives.

FEMALE NARRATORS OF A NATIONAL MYTH, 1860-1931

Women were especially prominent among the professional writers who – like teachers, governmental officials and protestant priests – took part in producing the Queen Louise myth. In this section I shall chronologically discuss five examples, starting with the very popular author of historical novels, Luise Mühlbach. She is followed by Elisabeth Halden, who in 1899 published a successful version for young female readers, and by Ella Mensch, who around 1900 criticized the romanticization of the myth and openly tried to establish a different myth. How the Queen Louise myth helped to legitimate right-wing female activism in the 1920s is negotiated in Sophie Hoechstetter's novel *Königin Luise* (1926). I conclude with Henny Porten's film version of *Luise, Königin von Preußen* (1931).

Queen Louise of Prussia, née Princess of Mecklenburg-Strelitz, was born in 1776. She married the Prussian Prince Frederick William in 1793 and became Queen in 1797. In 1806, after the defeat of Jena and Auerstedt, the Queen and her family fled to the eastern border where they resided both in Königsberg and Tilsit until their return to Berlin in 1809. In July 1807 she discussed the outcomes of the peace treaty of Tilsit with Napoleon but failed to gain better terms for Prussia. She died in 1810 at the age of 34.

Among her children were the later Kings Frederick William IV and William, who in 1871 became Emperor of the Germans.

During her lifetime, Queen Louise's biography was already idealized, and her dynastic role, nationalized by the contemporary concept of the nation's first family, translated into being the Prussian *Landesmutter* (mother of the nation) (cf. Wülfing/Bruns/Parr 1991: 97; Hagemann 2002: 350-357, 366-374; Förster 2008: 45-47). Being part of the ›origin myth‹ of the German nation state, Queen Louise was established as *the* ideal German woman and continued to be regarded as such throughout the nineteenth century and even the first half of the twentieth. This re-invention of her idealized biography was intensified tremendously by the accelerating media development in the second half of the nineteenth and the early decades of the twentieth centuries. Among the characteristics ascribed to the Prussian Queen were naturalness, modesty, solicitousness, piety, self-denial and readiness to make sacrifices both for her family and the nation. She never aimed at crossing gender boundaries and only did so when the nation was in need. Most of the time she remained a silent sufferer. This version of her biography was very prominent in Prussian schools throughout the nineteenth and early twentieth centuries, but other historical narratives differed substantially from this version (cf. Förster 2011: 181-190, 238-248).

Luise Mühlbach (1814-1873), whose real name was Clara Mundt, was – besides Alexandre Dumas and Eugene Sue – one of the most popular authors in public libraries throughout the second half of the nineteenth century (cf. Martino 1990: 419, 422). She wrote numerous historical novels, covering with her newly published books around a tenth of all yearly published ones, most of them featuring female figures. To date research has overlooked her historical writings, either focussing on her earlier social novels (cf. Tönnesen 1997) or – like Hartmut Eggert in his study on the historical novel – looking down on her subjective portrayal of historical figures (cf. Eggert 1971: 75-76). But Mühlbach reflected upon her position as an author, and formulated her own concept of historical novels. Crucial to Mühlbach's concept was the popularization of history. In her novel *Der alte Fritz und die neue Zeit* (1867) she articulated her aim to carry history from the study into everyday life, and to make what had only been specialist knowledge into common knowledge. In order to achieve this she asked for relative freedom in dealing with historical sources and argued in favour of an image of how the past might have been: »It only matters that these

words and actions express the mind and character of that particular historical figure and that we do not impute something to them that they could never
have done.«[2] (Mühlbach 1867, qtd. in Kurth-Voigt/McClain 1981: 929)
Aiming at popularizing history, she advocated telling lively tales of the
past, depicting historical subjects as human beings. Unlike Eggert who
criticized Mühlbach's privatization of history, I think it is high time to pay
attention to its potential in regard to both the possible identification with the
popular history displayed and strategies of emotionalization applied here.
Mühlbach herself held a functional view on this topic: Her novels, as she
wrote to Hermann Pückler-Muskau in February 1864, were meant to raise
patriotic consciousness in the German-speaking countries (cf. Tönnesen
1997: 212).

The following episode shows how – in Mühlbach's view – history
might have happened: In *Napoleon und Königin Luise* (1858) a Prussian
official betrays the fleeing Queen to the approaching French soldiers. This
official completely lacks national consciousness and drives the Queen's
horses away so that she only just manages a dramatic last-minute escape.
Finally in the coach she draws a dagger, ready to commit suicide because
she could not bear the dishonour of being a prisoner of the French:

»›My decision is made. I would rather die than fall into the hands of the French.‹
[...] The *chasseurs* were only two horses' length away and each second brought
them closer, even closer! [...] She held the little sparkling dagger in her right hand.
Breathlessly tired she expected her fate. Suddenly the coach drove with a thundering
noise across the streets. Now it stopped and it seemed as if an angel spoke when
Louise heard the words: ›This is Küstrin! We are safe.‹«[3] (Mühlbach 1860 [1858]:
83-84)

---

2   »Es kommt nur darauf an, daß diese Worte und Handlungen in dem Geist und
     Charakter jener historischen Personen gehalten sind, und daß man ihnen nichts
     andichtet, was sie nicht gethan haben könnten.«

3   »[M]ein Entschluß ist unabänderlich. Lieber sterben als die Schmach der Lä-
     cherlichkeit ertragen. [...] Kaum zwei Pferdeslängen nur noch waren die Chas-
     seurs entfernt, und jede Sekunde brachte sie näher, immer näher! [...] Fest in ih-
     rer Rechten hielt sie den kleinen blitzenden Dolch. In athemloser Ermattung,
     bleich wie eine Sterbende, erwartete sie ihr Schicksal. Auf einmal fuhr der Wa-
     gen mit donnerndem Geräusch über ein Straßenpflaster hin. Jetzt hielt er an, und

Mühlbach pictures a heroic Queen ready to sacrifice herself for the nation –
a role normally limited to the community of weapon-bearing male citizens
(cf. Frevert 1996; Hagemann 2002: 89). Later, she changes from the
wounded female – wounded because Napoleon had accused her of having a
liaison with Tsar Alexander – to an »aloof and invulnerable Queen«
(Mühlbach 1860 [1858]: 288). This Queen then meets Napoleon to discuss
the Treaty of Tilsit representing Germany – not Prussia! – thereby crossing
both gender and national boundaries. Throughout the novel, ›the nation‹ is
continuously used to legitimize the extension of the female sphere of public
and political action. Even if the Queen's thirst for revenge is not satisfied
but rather redeemed by her clemency, this thirst is described in detail in the
first place. To enhance suspense and (its immediate) relief Mühlbach uses
climactic and anticlimactic sentence constructions as well as the constant
threats to the Queen's life as »strategies of emotionalization« (Nusser 1991:
122), thereby advocating the reader's identification with the protagonist.
This identification is also endorsed by her stereotypical characterization
and the strong value judgements within the book and furthered by the re-
dundant narrative. In addition to such textual elements, the extremely short
loan period of only one week for books by favoured authors (at a time when
most readers borrowed books rather than buying them) probably encouraged avid, rather than reflective, reading, especially in the case of a book of
700 pages (cf. Jäger/Schönert 1980: 45).

In the 1860s, Luise Mühlbach used both the characteristics of the
popular novel and the national discourse to negotiate female spheres of
political action – rather successfully if judged by the presence of her books
in public libraries. This negotiation continued throughout the period of time
discussed in this article. During the Wilhelmine era children and adolescents were the main target group of the Queen Louise myth. Besides its use
in school and school festivals, the Queen was the subject of many newly
published books for young readers. However, the images of the Prussian
Queen that were presented in these various publications differed greatly.
Biographical novels described her as a role model for girls and young
women characterized by her motherliness, her care for those in need, her
religiousness and her eagerness to sacrifice herself for the nation (cf.

---

wie eine Engelsstimme tönte es Luisen, als sie die Worte hörte: Da ist Küstrin!
Wir sind gerettet.«

Augusti 1897: 5). This interpretation largely matched the one articulated in Prussian schools, yet biographical novels that stressed the Queen's exemplary character had rarely more than one print-run. The more fictionalized historical novels did not explicitly accentuate the Queen's virtues. They introduced a fictional character – often adolescent – who lived in the immediate vicinity of the Queen. This afforded the young readers a glimpse of the Queen's private life. Besides introducing eyewitnesses and a detailed description of the Queen's childhood and especially her youth, this fictional character was the means of supporting an affirmative response to the nationalist content of such novels. Furthermore, the historical novels included elements of historical romances and adventure stories (cf. Förster 2011: 181-190).

Elisabeth Halden's (1841-1916) *Königin Luise* is a prominent example of a hybrid historical novel (cf. Halden 1906).[4] First published in 1899 it had four print runs in 1910. Halden's depiction of the Prussian Queen differed considerably from interpretations in biographical novels: The Queen is interested in educating herself and takes political action after Napoleon transgresses Prussian territory in Ansbach-Bayreuth. Halden tells *in extenso* how the Queen, as head of a regiment, takes part in a military parade (cf. ibid.: 116-117). After Napoleon accuses her of adultery with the Russian Tsar, as in Mühlbach's novel, she does not embrace the role of a passive victim but decides to defend her honour herself – which, in those times, would have been her husband's task (cf. Frevert 1991: 223-224). Accordingly, the Queen longs to be ›a man‹ herself in order to be able to take revenge (cf. Halden 1906: 116). Similarly, her negotiations with the French Emperor are not – as is usually the case – a display of the victimized housewife; on the contrary, Queen Louise meets him as a sovereign who wants to better the fate of her country and her people (cf. ibid.: 165-166). Her distinct characterization as sovereign makes Halden's novel an exception among both the biographical and the historical novels for young readers. Her Queen is both proud and courageous, and takes political action after her negotiations with Napoleon have failed. The exiled monarch engages in supporting the Prussian reformers and ultimately manages to ›save‹ Silesia from French interests (cf. ibid.: 198, 238). The novel contra-

---

4   For a detailed summary of the novel cf. Askey (2007: 276-278). Halden's real
    name was Agnes Breitzmann.

dicts the then institutionalized version of the myth and introduces an autonomous, independent and active Queen to young readers. At the same time, it employs various means to further an affirmative reader response and therefore the identification with a female role model that differed considerably from the one taught in schools. Since Halden's other historical novels portray similar female figures (cf. Glasenapp 2003: 205), or at least young women who had to make their own living (cf. Kirch 2003: 132), we may assume that nationalist discourse served again as a means to broaden the female sphere. This was in turn supported by the devices of popular literature, particularly by the fictitious adolescent protagonist who serves as an eyewitness to this extension of the Queen's field of endeavour.

At the same time, the author Ella Mensch (1859-1935), who was among the first German women to receive a PhD in German Literature from Zurich University in 1886 and was a member of the German Female Teacher's Association, an important part of the bourgeois women's movement (cf. Budke/Schulze 1995: 259-260), fiercely criticized the Queen's public image as devoted housewife and mother as well as her portrayal as silent sufferer. Mensch's rather successful *Königin Luise von Preußen* – with its six print-runs within about fifteen years – is one of the rare examples of an openly articulated critique of the myth and of historical research on the Queen. The author argues against the myth in general and tries to establish a new myth by depicting Queen Louise as a gifted politician hindered by society in general, and her husband in particular, in unfolding her talents. Mensch even suggests that the conservative Reaction after 1815 could have been prevented if the Queen had not died young and had continued to advise her weak husband (cf. Mensch 1908: 24, 45, 72, 89). This version of the Queen Louise myth was not taken up in later adaptations. A similar reinterpretation is only to be found in an article by the German feminist Käthe Schirmacher (cf. Schirmacher 1927). But there were other activists who opposed the monopolization of the Queen. In 1910 members of the bourgeois women's movement criticized the Emperor's interpretation of his great-grandmother when he argued that there was one thing to learn from Queen Louise's biography: A woman's duty was to work quietly in the family, to raise obedient children and not to fight for ›so-called rights‹ or membership of political associations (cf. Krieger 1913: 142-144). Agnes Harder, head of the conservative German Women's Association (*Deutscher Frauenbund*) argued in favour of the Queen's political duty to the fatherland; the catholic teacher Cäcilie Movius accentuated her relevance within the Prussian reform movement.[5]

After the First World War, negotiations for female political participation took a new turn. When universal suffrage was introduced in January 1919 even conservative and right-wing parties such as the German National People's Party (*Deutschnationale Volkspartei*, DNVP) had to come to terms both with the female electorate and a small, albeit existing, number of female politicians such as Käthe Schirmacher. Notwithstanding the achievements of universal suffrage, women's political participation was highly contested within these parties and accordingly had to be legitimized (cf. Heinsohn 2010: 95-100; Streubel 2006: 259-292). DNVP's female politicians, but also members of the Queen Louise Association (*Bund Königin Luise*) referred to the myth in order to defend their public activities as duty to the downtrodden nation. By picturing the Queen as a female leader (*Führerin*) these right-wing activists took part in modernizing the myth, which is one of the reasons why the myth was still relevant in the 1920s and 1930s (cf. Förster 2011: 328-354; Süchting-Hänger 2002: 290-295).

There is one contemporary popular novel that can be read as a guidebook for right-wing female activists. Sophie Hoechstetter's *Königin Luise* exemplifies the contemporary discourse, led by right-wing female activists, on women's public and political work. Käthe Schirmacher published a very appreciative review of the novel in the *Frauen-Weckruf*, a right-wing women's journal (cf. Schirmacher 1927). Hoechstetter's characterization of Queen Louise more or less parallels the way she was pictured by the *Bund Königin Luise*: as a woman bound by her duty to the nation to cross traditional gender boundaries.

In *Königin Luise*, which first appeared on the occasion of the Queen's 125th birthday anniversary in 1926, Hoechstetter describes the political awakening of the Prussian Queen. Politicized by Prussia's ongoing conflict

---

5   The Social Democrats used the Emperor's Königsberg speech to open a debate on the Emperor's public statements in general. During the debate Eduard David and Georg Ledebour stressed that lower-class women were working out of economic necessity. They claimed working women could fend for their rights and still be loving and caring mothers. For the reactions to the Emperor's speech cf. Förster (2011: 235-238).

with Napoleonic France, she develops an intense national feeling (*National-gefühl*). This national feeling is a guiding star to her later actions. Because her husband Frederick William III remains passive in the face of the ›Napoleonic threat‹, his previously apolitical wife is forced to fill the gap he leaves behind. Pressed to take action by, amongst others, the Prussian Prince Louis Ferdinand, the Queen reluctantly but nevertheless determinedly supports the reformers at the Prussian court, such as Hardenberg and, later, Stein (cf. Hoechstetter 1926: 197). Thereby she comes permanently into conflict with the marital gender order and, consequently, not only with her husband but also with her own gender identity. When she urges her husband to defend the national honour by declaring war on Napoleon, she acts against her true, peace-loving, nature (cf. ibid.: 220).

The Queen's sense of duty to the nation forces her to take action, but she never actively claims political power. Only when the fatherland is in dire need of her help does the Queen emerge from the private sphere. The nation, therefore, serves as the ultimate justification for female political action while other positive male role models, like Prince Louis Ferdinand or Baronet Stein, initiate and sanction these actions. The Queen acts according to her sense of duty and not because she has the right to do so. In short, the Prussian Queen may only participate in political decision-making because her husband does not adhere to a highly-gendered concept of masculinity that requires the king to lead. Like in Halden's and Mühlbach's books, the Queen again regrets not being able to actively sacrifice her life to the nation (cf. ibid.: 197, 277-280, 287).

At the same time, Hoechstetter deploys elements of the melodramatic women's novel and historical romance (cf. Hughes 1993). For example, the ongoing conflict with the weak and jealous Frederick William III may have been intended to address the contemporary reader's experience. The Queen renounces her love for the Russian Tsar, »the only man who could enravish her soul to great passion« and is rewarded with the appointment of Prussian reformer Hardenberg as minister (cf. Hoechstetter 1926: 178).

When German film star Henny Porten promoted *Luise, Königin von Preußen* – a film that she had produced herself – in 1931, she declared she did not wish to make any political statement. »I do not want to know anything about politics, for I am a woman and politics is not for women«,[6] she said in framing her version of the Queen Louise myth. Her aim was to present the »fate of a woman and mother. Nothing else.«[7] In addition to this Porten accentuated how her own biography matched that of the Queen. Like Queen Louise she had had to suffer from severe blows but had never lost her ideals. Playing the Prussian Queen was the ›role of a lifetime‹ and she had wanted it for years (cf. Förster 2011: 372-374).

Luise, Königin von Preußen was directed by Carl Froehlich and featured Gustav Gründgens, a prominent German actor, as Frederick William III (cf. Belach 1986; Sykora 1991; Parr 2004; Förster 2011: 372-381). It combined militaristic scenes and critique against the treaty of Versailles (1919) with a pacifist ending, as well as an unfortunate love story with the motherly and later suffering Queen. The script was written by Walter von Molo, author of the very successful novel *Luise* (1919).[8] While Molo's novel showed a politically active Queen, the film displayed a motherly Queen that fitted Porten's melodramatic repertoire. Although troubled by her weak and undecided husband, the Queen forsakes the love of her life, Prince Louis Ferdinand. True to Porten's interpretation of her character, she is not politically involved, and her idea of the nation remains emotional and naive: »I adore Germany. It is something that makes me good. [...] Our love is German, our marriage is German, our children are German. [...] If Germany dies, I shall perish, too.«[9]

As a result of its hybrid character the film offered a broad range of topics that both male and female spectators could connect with. Notwithstanding the apolitical Queen who argues against war in general, the film itself was highly political. Moreover, the first film with sound that featured the Prussian Queen used sound techniques to promote nationalist ideas,

---

6   »Ich will nichts von Politik wissen, denn ich bin ja eine Frau und für Frauen ist das nichts.« (*Film-Kurier* 323, 3 October 1931, SDK/Filmmuseum Berlin/3085)

7   »Ich will ein Frauen- und Mutterschicksal zeigen. Nichts weiter.« (*Der Mittag* 245, 19 October 1931, SDK/Filmmuseum Berlin/3085)

8   *Luise* was part of Molo's *Fridericus* trilogy that sold half a million copies by the 1950s.

9   »Ich liebe Deutschland. Es ist etwas, was mich gut macht. [...] Unsere Liebe ist doch deutsch, unsere Ehe ist deutsch, unsere Kinder sind deutsch. [...] Du, wenn Deutschland stirbt, sterb' ich auch.«

particularly a scene showing the outcome of the Treaty of Tilsit (1807). While a voice-over reads out the lost territories to the beats of a drum, the outcome is visualized by a montage of clouds passing by, thereby suggesting they were short-lived. Audiences also read this as a comment on the Treaty of Versailles.

Despite its multifaceted offerings, Porten's film failed at least partly. Firstly, the film was a financial disaster: Porten's production company had to declare bankruptcy in March 1932. In addition to its high manufacturing costs, the film failed to receive the rating ›artistically valuable‹ which would have meant tax advantages. Moreover, Porten herself stated that many exhibitors had terminated contracts due to threats by national-socialist groups to destroy auditoriums. Secondly, the audience did not accept the Queen's pacifist speech in the closing scene but cheered to all militaristic and anti-French scenes. The last scene was later cut and the film shown without it. Thirdly, critics pointed to the aesthetic shortcomings of the film, especially Porten's rather static acting. Ludwig Marcuse wrote that the Queen looked like the »principal of an association for the betterment of fallen girls«.[10] In fact close-ups of Porten's suffering face and her empty stares were among the main measures employed to visualize the Queen's despair. Others criticized the film for openly displaying right-wing and anti-democratic ideas. Siegfried Kracauer argued that the film popularized the demands of the *Harzburger Front* despite its pacifist ending (cf. Kracauer 1993: 278). Fourthly, Porten's version was the antipode to the representations of an heroic and politically active Queen which were dominant during the 1920s and 1930s. That a female audience might identify with such a figure is highly questionable.

Conclusion

This overview of how female actors helped to construct the nation through popular images of Queen Louise has shown how the myth was continuously used to negotiate a female sphere of political and public action. The narratives discussed here offered versions of the myth to adult and young

---

10 »[W]ie die Vorsteherin eines Vereins zur Hebung gefallener Mädchen« (*Vossische Zeitung* 574, 5 December 1931, SDK/Filmmuseum Berlin/3085).

readers that differed decidedly from those taught in Prussian schools and publically disseminated during the German Empire. These versions were highly popular and successful on the media market, while the image of the Queen as an example of piety and self-denial raised considerably less interest. After the First World War, versions of a politically active Queen dominated the literary market and were eventually taught in schools. Considering the examples discussed as popular historiography broadens our findings on how women shaped nationalist discourses and how they participated in negotiating gender roles within the German nation state. Moreover, these sources provide us with information on how women took part in constructing collective memory. Including them will, therefore, add to those different shades of grey in history that Thomas Nipperdey so famously asked for (cf. Nipperdey 1998: 905).[11]

WORKS CITED

Askey, Jennifer Drake (2007): »Growing into a Nation: Queen Luise and the Lessons of Nationalism in Adolescent Fiction for Girls«. In: Waltraud Maierhofer/Gertrud Rösch/Caroline Bland (eds.), *Women Against Napoleon: Historical and Fictional Responses to his Rise and Legacy*, Frankfurt am Main: Campus, 265-280.

Augusti, Brigitte [Auguste Plehn] (1897): *Luise, Königin von Preußen: Ein Lebensbild, deutschen Frauen und Mädchen gewidmet*, Breslau: Hirt.

Belach, Helga (1986): *Henny Porten: Der erste deutsche Filmstar 1890-1960*, Berlin: Haude und Spener.

Blom, Ida/Karen Hagemann/Catherine Hall (eds.) (2000): *Gendered Nations: Nationalism and Gender Order in the Long Nineteenth Century*, Oxford: Berg.

Budke, Petra/Jutta Schulze (1995): *Schriftstellerinnen in Berlin 1871-1945: Ein Lexikon zu Leben und Werk*, Recklinghausen: Orlanda.

---

11 I would like to thank Sheena Goulty and Mairi Rivers for their meticulous comments on this article's language and Barbara Segelken, Christina Strunck and Nina von Zimmermann for their insightful and helpful remarks. All translations are my own.

Chartier, Roger (1989): »Texts, Prints, Readings«. In: Lynn Hunt (ed.), *The New Cultural History*, Berkeley/CA: University of California Press, 151-175.

Crivellari, Fabio/Marcus Sandl (2003): »Die Medialität der Geschichte: Forschungsstand und Perspektiven einer interdisziplinären Zusammenarbeit von Geschichts- und Medienwissenschaften«. *Historische Zeitschrift* 277, 619-654.

Eco, Umberto (1995): *Im Labyrinth der Vernunft*, Leipzig: Reclam.

Eggert, Hartmut (1971): *Studien zur Wirkungsgeschichte des deutschen historischen Romans 1850-1875*, Berlin: Klostermann.

Förster, Birte (2008): »Von der Halbwaise zur Landesmutter: Familie, Nation und Gender in der Königin Luise-Biographik von 1860 bis 1930«. In: Christian v. Zimmermann/Nina v. Zimmermann (eds.), *Familiengeschichten: Familienstrukturen in biographischen Texten*, Frankfurt am Main: Campus, 45-62.

Förster, Birte (2011): *Der Königin Luise-Mythos: Mediengeschichte des »Idealbilds deutscher Weiblichkeit«, 1860-1960*, Göttingen: V&R unipress.

Frevert, Ute (1991): *Ehrenmänner: Das Duell in der bürgerlichen Gesellschaft*, München: Beck.

Frevert, Ute (1996): »Nation, Krieg und Geschlecht im 19. Jahrhundert«. In: Manfred Hettling/Paul Nolte (eds.), *Nation und Gesellschaft in Deutschland: Historische Essays*, München: Beck, 151-170.

Genette, Gérard (1992): *Paratexte*, Frankfurt am Main: Campus.

Glasenapp, Gabriele v. (2003): »Ihre Geschichte: Historische Erzählungen für junge Leserinnen während der Kaiserzeit«. In: Gisela Wilkending (ed.), *Mädchenliteratur in der Kaiserzeit: Zwischen weiblicher Identifizierung und Grenzüberschreitung*, Stuttgart: Metzler, 165-217.

Hagemann, Karen (2002): *»Mannlicher Muth und Teutsche Ehre«: Nation, Militär und Geschlecht zur Zeit der Antinapoleonischen Kriege Preußens*, Paderborn: Schöningh.

Halden, Elisabeth [Agnes Breitzmann] (1906 [1899]): *Königin Luise*, Berlin: Meidinger.

Hardtwig, Wolfgang/Erhard Schütz (2005): *Geschichte für Leser: Populäre Geschichtsschreibung in Deutschland im 20. Jahrhundert*, Stuttgart: Steiner.

Heinsohn, Kirsten (2010): *Konservative Parteien in Deutschland 1912 bis 1933: Demokratisierung und Partizipation in geschlechterhistorischer Perspektive*, Düsseldorf: Droste.

Hoechstetter, Sophie (1926): *Königin Luise: Historischer Roman. Mit 24 Wiedergaben nach zeitgenössischen Bildern und einem Brieffaksimile*, Berlin: Bong.

Hügel, Hans-Otto (2007): *Lob des Mainstreams: Zu Begriff und Geschichte von Unterhaltung und Populärer Kultur*, Köln: Böhlau.

Hughes, Helen (1993): *The Historical Romance*, London: Routledge.

Iser, Wolfgang (1976): *Der Akt des Lesens: Theorie ästhetischer Wirkung*, München: Fink.

Jäger, Georg/Jörg Schönert (1980): »Die Leihbibliothek als Institution des literarischen Lebens im 18. und 19. Jahrhundert – ein Problemaufriß«. In: Georg Jäger/Jörg Schönert (eds.), *Die Leihbibliothek als Institution des literarischen Lebens im 18. und 19. Jahrhundert: Organisationsformen, Bestände, Publikum*, Hamburg: Hauswedell, 7-60.

Kirch, Silke (2003): »Reiseromane und Kolonialromane um 1900 für junge Leserinnen«. In: Gisela Wilkending (ed.), *Mädchenliteratur in der Kaiserzeit: Zwischen weiblicher Identifizierung und Grenzüberschreitung*, Stuttgart: Metzler, 103-164.

Korte, Barbara/Sylvia Paletschek (2009): »Geschichte in populären Medien und Genres: Vom historischen Roman zum Computerspiel«. In: Barbara Korte/Sylvia Paletschek (eds.), *History Goes Pop: Zur Repräsentation von Geschichte in populären Medien und Genres*, Bielefeld: transcript, 9-59.

Kracauer, Siegfried (1993): »Nationales Epos«. In: *Von Caligari zu Hitler: Eine psychologische Geschichte des deutschen Films*, Frankfurt am Main: Suhrkamp, 264-287, 317-318.

Krieger, Bogdan (ed.) (1913): *Die Reden Wilhelms II*, vol. 4: *1906-1912*, Leipzig: Reclam.

Kurth-Voigt, Lieselotte E./William McClain (1981): »Clara Mundts Briefe an Hermann Costenoble: Zu L. Mühlbachs historischen Romanen«. *Archiv für Geschichte des Buchwesens 22*, 917-1242.

Luise, Königin von Preußen (Deutschland 1931, Director: Carl Froehlich).

Martino, Alberto (1990): *Die deutsche Leihbibliothek: Geschichte einer literarischen Institution 1756-1914*, Wiesbaden: Harrassowitz.

Mensch, E[lla] (1908): *Königin Luise von Preußen: Ein Lebens- und Zeitbild*, Berlin: Seemann & Nachf.

Mühlbach, Luise [Clara Mundt] (1860 [1858]): *Napoleon und Königin Luise: Napoleon in Deutschland 2*, Berlin: Janke.

Nipperdey, Thomas (1998): *Deutsche Geschichte 1800-1918*, München: Beck.

Nissen, Martin (2009): *Populäre Geschichtsschreibung: Historiker, Verleger und die deutsche Öffentlichkeit (1848-1900)*, Köln: Böhlau.

Nusser, Peter (1991): *Trivialliteratur*, Stuttgart: Metzler.

Paletschek, Sylvia (2010): »Introduction: Why Analyse Popular Historiographies«. In: Sylvia Paletschek (ed.), *Popular Historiographies in the 19th and 20th Centuries: Cultural Meanings, Social Practices*, Oxford: Berghahn, 1-18.

Paletschek, Sylvia/Sylvia Schraut (eds.) (2008): *The Gender of Memory: Cultures of Remembrance in Nineteenth- and Twentieth-Century Europe*, Frankfurt am Main: Campus.

Parr, Rolf (2004): »›Das ist unnatürlich, schlimmer: bürgerlich‹ – Königin Luise im Film«. In: Roland Berbig/Martina Lauster/Rolf Parr (eds.), *Zeitdiskurse: Reflexionen zum 19. und 20. Jahrhundert als Festschrift für Wulf Wülfing*, Heidelberg: Synchron Wissenschaftsverlag, 135-163.

Ruchatz, Jens (2005): »Der Ort des Populären«. In: Gereon Blaseio/Hedwig Pompe/Jens Ruchatz (eds.), *Popularisierung und Popularität*, Köln: DuMont, 139-145.

Schirmacher, Käthe (1927): »Was ist an Königin Luise vorbildlich«. *Frauen-Weckruf* 18.3, 45-46.

Streubel, Christiane (2006): *Radikale Nationalistinnen: Agitation und Programmatik rechter Frauen in der Weimarer Republik*, Frankfurt am Main: Campus.

Süchting-Hänger, Andrea (2002): *Das »Gewissen der Nation«: Nationales Engagement und politisches Handeln konservativer Frauenorganisationen 1900 bis 1937*, Düsseldorf: Droste.

Sykora, Katharina (1991): »Ambivalente Versprechungen: Die Figur der Königin Luise im Film«. In: Barbara Determann/Ulrike Hammer/Doron Kiesel (eds.), *Verdeckte Überlieferungen: Weiblichkeitsbilder zwischen Weimarer Republik, Nationalsozialismus und Fünfziger Jahren*, Frankfurt am Main: Haag and Herchen, 137-168.

Tönnesen, Cornelia (1997): *Die Vormärz-Autorin Luise Mühlbach: Vom sozialkritischen Frühwerk zum historischen Roman*, Neuss: Ahasvera.

Wülfing, Wulf/Karin Bruns/Rolf Parr (1991): *Historische Mythologie der Deutschen 1798-1918*, München: Fink.

Creating Popular Music History

The Barbershop Harmony Revival in the
United States around 1940

FRÉDÉRIC DÖHL

BARBERSHOP HARMONY AS A CASE STUDY

Since at least the late eighteenth and early nineteenth centuries, the field of music history has been actively and substantially shaped by ideologies such as nationalism, chauvinism and racism, as well as political, economic and aesthetic influences, among others (cf. Hentschel 2006; Riethmüller 2011). First within art music and later, especially since the early twentieth century, within jazz, folk and popular music, achieving authority in the interpretation of music history and forming general knowledge and public opinion has become a central issue and primary concern, at least in Western cultures. This is not and has never been a solely intellectual discourse, even for art music. Today, a great number of magazines, newspapers, radio formats, blogs and other media productions are concerned with popularizing music in some way. While doing this they offer views about aspects of music history and try to support them, for example in reviews and short historical abstracts about composers, performers or genres. Many elements that are still dominant in our contemporary musical life originated in the earlier development, which started during Beethoven's lifetime (1770-1827). These factors gained further strength due to their mutual dependence and interaction. They include, to name just a few, the emergence of the concept of work and the idea of musical autonomy, romantic ideas of genius and ›art-as-religion‹ (*Kunstreligion*), the economic emancipation of composers and instrumentalists from the court and church, and the development of copyright law, bourgeois and public concerts and a modern media market dealing with music and musicians (cf. Berger 2007; Goehr 2007; Tadday 1993; Taruskin 2006).

To write an overall review of the methods of creating a particular image of music history in Western music and the motives implied would be a large-scale project, to say the least, due to the number of musical styles, subcultures and ideological influences that are involved, and the time scope that would need to be covered. Instead, this essay presents a representative case study that shows how effective and widespread the creation of a specific image of music history can become, especially (but not exclusively) within a closed musical subculture, and the extent to which this constructed image can differ from historical and musical facts. An aspect of music history from the ranks of American popular music will be discussed, namely the origins of Barbershop Harmony, a well-defined tradition of four-part *a cappella* music. This example was mainly chosen for two reasons: First, Barbershop Harmony functions as a counter example to dominant processes. Typically, the musicians are the ones who ›make (music) history‹, but at the end of the day, the historians, journalists, philosophers and marketing executives are the ones who write and shape it. Barbershop Harmony, by contrast, is a part of music history that was designed and established in general knowledge almost exclusively by the musicians who invented it and in the way they wanted it. Secondly, the story of Barbershop Harmony is about a piece of popular (music) history that proves to be mainly fiction, an excogitated history that nonetheless became very popular, especially in the United States, and widely accepted as actual music history.

The Musical and Aesthetic Definition of Barbershop Harmony

Barbershop Harmony is widely understood today as a historically informed performance practice. That is to say that for this style of music the history of music – or better: the history of a specific musical tradition – plays a central role within the concept of the music itself. As with the equivalent movement for historically informed performance practice in classical music – which became quite prominent during the last decades (cf. Taruskin 1995) – the musicians claim to strive for the preservation of a specific kind of old music in a special way: They want to perform it as closely to its original performance conditions as possible. With Barbershop Harmony we are therefore not only dealing with the history of a specific kind of popular music and how it evolved, but also with an understanding of the crucial role of music history within this kind of popular music, which is apparent, for example, in the introduction of strict musical rules.

Barbershop Harmony is precisely defined by its aesthetic approach as well as by its musical material. The *a cappella* singers sing four-part chords, with each singer having the same text in most cases. At least one third of all chords sung must be major chords with a minor seventh. The two other types of chords central to the style are major chords and diminished chords. There are strict rules as to what other chords are allowed. The movement is predominantly homophonic with strict limitations on exceptions. The melody is sung by the second voice, called the lead, harmonized by the tenor above and the bass below. The fourth voice, the baritone, fills the chord above the bass and below the tenor. There are also strict rules for which tones each voice should sing within a chord. For example, the bass normally features the root or the fifth of a chord. Barbershop Harmony is sung in all-male or all-female ensembles and features a just scale (instead of an equal tempered scale, which is, for example, used for the tuning of guitars and pianos). Depending on the function of each singer's tone in the chord, the other three singers tune to the frequency sung by the lead. Barbershop singers strive for a specific ideal of sound: Based on the rules and sung correctly with unified articulation, a quartet is able to create an expanded sound which is described by terms such as ›angel voice‹ or ›fifth voice‹. Together, the four singers create an effect greater than the sum of the individual voices.[1]

---

1 There is a measurable acoustic effect related to the natural overtones each tone possesses (cf. in detail Averill 1999; Kalin 2005). The effect on the ears is similar to the ability of our eyes to see moving pictures: It is an illusion. Just as the eyes start to see pictures moving when they are shown with a specific speed, our ears start to combine overtones that are produced by several voices, and on this basis calculate ›additional voices‹, as if they were actually being sung by a

Becoming a Musical and Socio-Cultural Stereotype

Thanks to its distinctive sound, Barbershop Harmony possesses such a strong musical identity that during the 1940s, immediately after its formation within the ranks of the Barbershop Harmony Society (back then called the Society for the Preservation and Encouragement of Barbershop Quartet Singing in America or SPEBSQSA), it became a musical stereotype (cf. Döhl 2009a: 200-208). It was quickly picked up outside the subculture, for example in Gene Kelly's famous movie *An American in Paris* (1951) or in the very successful Broadway show *The Music Man*, which won the Tony Award for Best Musical in 1957 (beating Leonard Bernstein's *West Side Story*) and was filmed with equal success in 1962. Prominent adaptations such as these helped to establish Barbershop Harmony as an independent style of popular music and as a musical stereotype accompanied by strong socio-cultural and visual stereotypes including turn-of-the-century clothing and beards, that are still regularly, and mostly in satirical contexts, featured in well-known American cartoons, movies and television shows such as *Diagnosis: Murder*, *The Simpsons*, *Friends* or *Scrubs*. The adaptations also helped to spread the word about ideas of music history that are crucial to the formation of the concept of Barbershop Harmony and the subculture devoted to it, and promoted their consolidation in general knowledge and public opinion.

Music History as Fiction

Current musicological research has shown that Barbershop Harmony is not a historically informed performance practice in the way that it has been understood within the subculture as well as for decades in history books, journalistic commentaries or adaptations in other parts of American popular culture. The style of music practiced since the 1940s (and since the 1960s

---

fifth or sixth singer. The sound created is much richer than it would be without these musical features, a specific kind of ›glimmering‹ that can create a very powerful impression.

exclusively) under the name of Barbershop Harmony did not exist at the point of time in music history, around 1900, when it was commonly believed to have originated. Based on a false image of the past, the people who wrote and institutionalized the history of Barbershop Harmony (including the formation of the organizations and contests that are essential to this subculture) created a faulty historical construct.[2]

This matter is of particular interest because, as mentioned earlier, Barbershop Harmony is widely understood today as a historically informed performance practice. Its practitioners claim to strive for preservation: They intend to perform a specific kind of old music as closely to its original performance conditions as possible.[3] If one strives for a historically informed performance practice, the aim must be to specifically reconstruct the kind of old music in which one is interested as precisely and correctly as possible, and perform it like that. When the historical information collected is incorrect or is invented because historical evidence for what is believed to have taken place in the past is lacking, the music instead reflects a rear projection of present opinions. This is precisely what happened during the so-called Barbershop Harmony revival of the late 1930s, ›so-called‹ because the music ›revived‹ here did not exist in the era in which it was believed to have existed (cf. in detail Döhl 2009a). Barbershop Harmony was invented by mistake.

Recent research strongly suggests that what was known as ›barber shop‹ before and after the revival (around 1940) is, from a musical point of view,

---

2   Initiated by the research works of musicologists such as Val Hicks (1988) and Lynn Abbott (1992), for the first time a noteworthy and continuously increasing scholarly interest in the history and current status of Barbershop Harmony is evident. Apart from studies from an acoustic perspective (cf. Averill 1999; Kalin 2005) and an anthropological/sociological point of view (cf. Döhl 2009b; Garnett 1999, 2005a, 2005b; Kaplan 1993; Mook 2004, 2007; Stebbins 1992, 1996), studies about the institutions of this subculture (cf. Ayling 2000; Hicks 1988) or early sound recordings can be identified (cf. esp. Brooks 2005; Gracyk 2000, 2006; Henry 2000), and much attention is also being paid to the origins of this American tradition (Abbott 1992; Abbott/Seroff 1996, 2002; Henry 2000; Averill 2003; Döhl 2008, 2009a).

3   For a discussion of the possibilities and limits of ›original performance‹ in general cf. Taruskin (1995).

not at all the same thing. Since there is no evidence that Barbershop Harmony existed under a different name before the First World War, the consequence has to be that the common view regarding this vocal polyphonic style as a kind of historically informed performance practice is unfounded. Around 1900, but partly also still in the middle of the twentieth century, the common phrase ›barber shop chord(s)‹ did not stand for a specific form of four-part *a cappella* music, especially not in such an exclusive understanding as it is today. Rather, the term was a label for a specific harmonic style based on the chords mentioned earlier that, since the 1940s, have been typical of Barbershop Harmony and thus gave this form of *a cappella* music its name. But around 1900, ›Barbershop chords‹ was just a name for a harmonic concept, just as ›Ragtime‹ (from ragged time, meaning syncopated rhythm) was the name of a rhythmic style. Therefore, in those days ›barber shop chord(s)‹ could be produced by singers as well as by instrumentalists, in very different styles of singing from pop to opera, by accompanied singers or *a cappella*, from solo up to quintet and octet, and by professional musicians or amateurs (cf. Döhl 2009a: 64-158). Such variety is incompatible with the modern concept of Barbershop Harmony as an aesthetic concept that leaves little margin for deviation. The term was adopted for quite different kinds of singers in those years, for example professional vaudeville ensembles including the Manhattan Comedy Four and The Boston Quartet, the American popular-music legends Bert Williams and George M. Cohan, both performing solo, student groups in Harvard, Princeton and Yale, a quartet composed of professional players of the reigning baseball champions the Boston Red Sox, who were touring as singers in the off season, and even a bunch of murderers on their way to prison. In sources collected by current research, there is even a review of a vocal quartet performance that was composed of members of the New York Metropolitan Opera. These were in fact dramatic singers of the Richard Wagner repertoire, whose rendition of a song in a special edition of an operetta by Strauss in 1906 was reviewed in the *New York Times* under the heading »Barber Shop Chords« (cf. ibid.: 108). The sound these four Wagnerian singers produced must have been quite different to the ideal of singing preferred in modern Barbershop Harmony that tends to avoid artificial vocal techniques (for example vibrato) that are common in classical music. The term was likewise used for piano, mandolin and ukulele players. The author of the most commonly known reference to the term barber

shop/barbershop from the years prior to the First World War, the song
»Play That Barber Shop Chord« (1910), actually borrowed it from African-
American mandolin players whom he met around 1904/05 (cf. ibid.: 79).[4]

Even musicologists such as Daniel Gregory Mason and established
American composers of art music such as Aaron Copland and Virgil Thomson described very different kinds of music with the phrase ›barber shop
chords‹, including ragtime, jazz and even early French contemporary art
music such as the ballets of Darius Milhaud. In the 1930s, the initiators of
›Barbershop Quartet Contests‹ started their initiatives by permitting and
regularizing the use of instruments. Publishers in the 1930s did not care
whether Barbershop Harmony was performed by three, four or five singers,
accompanied or *a cappella* – as is evident from many covers of sheet music
from these times; nor did most people in interviews, when they were asked
about the American vocal quartet scene of their youth around 1900. The
originally widespread conception of the term barber shop/barbershop is still
visible in sources from the 1940s and early 1950s when people used the
term for recordings of well-known vocal groups such as The Mills
Brothers, The Hi-Lo's and The Chordettes, whose music intersects with
Barbershop Harmony (through the use of specific chords, a homophonic
texture and so on) but differs from the concept in key aspects (namely the
use of accompanied music, not four-part as far as possible, solo passages
and a melody with outside voices etc.). In the course of the 1950s, the difference to the now newly established strict concept of Barbershop Harmony
by the Barbershop Harmony Society and its affiliated organizations was
more clearly perceived, as is evident, for example, in *Time Magazine*'s
naming of The Hi-Lo's as a »neo-barbershop group« (»Music: Up from the
Barbershop« 1957).

However faulty a historical construct it may be, the image of the origins
of Barbershop Harmony in the early twentieth century became so strong

---

4   It is unknown whether the musical term barber shop/barbershop is related to the
    actual barber's shop, which was a social gathering place for the male community
    prior to the First World War, especially on weekends. All kinds of activities, in-
    cluding music making, were popular pastimes there. Indeed, some sources sug-
    gest this plausible interpretation. For example, Lewis Muir, the author of »Play
    That Barber Shop Chord«, borrowed the term from mandolin players whom he
    actually met performing in a barber's shop (cf. Döhl 2009a).

that it was able not only to form the basis for the musical and socio-cultural rules of a powerful, well-organized and highly active subculture, but also to create a musical and socio-cultural stereotype that became part of American general knowledge (cf. Averill 2003) and to shape public opinion about American popular music around 1900 in a way that differs widely from the actual music history of this era (cf. Brooks 2005; Döhl 2009a) but was nonetheless very influential. The quick establishment in the 1940s of the musical and socio-cultural stereotype of Barbershop Harmony – elderly white male singers singing popular turn-of-the-century songs in a specific way during their leisure hours – led to a rear projection for the era around 1900 that excluded Afro-American musicians[5] as well as European immigrants and, especially, women (cf. Döhl 2008, 2009b) from the assumed origins of the style, and hence from the general image of American popular music around 1900. Because of the power of the stereotype, this effect can even be identified outside the subculture in general knowledge and public opinion as well as in books dealing with American music history around 1900.

Judging the Motives

Was the faulty historical construct of Barbershop Harmony intended, for example to legitimate the exclusion of African-American singers from the subculture in the early 1940s? In the end, there are no sustainable indications that would confirm such suspicions, at least in regard to the formation of the musical and aesthetic concept that is the core of Barbershop Harmony – although the exclusion of African-Americans did take place (cf. Averill 2003; Döhl 2009b). But how could this kind of historical rear projection happen by mistake? And even more, how could it remain undiscovered, even unquestioned, for so long? An answer needs to consider several aspects, including the dependence of Barbershop Harmony on a specific version of popular history that ruled the American public opinion of the 1930s:

---

5   This recently started to change due to studies such as Abbott (1992); Abbott/Seroff (1996, 2002); Averill (2003); Henry (2000).

(1) The subculture in which the singing of Barbershop Harmony has been concentrated until today arose in the late 1930s United States out of a general and strong nostalgic movement which was caused by the Great Depression (cf. Averill 2003). This movement was focused on the *fin de siècle*, or the ›Gay Nineties‹ as it is called in the United States. These years are remembered as happy times in America's socio-cultural memory. Being part of this general movement, the people who formed Barbershop Harmony did not strive to invent something musically new to answer socio-cultural changes as did, for example, Rock'n'Roll, Punk, HipHop or Techno later in the twentieth century. Rather, they wanted to recreate turn-of-the-century music to reestablish something of the ideal world it allegedly represented. The revivalists of Barbershop Harmony, as they called themselves, were elderly, established, middle-class businessmen who remembered their childhood days and the music that surrounded them.

Around 1900, a huge scene consisting of four-part, all-male vocal quartets had indeed existed, sometimes performing accompanied, sometimes not. These groups were formed in a wide range of performance practices and situations. Vocal groups were central elements of popular music theatre, in vaudeville and minstrel shows, and toured the whole country with their companies. They were the major protagonists of the early years of recording, too, because the format of close-harmony singing was favored by the limited technical recording conditions of those days. Groups such as the American Quartet or the Haydn Quartet were popstars of their age and Bill Murray, lead singer of these formations, was the first musician apart from Caruso who was able to live solely from the royalties he earned from his recordings (cf. Döhl 2009a: 152). On the other hand, accompanied and unaccompanied multi-part singing still played a large part in the leisure time of ordinary people, also outside the churches and choral societies. One must remember that these people were the last generation before recordings, radio stations and – a little later – movies made it possible for most people to consume music without anybody being needed to perform in real time. Four-part vocal groups were everywhere in the United States around 1900, also strongly represented within youth culture, and that was what the revivalists of Barbershop Harmony remembered around 1940.[6]

---

6   For a list of more than 500 turn-of-the century vocal quartets cf. Döhl (2009a: 247-264).

They also remembered the word ›barbershop‹ that was introduced to popular music during the 1890s and how it became more or less exclusively associated with the four-part vocal groups.

The revivalists did not support their quest into the musical past with research. They relied on their memories and actively ignored the fact that their idea of the turn-of-the-century vocal quartet music contradicted other opinions established and practiced in parallel revival movements of the late 1930s.[7] Barbershop Harmony and the question of its origins around 1940 can therefore to some extent be considered a case of oral history; the problems with historical accuracy that were diagnosed earlier are typical of oral history when people have to remember experiences from their early days, even more so when there are no sources at hand to support their memories (cf. Niethammer 1985).

(2) Driven by nostalgia, the revivalists wanted to establish a historically informed performance practice. That is also the reason why the core of the repertoire sung by barbershoppers still includes the popular ballads of the turn of the century that had widespread success in those years: songs such as »Sweet Adeline« or »Take Me Out to the Ball Game« which are considered folk songs in the United States today. To achieve that aim, the revivalists had to musically define what was and was not to be considered Barbershop Harmony. Without defining that kind of standard, they would have lost legitimacy for their attempt to recreate and preserve a characteristic form of music making. Thus, all revivalist movements of the 1930s started by creating musical rules. In the case of the Barbershop Harmony Society, the most important organization, these rules grew in number over the next few years. In 1941, the rules were first summarized in writing and circulated within the subculture (cf. Henry 2000: 3-5); the current version contains about 200 pages. The strict concept of historically informed performance practice strengthens an idea about the musical past once it is established – even more if no research or sources exist that support any other view.

(3) As was the fashion in the 1930s, all revivalist groups established singing contests. These contests still form the core of the whole subculture. Most singers participate from time to time either actively or passively. The musical greats, singers and arrangers alike, are born here. This system of

---

7   For these parallel movements cf. Averill (2003: 91-98) and Döhl (2009a).

contests has helped to establish and confirm the rules and the image of musical history that is crucial to it. One must follow the rules in order to compete successfully, and must compete to take part in the musical and social life of the subculture. As a judge active today within the ranks of the Barbershop Harmony Society once summarized: »What barbershop IS is determined by the judges, primarily by the music judges.« (Greg Volk, qtd. in Döhl 2009a: 28)

(4) Thanks to the singing contests, the subculture immediately became and still is highly institutionalized. Nearly everybody interested in performing this music regularly or seriously joins the organizations formed after 1938. Combined, all present organizations worldwide comprise about 70,000 singers. The most important, self-appointed umbrella organization is the Barbershop Harmony Society based in Nashville. Like all monopolistic organizations, the barbershop communities tend to defend their opinions like keepers of the grail, including the question as to what Barbershop Harmony is and is not, and where its origins lie. They actively try to impose their definition of the history of this music inside and outside the subculture, for example through education programs or articles like the ones found in Wikipedia. This further strengthens the idea of the musical past that is at the core of Barbershop Harmony.

It is through an interplay of several aspects, then, that a faulty historical construct was able to be accepted as musical history for decades: nostalgia as a catalyst; the concept of a historically informed performance practice founded on oral history; singing contests as a socio-cultural frame for performances; a subculture with a centralistic institutional structure that precluded alternative, outside movements devoted to the same music; an absence of relevance for the mainstream intellectual and economic music (history) market; a quickly established musical and socio-cultural stereotype in general knowledge; and regular adaptations of the stereotype in other parts of popular culture.

CONCLUSION

The question arises as to why nobody within the subculture has challenged the historical construct that forms the basis of Barbershop Harmony, if only by asking why there are so few sources available to support this image of the past. An organization like the Barbershop Harmony Society has to be conservative and dogmatic, representing as it does a musical community that is based on a specific version of musical history as the foundation of their musical practice. If one were to attempt to challenge this foundation, one would challenge the whole subculture, including its contest system and musical rules, its social beliefs and the musical identity of the people who are part of it. At the least one would have to reestablish the historical focus of this performance practice and shift it from 1900 to 1940. This would not be a problem from the point of view of the concept of historically informed performance practice: Despite the fact that more time (70 years) has passed between today and the actual origins of Barbershop Harmony around 1940 (compared to the 40 year difference between the Barbershop Harmony revival and the gay nineties), the music itself has not changed since the 1940s. However, since Barbershop Harmony is a subculture existing outside of any musical mainstream and lacking economic importance or political implications, any questions have to arise from inside in order to be accepted. The hesitation on the part of barbershoppers to challenge their own foundation in the past and present is not surprising: The people in the subculture are in it because of a specific kind of music and social system. Why should anybody except for scholars have an interest in asking questions about the historical correctness of its foundations? Things are no different with the research leading to this article, which happened largely by accident. While performing Barbershop Harmony in student groups, the author's interest in the origins of this musical tradition evolved naturally, and while trying to find out more, it was unexpectedly discovered that nobody really knows much about the history of the style and that there are many different and contradictory theories circulating (for an overview cf. Döhl 2009a: 32-41, 51-56). The discoveries made in this article, however, are ›interesting‹ to say the least, for a musical practice that claims to be a historically informed performance practice, a preservation of a part of musical history that strives to be as close as possible to its origins. Barbershop Harmony thus becomes more than a curiosity of American popular music in the twentieth century. It is a brilliant case for showing how musical history can be written (and has often been written) as a powerful piece of historical fiction with which many people can identify.

WORKS CITED

Abbott, Lynn (1992): »Play That Barber Shop Chord: A Case for the African-American Origin of Barbershop Harmony«. *American Music* 10.3, 289-325.

Abbott, Lynn/Doug Seroff (1996): »They Cert'ly Sound Good to Me: Sheet Music, Southern Vaudeville, and the Commercial Ascendancy of the Blues«. *American Music* 14.4, 402-454.

Abbott, Lynn/Doug Seroff (2002): *Out of Sight: The Rise of African American Popular Music, 1889-1895*, Jackson/MS: University Press of Mississippi.

Averill, Gage (1999): »Bell Tones and Ringing Chords: Sense and Sensation in Barbershop Harmony«. *The World of Music* 41.1, 37-51.

Averill, Gage (2003): *Four Parts, No Waiting: A Social History of American Barbershop Harmony*, Oxford: Oxford University Press.

Ayling, Benjamin Charles (2000): *An Historical Perspective of International Champion Quartets of the Society for the Preservation and Encouragement of Barber Shop Quartet Singing in America, 1939-1963*, Ann Arbor/MI: UMI ProQuest Digital Dissertations.

Berger, Karol (2007): *Bach's Cycle, Mozart's Arrow: An Essay on the Origins of Musical Modernity*, Berkeley/CA: University of California Press.

Brooks, Tim (2005): *Lost Sounds: Blacks and the Birth of the Recording Industry, 1890-1919*, Urbana-Champaign/IL: University of Illinois Press.

Döhl, Frédéric (2008): »Mythos Barbershop: Folgen einer Musikgeschichte als Wunschbild«. *Archiv für Musikwissenschaft* 65.4, 309-334.

Döhl, Frédéric (2009a): *...that old barbershop sound: Die Entstehung einer Tradition amerikanischer A-cappella-Musik*, Stuttgart: Franz Steiner Verlag.

Döhl, Frédéric (2009b): »Soziale Distinktion in der amerikanischen Musikgeschichte: Die Entstehung der Barbershop Harmony«. In: Anne Ebert/Maria Lidola/Karoline Bahrs/Karoline Noack (eds.), *Differenz und Herrschaft in den Amerikas: Repräsentationen des Anderen in Geschichte und Gegenwart*, Bielefeld: transcript, 93-102.

Garnett, Liz (1999): »Ethics and Aesthetics: The Social Theory of Barbershop Harmony«. *Popular Music* 18.1, 41-61.

Garnett, Liz (2005a): *The British Barbershopper: A Study in Socio-Musical Values*, London: Ashgate.

Garnett, Liz (2005b): »Cool Charts or Barbertrash? Barbershop Harmony's Flexible Concept of the Musical Work«. *Twentieth-Century Music* 2, 245-263.

Goehr, Lydia (2007): *The Imaginary Museum of Musical Works: An Essay in the Philosophy of Music*, 2nd ed., Oxford: Oxford University Press.

Gracyk, Tim (2000): *Popular American Recording Pioneers, 1895-1925*, New York/NY: Haworth Press.

Gracyk, Tim (2006): »Barbershop Quartets on Early 78s«. In: *Tim's Phonographs and Old Records* (http://www.gracyk.com/barbershop.shtml). Accessed 22 November 2010.

Henry, James Earl (2000): *The Origins of Barbershop Harmony: A Study of Barbershop's Musical Link to Other African-American Musics as Evidenced Through Recordings and Arrangements of Early Black and White Quartets*, Ann Arbor/MI: UMI ProQuest Digital Dissertations.

Hentschel, Frank (2006): *Bürgerlich Ideologie und Musik: Politik der Musikgeschichtsschreibung in Deutschland 1776-1871*, Frankfurt am Main: Campus.

Hicks, Val (1988): *Heritage of Harmony: Society for the Preservation and Encouragement of Barber Shop Quartet Singing in America*, Friendship/WI: New Past Press.

Kalin, Gustaf (2005): »Format Frequency Adjustment in Barbershop Quartet Singing«. In: *KTH – Speech, Music and Hearing* (http://w2.nada.kth.se/publications/masterprojects/2005/kalin.pdf). Accessed 22 November 2010.

Kaplan, Max (ed.) (1993): *Barbershopping: Musical and Social Harmony*, Rutherford/NJ: Fairleigh Dickinson University Press.

Mook, Richard (2004): *The Sounds of Liberty: Nostalgia, Masculinity, and Whiteness in Philadelphia Barbershop, 1900-2003*, Ann Arbor/MI: UMI ProQuest Digital Dissertations.

Mook, Richard (2007): »White Masculinity in Barbershop Quartet Singing«. *Journal for the Society of American Music* 1.3, 453-483.

»Music: Up from the Barbershop« (1957): In: *Time Magazine* 17 June 1957 (http://www.time.com/time/magazine/article/0,9171,867728,00.html). Accessed 22 November 2010.

Niethammer, Lutz (ed.) (1985): *Lebenserfahrung und kollektives Gedächtnis: Die Praxis der »Oral History«*, 2nd ed., Frankfurt am Main: Suhrkamp

Riethmüller, Albrecht (2011): *Musik und Ideologie*, Laaber: Laaber.

Stebbins, Robert A. (1992): »Coasts and Rewards in Barbershop Singing«. *Leisure Studies* 11.2, 123-133.

Stebbins, Robert A. (1996): *The Barbershop Singer: Inside the Social World of a Musical Hobby*, Toronto: University of Toronto Press.

Tadday, Ulrich (1993): *Die Anfänge des Musikfeuilletons: Der kommunikative Gebrauchswert musikalischer Bildung in Deutschland um 1800*, Stuttgart: J.B. Metzler.

Taruskin, Richard (1995): *Text and Act: Essays on Music and Performance*, New York/NY: Oxford University Press.

Taruskin, Richard (2006): »Is There a Baby in the Bathwater?«. *Archiv für Musikwissenschaft* 63.3, 163-185 (Part I), 63.4, 309-327 (Part II).

»Quick, accessible to everyone and delightful«

History and Art History in Popular Italian Magazines of the 1960s

ANTONIE R. WIEDEMANN

A FIRST APPROACH TO A NEGLECTED GENRE: POPULAR HISTORICAL MAGAZINES IN ITALY

The aim of this contribution is to provide a first approach to the study of popular historical publications in Italy in the second half of the twentieth century, especially in the 1960s. During these years, many popular publications regarding history and art history were published in Italy with the intention of spreading historical knowledge. The success of these products is evidence of an important moment of public interest in history. In this paper the focus will be on a case study of two important magazines. I will also focus on the genre of the so-called *fascicoli*, taking into consideration not just the contents, but also the readers and the role of the publishers.

Although there were a large number of historical magazines and books being addressed to the general public in Italy after the Second World War, this phenomenon has so far not been studied in an exhaustive manner. A first attempt was delivered by Silvia Pizzetti in 1981, who published an introduction to the use of history in popular magazines, but her work lacks an exhaustive analysis of the social and historical context. The relatively poor state of research regarding popular history,[1] especially in print media, might be due to the Italian academic culture which dictates that disciplinary boundaries should not be crossed. Historical didactics more often centre on institutional problems or on the study of school textbooks (cf. Pivato 2000; Cajani 2001; Federico 2004) rather than researching collective consciousness and historical memory.[2] In addition, most studies in methodology or the history of Italian historiography are mainly focused on academic history (cf. Ridolfi 2008; Di Rienzo 2004), whereas media studies tend to reflect on the representation of history in television or films (cf. Grasso 2006). In the field of publishing and book studies, attention has mostly been directed toward the study of important publishers rather than readers, although more recent studies appear to deepen these aspects of reception.[3] With regard to popular publications on the history of the arts, the state of research in Italy is even poorer. Studies on the development of the arts focus more on technical aspects as researched in museums, for instance, and neglect considerations of the role of art for the Italian collective consciousness,[4] whereas in Germany, for example, first studies in this direction have been undertaken.[5] This is more astonishing since art history has been studied in schools in

---

1 The volume by Legnani (2000) gives a broad overview of popular history in contemporary Italy, but it is striking that the ›products‹ he analyzes do not really consider the dissemination of history through non-professionals, with the exception of historical novels. He neither considers historical films nor popular magazines.

2 A first approach towards a discussion of historical narratives, media and memory was recently delivered by Dario Petrosino (2010).

3 The recent collection of essays on the history of popular publishing in Italy entitled *Libri per tutti* covers a wide range of historical periods from the sixteenth century to contemporary times, but does not cover the period between 1945 and 1990 (cf. Braida/Infelise 2010).

4 Even in authoritative publications such as *I luoghi della memoria* by Mario Isneghi (2010), with contributions for example on the role of the opera for the Italian collective consciousness, the impact of art was not considered.

5 In particular, the so-called *Kunsterziehungsbewegung* and the attempts of aesthetic education around 1900 have been discussed for example by Hein (1991) and Krebs (2001).

Italy since the early twentieth century.[6] The following pages should therefore be understood as a first attempt at an analytical approach to some of the most popular historical magazines in Italy. This is not meant to be an exhaustive review on the subject, but rather an attempt at contextualizing the phenomenon within the Italian society of the 1960s.

THE CASE OF *STORIA ILLUSTRATA* AND *HISTORIA*

The two popular history magazines to be analyzed here are *Storia Illustrata*, published by the well-known publisher Arnoldo Mondadori, and *Historia,* published by Cino Del Duca.[7] For the period in consideration (1957-1970), these two periodicals were the only popular magazines in Italy which dealt with history as their main subject, which was also prominently displayed on their covers (cf. figs. 1 and 2).[8] Both were first published in 1957, during a crucial period of the Italian economic boom. In fact, the late 1950s can be considered a moment of growth, with an average increase of the GDP around 5.3 percent between 1951 and 1958, achieving 8.3 percent in 1961 (cf. Colarizzi 2000: 350). They were the first historical magazines in Italy after the Second World War and considering that both continued to be published until the 1990s,[9] they must have been well accepted by readers.

At first glance, the magazines are very similar in their approach to history,[10] except for the fact that they come from different backgrounds.

---

6   For a history of art history as a school subject see the collection of articles edited by Ferretti (2003), especially the contributions by Franchi and Nicolini.

7   My analysis is based on a sample of 20 issues of each magazine between 1958 and 1970.

8   Since on this occasion the focus is put on popular historical magazines and fascicules as a genre, articles in other magazines are not contemplated.

9   As Angelo D'Orsi emphasizes, the popularization of history in Italy since the 1990s occurs mostly in newspapers, radio, television and film, and no longer in magazines (cf. D'Orsi 2002: 146).

10 In this context, the slight differences concerning political orientation and the approach to history noticed by Silvia Pizzetti (1981: 191-226) are negligible for the purposes of the present analysis.

Even the editorials give evidence of this similarity. In the first edition of *Storia Illustrata,* the editor in chief Nando Sampietro – also editor of the Italian version of *Life Magazine, Epoca* – declared the aim of the magazine to be to »give a lecture to the reader that should be useful, but still quick, accessible to everyone and [...] delightful« (*Storia Illustrata* 1957.1: 5; my translation). History is considered »the truest and most beautiful and most poetic novel« (ibid.).

Figs. 1 and 2: Front covers of Storia Illustrata *and* Historia.

In an attempt to justify this approach, which could be considered somehow superficial, Sampietro not only quotes the historian and national poet Giosuè Carducci, who had expressed the intention of writing a history of Italy's *Risorgimento* period that had to be »simple and plain«. He also declares a moderate patriotism and the desire to »like our country« and not to contribute to the »self-destruction of certain publications« (ibid.) as reasons behind the approach – which can be interpreted as a not so well hidden attack on leftist historiography in publications of the communist party (cf. Romeo 1987).

The idea of history told in a narrative fashion is also expressed by Alessandro Cutolo, editor of *Historia*. In his first editorial, Cutolo indicates that the intention of his magazine is to present history as a narration. Explaining the reasons behind the creation of his new magazine, he declares that it is basically an Italian version of the French magazine *Historia*, which had been published with success in France (35,000 copies) for many decades (cf. *Historia* 1957.1: 5). Indeed, many of the articles in the Italian publication were translated directly from French (cf. for example ibid.: 5). Cutolo also illustrates the topics that were to be treated in his magazine: »Alongside dense concepts, there will be space for an anecdotal, colourful representation of society, and of the intellectual, artistic, social, economic and scientific life.« (Ibid.: 5) As a matter of fact, the tendency to write history as a sequence of anecdotes in *Historia* is rather evident. We can find articles such as »La Sangiovannara«, which describes a popular heroine of the Liberation of Naples at the time of Garibaldi's arrival (*Historia* 1960.1: 48), or pieces of the calibre of »Hitler believed in horoscopes« (*Historia* 1965.1: 82).

The idea of narrating history is repeated several times in both editorials. It seems that the term *narrare* is used by both the publishers of *Historia* and those of *Storia Illustrata* with the aim of underlining the popular approach of their magazines and distinguishing themselves from academic historians: »We do not want to annoy our kind reader. We do not want to send them back to school and bore them. We want to entertain our public. These pages will not have the tone of a lesson, but of a conversation, of an account.« (*Storia Illustrata* 1957.1: 5) Often the contributions explicitly underline the attempt to write history using conventional categories of literature and especially of crime novels,[11] as in the section of *Storia Illustrata* entitled »Crime in History« (cf. for example *Storia Illustrata* 1965.4: 534-557 or 1965.2: 224-229). Even in one of the rare articles written by a professional historian,[12] entitled »Metternich tra Napoleone e Mazzini«, the style used reminds one strongly of the incipit of a monumental film: »End of the 18th century. The ancient Hapsburgian monarchy experiences the moment of its greatest power. Its boundaries reach from the river Po to the Danube, from Bohemia to the Balkans, covering different races, Germans and Slavs, Latins and Magyars.« (*Storia Illustrata* 1965.3: 352)

The tendency to tell history as a story was even exercised regarding contemporary history, as well as in autobiographical interpretations: In

---

11 For a broad discussion on the correlations between history and crime fiction see Korte/Paletschek (2009) and Saupe (2009).

12 The article was written by Franco Valsecchi, who at the time was a professor of modern history at the university of Rome.

Storia Illustrata, for example, we can find several articles written by eye-witnesses. Rolando Balducci reveals the secrets of young Mussolini between 1910-1914 (cf. *Storia Illustrata* 1965.1: 106) and Raffaele Cadorna, son of the famous general Luigi Cadorna, tells from his ›privileged‹ point of view a very moderate history of the *Resistenza*, trying to create a coherent narration of what could be considered one of the most intensely discussed topics of Italian contemporary history (cf. *Storia Illustrata* 1965.4: 471-499). The appealing and engaging language of the popular history magazine might also be due to the fact that most of the articles were written by professional journalists.[13]

With regard to structure, the similarities between the two magazines are also quite apparent. In both cases, the design was inspired by the illustrated women's or society magazines of the 1950s. A large amount of space is given to letters and questions from readers, and both provide regular columns such as »History of a Capital« or »History in a Newspaper«. Whereas *Historia* started its campaign with the slogan »100 pages for 100 lire«,[14] *Storia Illustrata* had more pages, but also a higher price (160 pages and 200 lire) from the beginning. Nevertheless, they were sold at very affordable prices for a broad range of readers.[15]

FROM HISTORY TO SOCIETY

In terms of the magazines' content, it is hardly surprising that on average most articles are concerned with the twentieth century, while a large number are also concerned with the nineteenth century. At first glance, we could define Italian history from the *Risorgimento* period to the Second

---

13 Journalists writing for *Storia Illustrata* included some of the most famous names, such as Giovanni Ansaldo, or Indro Montanelli, who could be defined as a semi-professional historian (cf. Petrosino 2010). In the competitor magazine, *Historia*, famous journalists' names are lacking. This difference between the two publications can be attributed to the superior economic power of *Storia Illustrata*'s editor Arnoldo Mondadori.

14 100 Lire in the 1960s corresponded to the price of a bottle of milk or two bus tickets.

15 The exact number of sold copies is difficult to ascertain.

World War as a topic privileged by the magazines, whereas the early-modern age, as well as medieval and ancient history, are covered by a minimal number of contributions. Furthermore, it is quite remarkable that while the articles on the nineteenth and twentieth centuries mostly cover political or military topics, those regarding earlier periods largely focus on curiosities and on the history of culture and society. An interesting example in this respect might be the piece »Profilo di Siena – Seno di Venezia« (*Storia Illustrata* 1965.1: 302-311) which considers the history of female beauty. The article is supported by reproductions of famous female figures and portraits from Prassitele to Canova.

In terms of the evolution of the themes covered by the magazines over the first decade of their publication, it is evident that the percentage of articles about the twentieth century even increased, with a strong focus on the not so distant events of fascism and the Second World War. With regard to the topics treated, both magazines seem to focus on the military, especially in *Storia Illustrata*, with a predilection for details that might not contribute to the general comprehension of historical subjects but gives authority to whoever is writing. The representation of history through important personalities might be seen as a way to reduce the complexity of historical contexts and developments. Generally, articles regarding recent history and politics are highly descriptive and tend to avoid clear positions (also cf. Pizzetti 1981: 197).

It is also remarkable that there are almost no links to other kinds of popular historical productions of the 1960s such as the numerous Italian colossal movies or the more committed productions of these years such as Luchino Visconti's *Gattopardo*. It could be suggested that the editors tried to maintain a middle position between the academic and a more openly popular approach.

From the second half of the 1960s, more and more articles were no longer strictly concerned with history, but had a wider scope, encompassing contemporary politics and society. In 1970, for example, *Historia* had a cover story on the war in Vietnam (cf. *Historia* 1970.1) or, already in 1965, on the conflict between Indonesia and Malaysia (cf. *Historia* 1965.2). Additionally, a report on the island of Madeira can be found in *Storia Illustrata* (cf. *Storia Illustrata* 1970.3). This evolution towards topics that went beyond historical subjects could have been motivated by the fact that, due to the political situation in the second half of the 1960s, readers had become more and more politicized[16] and the interest in history generally declined. In these political articles background information is also neglected.

READING POPULAR HISTORY MAGAZINES IN 1960S ITALY

In order to gain a deeper understanding of the effects these magazines might have had on the imagination of history, it is necessary to understand what kind of public these were directed toward. For the readers of *Storia Illustrata* we have some data, thanks to research done by the Italian opinion polling institute Doxa in 1963. Its results convey a clear image of the readers of historical magazines: Most of them were male (almost 75 percent), employees, technicians, self-employed individuals and students, identifiable at large in the moderate Italian middle class of the time. The majority of the readers were real *aficionados*: 80 percent of the readers bought every issue, read it for more than two hours and kept it afterwards (cf. Istituto Doxa 1963: 95-107).[17]

The great number of letters published underlines the tight relationship between the readers and the editors and gives an idea of the expectations the readers had of the magazines. Many readers wrote in order to ask questions or make assertions, especially regarding topics related to recent history; very often it seems that the magazine was consulted as a kind of authority by its readers. A high percentage of these letters regard questions about single events or, very often, specific weapons, often from readers who were involved in the recent wars themselves (cf. for example *Historia* 1965.1: 7 or *Storia Illustrata* 1970.2: 5). Reading the letters from the consumers of these magazines we realize that some of them found it difficult to separate literature from history,[18] whereas others seem to be focused on

---

16 For a short but precise overview of the social and political movements in the second half of the 1960s cf. the chapter »Protesta sociale e protesta studentesca« (Colarizzi 2000: 390-397).

17 This is also supported by the magazines themselves. Often within the magazines one can find advertisements for collectors of the issues.

18 For example, on the same page in the January 1965 issue of *Historia* there is a letter from a reader asking for historical information on some figures in the

dates in an almost pedantic way. In general, however, the readers are looking for one historical truth, and not for different aspects.

It seems therefore that the interest in the past – which, as we have seen, was mostly an interest in contemporary history – could also have been motivated by the need to elaborate personal history, i.e. a past that, in the middle of the economic boom with its radical social changes, had to be set aside and could find an expression in these magazines. For younger readers, the interest could also have been motivated by the fact that contemporary history was (and is) barely treated in Italian schools (cf. Gioia 2000). The veneration of the myth of the heroes of the Italian Unification[19] and the very moderate and patriotic description of controversial arguments such as the Italian *Resistenza*[20] (cf. Colarizzi 2000: 382) express a desire for a more patriotic image of the nation than that offered by the difficult 1960s, especially for the moderate Italian lower middle class, to which most of the readers of *Historia* and *Storia Illustrata* belonged.

Regarding the historical periods treated by these magazines, it is interesting to compare them with the events that Jacques Le Goff has identified as most important for the Italian collective consciousness (cf. Le Goff 1974: 540-541). It is striking that Rome, the medieval cities and the Renaissance, which Le Goff considered as crucial moments for the Italian collective identity, are barely treated in the magazines, whereas historical events from the beginning of the Italian Unification to the Second World War are predominant. This is of particular interest considering how for twenty years the fascist propaganda had tried to impose a tight connection between the Roman past and the present. Additionally, the historical events

---

poems *Orlando Furioso* and *Orlando Innamorato*, and on the next page a letter from a reader concerning the exact number of dioceses in northern Italy.

19 Analyzing the importance of the *Risorgimento* as a myth of the Italian nation, Maurizio Ridolfi underlines the strong correlation between popular-history making and institutional communication, trying to create an official image of the Italian Unification process at the beginning of the 1960s when Italian society was in the midst of heavy social changes (cf. Ridolfi 2010: 45).

20 As Simona Colarizzi has underlined, the unifying value of the myth of the *Resistenza*, considered a national liberation and second *Risorgimento*, remained almost undiscussed until 1968, when the partisan war began to be considered a *Rivoluzione tradita*, a betrayed revolution (cf. Colarizzi 2000: 382).

and persons evoked in the process of nation-making in the nineteenth century, such as Dante as a national poet (cf. Raphael 2005) are not treated to an extent that reflects Le Goff's evaluations.

POPULAR PUBLICATIONS ON ART HISTORY

Apart from these two magazines, another type of popular historical publication was able to gain significant success among Italian readers of the 1960s: the so-called *fascicoli,* or fascicules. These little books promoted the circulation of culture and history among those who would not usually go to bookshops to buy more expensive and ›difficult‹ books on the same topics. The booklets were offered in *edicola*, newsstands, at a low price[21] and produced on a large scale. The pioneers of these products were Fratelli Fabbri Editori who started publishing books for children immediately after 1945 and sold them at newsstands, because of the low number of bookshops all over the territory.

The first important success of Fabbri was an encyclopaedia for children, *Conoscere*; sold in several issues and six editions from 1958 to 1963, it achieved the incredible number of three million complete series sold (cf. Carotti 2006: 23; Fabbri 2008: 29).[22] This successful model was later also applied to the history of the arts. In fact, between 1961 and 1966 Fabbri published several series in this field.

Perhaps inspired by the *L'Arte per tutti* volumes published by the fascist Istituto Luce, the most famous of these *fascicoli*, the *Maestri del Colore,* has been a pioneer model, and not just because of the innovative method of distribution through newsstands and the relatively low price. These booklets consisted of a short introduction on an artist[23] – such as Mantegna (fig. 3) – and around 15 pages of high-quality photo prints of his most important works. In this context it is necessary to point out that the

---

21 The prices ranged from 250 to 600 Lire.

22 One encyclopaedia consisted of 200 individual issues.

23 This comprised around five pages of biography and a critical introduction to the work of the artist.

authors of these popular publications were mostly art professionals, such as Terisio Pignatti or Giovanni Previtali,[24] and not journalists.

Fig. 3: Front cover of Maestri del Colore, *issue on Mantegna.*

This professional effort was appreciated by one of the most famous Italian art historians of the time, Roberto Longhi; he considered these publications a »violent, but necessary opening of specialist knowledge to a large, indeterminate public« (Previtali 1982: 102).[25] The impact and success of these little books is emphasized by the number of copies sold: two millions of each series, each consisting of 150 single fascicules (cf. Fabbri 2008: 31),[26] although these numbers need to be taken with reservation.

---

24 The volume on Botticelli, written by Mina Bacci, was recently in the centre of a scandal that is evidence of the importance of these popular publications of the 1960s for Italian ›general‹ culture. The politician and art historian Vittorio Sgarbi published a monograph on Botticelli, plagiarizing the introduction of Bacci's volume of the *Maestri del Colore* (cf. Erbani 2008: 1).

25 The high quality of the *Maestri del Colore* series is also indicated by the fact that they can still be found in the bibliography for first-year university courses.

26 Since these numbers have been given by the publisher, they must be considered with caution. The enormous success of the series is also evidenced by a second,

For many Italians in the 1960s, these *fascicoli* represented a chance to approach the history and beauty of their own country in a manner that was previously unthinkable. As the journalist Gaetano Afeltra remembers: »These issues were not only an important cultural instrument. Mostly for Southern Italy, they represented a way to promote and appreciate beauty. In many homes the photo prints of the booklets were put in a frame and hung up on the wall with naïve enthusiasm.« (Righetti 2001: 37)

This eloquently demonstrates that these products were an answer to a general interest in the cultural history of one's own nation that developed in Italy during the economic growth of the 1950s and 1960s. In fact more than 50 percent of the issues were dedicated to Italian artists; other publications of the same period were entirely devoted to the history of Italian monuments. The public's appreciation for these publications is also proved by the fact that, following the pioneers of the *Maestri del Colore*, numerous similar series were released between 1966 and 1970, for instance *I tesori* (Sansoni) and *Forma e Colore* (Sansoni), but also more strictly historical publications such as *I Grandi di Tutti i Tempi* (Mondadori). However with the beginning of the 1970s the boom of these publications came to an end (cf. Cadioli/Vignini 2004: 114).

In this specific area of cultural and historical popularization, a boom of interest on the part of the public was combined for a short period with an opening of the academic world towards a popularization of specialist knowledge. It is not surprising that this happened precisely at a moment when the universities were going through a period of radical change.

The success of these publications could be interpreted as the result of a will to complete the social and economic rise of new social classes with a growth of culture, or at least with the demonstration of culture. It is important to emphasize that the history of art, which might seem to be a very particular sector of historical interest, was crucial for the development of the Italian collective identity, as Jacques Le Goff indicates in his previously quoted essay: »[T]here are few national histories in which art has such a big part as in the history of Italy« (Le Goff 1974: 537).

---

unaltered edition of the *fascicoli* in the 1990s and the translation of the series in Spain, for example.

PUBLIC HISTORY AND 1960S ITALIAN SOCIETY

A variety of reasons can be put forward for the success of historical magazines and *fascicoli* at the end of the 1950s and throughout the 1960s in Italy. First of all, there was a general desire for cultural legitimization on the part of a new middle class of probably mostly Northern Italian employees that had a strong will to accompany their economic rise with access to the cultural life of the higher classes.

The starting point was not just the achievement of a basic level of literacy – which in Italy was still a problem until the 1960s[27] – but also the unprecedented possibility of accessing cultural content at relatively low prices due to cheaper production techniques and the Italian economic boom. Indeed, publishers such as Mondadori, Cino del Duca and Fabbri were able to interpret this need for culture and exploit it for commercial success. Publishers decided to produce cultural products in a way that made it possible for anybody to build a little library, including parts of the society that were not even familiar with bookshops (cf. Ragone 1997: 469; Cadioli/Vignini 2004: 102). By selling magazines and *fascicoli* at newsstands and thus offering information piece by piece at low prices, these publishers opened the market of cultural publications to parts of society that until then had never been taken into consideration by the academic elite, which only in a few cases and for a short period collaborated in the production of these media of popularization.

Regarding the case of strictly historical magazines, we can see that the interest in the past already appears to decline at the end of the 1960s and the beginning of the 1970s when we can observe how the topics treated are of a more and more political nature. Whether this is a result of the radicalization of the public debate in the second half of the 1960s or simply an editorial choice, made with the aim of reaching a broader public, cannot be determined here. Still, it is striking that the decline of interest in history at the end of the 1960s coincides with a decline in the use of historical topics in advertising, as noted by Mike Seidensticker for German journals (cf. Seidensticker 1995).

---

27 In 1951 in Italy there was still a 30 percent rate of illiteracy in Italy, a number that decreased significantly to 8.9 percent by 1961 (cf. Turi 1997: 396-397).

For the 1960s, the publications considered in this contribution allegedly functioned both to commemorate and to orientate at a moment when Italian society was experiencing important changes in terms of economic growth, internal migration and a radicalization of politics, to mention only some of the most evident changes of those years. Following Gabriele Turi, the 1960s in Italy can be defined as »the climax of a long process of nationalization and, at the same time, the beginning of a period of splits and centrifugal tendencies in Italian society« (Turi 1993: 10). According to the statistical data provided by Istituto Doxa it seems that the readers of these magazines belonged mostly to the lower middle class that was less concerned with economic growth and more worried about the social changes that were taking place, a fact that created a strong desire to slow down on modernity and democracy and look back to the past, as can be seen with the attempt to elaborate history. Therefore we can consider these popular history magazines as significant for creating what Aleida Assmann has defined as the ›functional memory‹ of a cultural collective (cf. Assmann 1999).

Works Cited

Assmann, Aleida (1999): *Erinnerungsräume: Formen und Wandlungen des kulturellen Gedächtnisses*, München: Beck.

Braida, Ludovica/Mario Infelise (2010): *Libri per tutti: Generi editoriali di larga circolazione tra antico regime e età contemporanea*, Milano: UTET.

Cadioli, Alberto/Giuliano Vignini (2004): *Storia dell'editoria italiana*, Milano: Bibliografica.

Cajani, Luigi (2001): »Controversial History for Italian Schools«. In: Karl Pellens et al. (eds.), *Historical Consciousness and History Teaching in a Globalizing Society*, Frankfurt am Main: Peter Lang, 51-57.

Carotti, Carlo (2006): »Le dispense dei Fratelli Fabbri«. *La Fabbrica del Libro* 2, 22-26.

Colarizzi, Simona (2000): *Storia del Novecento italiano: Cent'anni di entusiasmo, di paure, di speranza*, Milano: BUR.

Di Rienzo, Eugenio (2004): *Un dopoguerra storiografico: Storici italiani tra guerra civile e prima Repubblica*, Firenze: Le Lettere.

D'Orsi, Angelo (2002): *Piccolo manuale di storiografia*, Milano: Bruno Mondadori.

Erbani, Francesco (2008): »Sgarbi e il plagio su Botticelli«. In: *Repubblica* 2 December 2008, 1.

Fabbri, Giovanni (2008): »Ricordi … (in breve)«. *La Fabbrica del Libro* 1, 25-32.

Federico, Valentina (2004): »Insegnare la storia in un mondo globale: Una riflessione sui manuali di storia a livello internazionale«. *Storia e Società* 2, 385-390.

Ferretti, Massimo (ed.) (2003*)*: *La storia dell'arte nella scuola italiana: Storia, strumenti, prospettive*, Roma: Carocci.

Franchi, Elena (2003): »Dalle cattedre ambulanti all'insegnamento ufficiale: L'ingresso della storia dell'arte nei licei«. In: Ferretti (ed.), *La storia dell'arte nella scuola italiana*, 5-20.

Gioia, Annabella (2000): »Contemporaneità e trasmissione del sapere storico«. *Italia Contemporanea* 219, 346-350.

Grasso, Aldo (2006): *Fare storia con la televisione: L'immagine come fonte, evento, memoria*, Milano: Vita e Pensiero.

Hein, Peter Ulrich (1991): *Transformation der Kunst: Ziele und Wirkungen der deutschen Kultur- und Kunsterziehungsbewegung*, Köln: Böhlau.

Historia (1957-1970), Milano: Cino del Duca Editore.

I maestri del colore (1962-1966), Milano: Fratelli Fabbri Editore.

Isneghi, Mario (ed.) (2010): *I luoghi della memoria: Simboli e miti dell'Italia unita*, Bari: Laterza.

Istituto Doxa (1963): *I lettori di otto periodici italiano: Studio statistico sulle caratteristiche demografiche, economiche, sociali e culturali per conto di Arnoldo Mondadori Editore*, Milano: Arnoldo Mondadori Editore.

Korte, Barbara/Sylvia Paletschek (eds.) (2009): *Geschichte im Krimi: Beiträge aus den Kulturwissenschaften*, Köln: Böhlau.

Krebs, Diethart (2001): »Kunsterziehungsbewegung und Kulturreform«. In: Kaspar Maase/Wolfgang Kaschuba (eds.), *Schund und Schönheit: Populäre Kultur um 1900*, Köln: Böhlau, 378-397.

Legnani, Massimo (2000): *Al mercato della storia: Il mestiere di storico tra scienza e consumo*, Roma: Carocci.

Le Goff, Jacques (1974): »Il peso del passato nella coscienza collettiva degli italiani«. In: Fabio Luca Cavazza/Stephen R. Graubard (eds.), *Il caso italiano*, Milano: Garzanti, 534-552.

Nicolini, Simonetta (2003): »Il manuale: Un modello per imparare la storia dell'arte, dall'epoca della riforma Gentile fino agli anni Sessanta«. In: Ferretti (ed.), *La storia dell'arte nella scuola italiana*, 21-38.

Petrosino, Dario (2010): »Appunti e spunti per un dibattito su narrazione storica, trasmissione della memoria e media«. *Storia e Futuro* 23, 1-18.

Pivato, Stefano (2000): »Il mercato della storia«. *Italia Contemporanea* 220/221, 543-549.

Pizzetti, Silvia (1981): *I rotocalchi e la storia: La divulgazione storica nei periodici illustrati (1950-1975)*, Roma: Bulzoni.

Previtali, Giovanni (1982): *L'arte di scrivere sull'arte: Roberto Longhi nella cultura del nostri tempo*, Roma: Editori Riuniti.

Ragone, Giovanni (1997): »Tascabile e nuovi lettori«. In: Turi (ed.), *Storia dell'editoria nell'Italia contemporanea*, 449-447.

Raphael, Lutz (2005): »Von der liberalen Kulturnation zur nationalistischen Kulturgemeinschaft: Deutsche und italienische Erfahrungen mit der Nationalkultur zwischen 1800 und 1960«. In: Christoph Dipper (ed.), *Deutschland und Italien 1860-1960: Politische und kulturelle Aspekte im Vergleich*, München: Oldenbourg, 243-275.

Ridolfi, Maurizio (2008): *La storia contemporanea attraverso le riviste*, Soveria Mannelli: Rubattino.

Ridolfi, Maurizio (2010): »Risorgimento«. In: Mario Isneghi (ed.), *I luoghi della memoria*, 1-47.

Righetti, Donata (2001): »Dino Fabbri, il D'Artagnan dell'editoria che portò i classici in edicola«. In: *Corriere della Sera* 12 December 2001, 37.

Romeo, Rosario (1987): »La storiografia marxista nel secondo dopoguerra«. In: Romeo Rosario (ed.), *L'Italia liberale: Sviluppo e contraddizioni*, Milano: Il Saggiatore, 103-170.

Saupe, Achim (2009): *Der Historiker als Detektiv – der Detektiv als Historiker: Historik, Kriminalistik und der Nationalsozialismus als Kriminalroman*, Bielefeld: transcript.

Seidensticker, Mike (1995): *Werbung mit Geschichte: Zur Ästhetik und Rhetorik des Ästhetischen*, Köln: Böhlau.

Storia Illustrata (1957-1970), Milano: Arnoldo Mondadori Editore.

Turi, Gabriele (1993): »Introduzione«. In: Simona Soldati/Gabriele Turi (eds.), *Fare gli italiani: Scuola e cultura nell'Italia contemporanea*, vol. 1: *La nascita dello Stato nazionale*, Bologna: Mulino, 9-33.

Turi, Gabriele (ed.) (1997): *Storia dell'editoria nell'Italia contemporanea*, Firenze: Giunti.

Don Juan de Austria in European Historical Culture

The Twentieth-Century Metamorphosis of a Popular Hero

FERNANDO SÁNCHEZ-MARCOS

INTRODUCTION

Undoubtedly, Don Juan de Austria or John of Austria (1547-1578)[1] is a historical figure of the sixteenth century who has attracted a great amount of attention from both his contemporaries and posterity.[2] In his lifetime, a rare combination of circumstances arose which invested his life with a heroic, legendary and enigmatic aura. The fascination aroused by his figure and his political and military career, associated primarily with the sea battle of Lepanto (1571), has led to numerous textual and iconic representations related to his life and the scenarios in which it unfolded, which continue to be appropriated even today (one such representation is shown in fig. 1).

---

1   The most usual name for him in English is now John of Austria; in German Juan d'Austria is more common than Johann von Österreich; Jean d'Autriche or Juan d'Autriche are used in French and Giovanni d'Austria or Juan d'Austria in Italian. The issue of names could in itself be an interesting subject.

2   In his own time, after Lepanto, many sites of memory dedicated to praising his victory appeared, such as the colossal statue erected in Messina in 1572 by Andrea Calamecca or the epic poem *La Austríada*, composed by Juan Rufo (1584). I will return to *La Austríada* below.

Fig. 1: Statue of John of Austria in his native city (Regensburg), erected in 1978. This is a copy of another statue by Andrea Calamech (1572), which is in Messina.

Photograph taken by Adrian Smith.

My main interest here is to offer a case study on twentieth-century European historical culture. I will analyse the changes and continuities which one can see in the public image of John of Austria over the course of the century. In particular I will focus on studying the metamorphosis that historical culture, i.e. the articulated historical representations operating on public opinion,[3] has undergone as regards John of Austria from the early twentieth century up until today.[4]

---

3   I also assume the definition of historical culture proposed by Maria Grever as an »umbrella concept, including: Narratives (internal side) meaning the circulation of specific contents of historical knowledge, interests and the development of personal historical consciousness; infrastructures (external side) which facilitate and structure the production, consumption, appropriation and transmission of specific historical contents« (»Historical Culture, Plurality and the Nation

Don Juan de Austria's Life and Political Career

Before considering the creation and transformation of the historical culture related to John of Austria, it seems appropriate to remember the main discussions that his figure has generated in academic history.[5] Lorenzo van der Hammen, who wrote the first biography of John of Austria in 1627, said about his life that »lo mas es lo que se ignora« (»the greatest part is that which is unknown«).[6] Today we know much more about John of Austria and we can put forward more diverse assessments of his activities.

John of Austria was born, almost incognito, in Regensburg in 1547, the fruit of a liaison between the Emperor Charles V and Barbara Blomberg. The Emperor, widower of his only wife Isabel of Portugal, had been in the city from April to August 1546 for the celebration of an Imperial Diet (5 May to 24 July) that aspired to solve, among other difficulties, the political-confessional problems. Blomberg was then an attractive, young, unmarried woman, the daughter of a family of the petty bourgeoisie and apparently a

---

State«, lecture at Freiburg i. Br., 11.12.2008, manuscript qtd. in Korte/Paletschek (2009: 11).

4   For previous works cf. Blanco Fernández (2001: 165-182); Molinié-Bertrand (2001: 193-203); Sánchez-Marcos (2000a).

5   For a fairly extensive list of published sources, studies and novels referring to John of Austria, ranging from L. van der Hammen (1627) via the classic studies of the nineteenth century (such as those by W. Havemann, L.P. Gachard and W. Stirling-Maxwell) to works of the first years of the current decade, cf. Kahl (2005). The relatively recent biographies by Bartolomé Bennassar (2001) and Marita A. Panzer (2004) also contain extensive bibliographies. John of Austria's adult life is closely intertwined with that of Philip II; for that reason, recent research works on the latter, such as the monumental study by Geoffrey Parker (2010), are indispensable for acquiring indepth knowledge of the world in which the former lived. Parker's work includes 58 pages of »Sources and Bibliography«. He also includes the numerous volumes edited by the Sociedad Estatal para la Conmemoración de los Centenarios de Felipe II y Carlos V in the context of the commemorations of Philip II and Charles V, held in 1998-2000 (cf. http://dialnet.unirioja.es/servlet/editor?codigo=3445. Accessed 14 July 2011).

6   Van der Hammen in his »Note from the Author« (1627: 328).

good singer. The hypothesis that the birth of her son took place on 24 February, the same day of the year that Charles V had been born on in 1500, is plausible although by no means proven.

To avoid the dishonour which having or being a bastard then involved, Blomberg agreed to marry Hieronymus Kegel, a member of the Emperor's courtly entourage. For this reason her son soon came to be called Jeromín (a diminutive of Hieronymus or Jerome). The paths of Jeromín/John of Austria and his mother were not to cross again until years later. Barbara Blomberg was widowed in 1569, when Charles V had already died. She continued to live in Germany and to receive a pension from Philip II, although her behaviour was far from that which the Emperors and, afterwards, John of Austria himself, might have desired of her. Only after much pressure and some turbulent interviews with her son, who had become very important, did Blomberg resign herself to going to Spain, where she died in a small village (Colindres) in Asturias.

Charles V soon decided that his offspring was to be taken to Spain. He charged a close associate and friend, Luis (Méndez) de Quijada (or Quixada), with this role. Jeromín spent his early childhood in Leganés, a village near Madrid, in the house of a Flemish musician (Frans Massis) and his wife (Ana de Medina). Later on, he went to live in the castle that Quijada and his wife, Magdalena de Ulloa, possessed. The latter was an adoptive mother for John in his crucial adolescent years and instilled Christian morality in him.[7] After his abdication and retirement to the Monastery of Yuste (Extremadura), Charles V wanted to be near his son. He was probably encouraged by the news he received from Quijada on the physical and mental qualities of Jeromín: He was a healthy boy, handsome, alert and courageous, who did not know he was the Emperor's son until the latter died in 1558. Shortly after, John was publicly recognised as a natural son of Charles V,[8] in accordance with the king's will, and joined the Spanish court of his half-brother Philip II. On 12 October 1559, the king himself conferred the coveted insignia of the Golden Fleece upon him.

---

7   On the environment that surrounded John of Austria in these years cf. the collection of studies in Diputación Provincial de Valladolid (1998).

8   John was the new name assigned to Jeromín by Philip II, as homage to a son of Charles and his wife Isabel of Portugal who had died at an early age.

At one point, Charles V had thought that John of Austria be destined for an ecclesiastical career, but the boy's fiery temperament and military inclinations took his life in another direction. During his years of military and humanistic training at Philip's court, he had as companions the unfortunate Prince Don Carlos (1545-1568), then son and heir of Philip II, and Prince Alexander Farnese (son of an illegitimate daughter of Charles V and, in success and fame, the very antithesis of Don Carlos). These two figures, although almost the same age as John, were his nephews, and their lives – especially that of Alexander – were intertwined at key moments with that of their uncle.

The public life of John of Austria, which unfolded in the midst of the confessionalisation efforts of a hegemonic Spain within a divided Europe, is marked by the Mediterranean conflict between the Catholic nations and the Ottoman Empire. Although he never left Europe, his mentality, like that of his contemporaries, was also imbued with the awareness that the Spanish Monarchy had carried out a victorious overseas expansion in America. In fact, the conflict between Spain and Elizabethan England, partly due to the contention for the Atlantic, was one of the realities that framed both John's public activities and his aspirations during the final years of his life. Regarding his public activities, his political-military undertakings in the Netherlands stand out, whose northern provinces, in revolt against Philip II since 1566, were supported by England. In terms of aspirations, I refer to his rather fanciful project to become king-consort of Mary Stuart of Scotland, displacing Elizabeth from the throne of England.

John's love of arms and his desire for glory were manifested in 1565, when he decided, without previously consulting Philip II, to leave the cortege that was accompanying Queen Elisabeth of Valois (which was heading for Bayonne) in Segovia and to go to Barcelona.[9] From there, John wanted to take part in the defence of the island of Malta, which was besieged by the Ottoman fleet.[10] Although he had to stop in Zaragoza because of illness, John was determined to continue to the Catalan capital. In Barcelona,

---

9   On the policies of Philip II in relation to France cf. Vázquez de Prada (2004).

10 The siege and defence of Malta aroused passionate interest among contemporaries. One of the accounts of the siege, the one by Francesco Balbi de Corregio, published in Italian in 1565, appeared in Spanish in 1567 and 1568 with a dedication to John of Austria (cf. Baró i Queralt 2009: 55-66).

where he was feted by the Viceroy, he received (and obeyed) a formal order from Philip II to return to Madrid. This adventure, even if truncated, gave John great popularity at court (especially among young nobles) and beyond.

On 18 January 1568, a dark episode took place in the Alcázar (citadel) of Madrid that has helped to fuel a negative image of Philip II and with which John was not totally unconnected. That day, the king, convinced that his heir Carlos was conspiring against him, arrested and imprisoned the Prince, who had repeatedly exhibited symptoms of mental instability. John, because of his frequent dealings with Carlos, was involved in a confrontation between father and son which had been growing *in crescendo* and had personal and political connotations. Although he had sought to ease the situation, there came a point at which he considered it his duty to warn the king of his son's plans.[11]

After John's flight to Barcelona in 1565, Philip II found a way to channel the former's fervour for war by appointing him supreme commander of the armies that were fighting in eastern Andalusia to quell the uprising of the Moriscos (descendants of Muslims) of Granada. These Moriscos had taken up arms against the Christians when an attempt was made to implement a decree which abolished freedom of expression of identity that had been promised before the conquest of the kingdom of Granada by the Catholic monarchs. In this (second) war of the Alpujarras, John had his baptism of fire and lost his adoptive father, Luis de Quijada, who was mortally wounded in combat. The successes of the army commanded by John of Austria were celebrated by a Catholic monarchy that was imbued with a crusade mentality and which, moreover, feared that the Moriscos were the fifth column of Ottoman rule. From a present-day perspective, the intolerant behaviour and ›ethnic cleansing‹ interventions arranged by both lay and clerical leaders of the monarchy against the Moriscos are frequently highlighted.

In 1571, the year after the war of the Alpujarras ended (victoriously for John), Philip II decided to join the Holy League led by Pope Pius V, even though the Spanish monarchy had already been waging a war in the Netherlands since 1566. What was at stake in the Mediterranean was the defence of Christianity against the Ottoman offensive that had managed to invade

---

11 Parker (2010: 396-438) offers a balanced and very well-documented interpretation of this episode and »the enigma of Don Carlos«.

Cyprus, a Venetian possession. On the initiative of Pius V, John of Austria was named supreme commander of the large fleet (about 200 vessels), made up of Venetian, Spanish and Holy See galleys. The Battle of Lepanto (north of the Gulf of Corinth) took place on 7 October 1571, between the Christian and Ottoman fleets. The squadron commanded by the son of Charles V won a clear victory, more important in symbolic terms (as it showed that the Turks were not invincible) than for its material impact, as the great historian of the Mediterranean, Ferdinand Braudel, has pointed out (cf. Braudel 1966: 396-398).[12] Thanks to Lepanto, at the age of twenty-four, John entered not only the history of Spain and Europe, but also universal history.

After Mars, Venus. When he returned to Italy, John enjoyed huge popularity, to which his youthful good looks, his being single, and his courage displayed in spectacles of risk such as bullfighting also contributed. In Naples he had one lover, Diana Falangola, by whom a daughter would be born. A few years earlier, Maria de Mendoza, a young lady from an Andalusian noble family, had been his lover. Maria even followed John to the Alpujarras. As a result of this co-habitation, there came into the world a girl whose existence had an unexpected consequence which will be dealt with below.

In 1571, when John of Austria was cheered and celebrated loudly, all his dreams seemed possible. *Etiam major* (Even greater) was his motto. To what larger enterprise could he aspire? To restore Morea to Christianity? To be crowned King of England and Ireland by means of an armed intervention and marriage to Mary Queen of Scots? These are some of the projects that John and his entourage entertained in the years after Lepanto, with some support from the papacy. But the prudence of Philip II towards his half-brother, as well as stubborn realities, constricted his activity.[13] The Holy League was soon dissolved. The last major seaborne victory achieved by the fleet commanded by John was the ephemeral conquest of Tunis in

---

12 Cervantes wrote in his *Novelas ejemplares* that Lepanto was »La más memorable y alta ocasión que vieron los pasados siglos, ni esperan ver los venideros« (»the grandest occasion the past or present has seen, or the future can hope to see«) (cf. Cervantes 1613: »Prologue to the Reader«).

13 On »Le problème des relations personelles entre Philippe II et Don Juan d'Autriche« cf. Bennassar (2000).

1573. It was soon recovered by the Muslims, but John's stay there has bequeathed to us a lasting artistic image: the portrait in which he appears with a lion at his feet; a lion he had adopted as a pet when it was a cub.[14]

»España, mi natura; Italia, mi ventura; Flandes, mi sepultura« (»Spain, my nature; Italy, my happiness, and Flanders, my grave«). This aphorism, celebrated in the Spain of the Golden Age, was also fulfilled in John of Austria's life. In 1576, Philip II named him, with flattering words, Governor General of the Spanish Netherlands, to succeed the deceased Luis de Requesens y Zúñiga. John, who was then in Italy, accepted the position reluctantly, and only went to Flanders after many detours and false promises from the court in Madrid that his aspirations to the throne of England would be supported. In the Netherlands, after the sack of Antwerp by some rebellious *tercios* (Spanish infantry units) just after his arrival, and without resources to continue an exhausting, bogged-down war, John initially adopted a peacemaking line. He accepted the withdrawal of the *tercios* by the so-called ›Perpetual Edict‹ (2 February 1577) and was able to enter Brussels. Afterwards, disappointed and feeling that he had made a mistake, he changed his attitude. He took the fortress of Namur and planned to resume the war, but despite the victory of Gembloux in January 1578, fortune eluded him.[15]

One of John's last sorrows was the news that the secretary he had sent to Madrid to seek support for his projects, Juan de Escobedo, had been killed near the royal Alcázar, on 31 March 1578. That assassination had been plotted by Antonio Pérez, then secretary to Philip II and later his staunch enemy. Pérez had managed to exacerbate Philip II's distrust of his brother and the king's acquiescence towards the conspiracy. This sinister plot, in which the attractive and intelligent princess of Eboli also took part,

---

14 Alonso Sánchez Coello: Don Juan d'Austria. Portrait (oil on canvas), Monasterio de El Escorial, Spain.

15 *La crónica sobre Don Juan de Austria y los Países Bajos* (1576-1578) is an important source on these years. It was written in 1601, by Martin Antonio Del Río, a scholar born in Antwerp, attached to John of Austria (cf. Del Rio 2003 [1601]).

is still the subject of debate and speculation.[16] It has also inspired many artistic productions, as will be demonstrated.

When he was campaigning, John of Austria died of dysentery in improvised accommodation (a pigeon loft) in Bouges, on 1 October 1578. After being honoured by his troops, his body was transferred to El Escorial. The epitaph on the sarcophagus containing his remains was composed by his nephew and friend Alexander Farnese, who was also his successor as Governor General of the Spanish Netherlands. This text summarises the historical impact made by John in the opinion of many of his contemporaries. It reads:

»To the Most Serene Prince John of Austria, | After having subjected the rebellious Moors in Andalusia; | and having put to flight and completely destroyed an | immense Turkish squadron before Patras; while | serving the King in the Netherlands, his life was taken | in the very prime of life by a continuous fever | in the castle of Bouges; to my beloved uncle, | I, Alexander Farnese, Duke of Parma and Piacenza | and successor to him in the governorship by | order of Our Highness Philip, | most powerful King | of Spain and the Indies, | dedicate this memorial on his funerary monument. | In the Year of Our Lord, 1578.«[17]

Leopold von Ranke ended his musings on John of Austria with this appropriate reflection:

»But so is this world. It stimulates man to develop all his abilities; it encourages all his hopes. Afterwards the individual does not moderate himself: feeling powerful, the man pursues the most glorious prizes of honour or possessions. The world does

---

16 Gregorio Marañón, Henry Kamen and Geoffrey Parker are some relevant names in relation to these debates.

17 »D.O.M.S. | Serenissimo Principi Joanni Austriaco | D. CAROL. V. IMPER. FILIO | Post Mauros in Bethica rebellantes subiugatos: | Turcorumque maximam classem apud Patras eo | duce fundltus fugalam deletamque; cum in | Belgio Proregem ageret, in castris Bou-granis continua febre in ipso juventutis | flore sublato: auunculo amantissimo | Alexander Farnesius Parma Pla- | centiaque princeps in imperio suc- | cessor ex mandato D. Philippi | Hispaniarum ac Indiarum | Regis pontentissimi hanc | altaris tabulam cenota- | phii loco. P. C. | MDLXXVIII.«

not award them to him: it enchains [man] to his limitations and allows him to disappear.« (von Ranke 1930 [1827]: 133)[18]

But after his death in 1578, did Don John of Austria really disappear? Does he not in some way survive in academic history and perhaps even more in the popular historical culture of the twentieth century? It is precisely this survival that will concern me from this point onwards.

THE SHAPING AND RE-SHAPING OF POPULAR HISTORICAL CULTURE

The case of John of Austria permits us to examine the usefulness of some concepts, sources and methods of studying popular historical culture. In the following I will diachronically analyse the continuity and changes in the public image of this many-sided and high-profile character of European history.

To advance a fundamental concept, there is a significant transition in European historical culture between the early twentieth century, when John of Austria was known and exalted above all as the last Crusader or the defender of Christendom against the Muslim Ottoman Empire, and the last decades of the century, during which his heterodox condition was sometimes emphasised. We find examples of the first approach in the novel *Jeromín* by Father Coloma, or in the famous poem by G. K. Chesterton entitled »Lepanto« (1911),[19] in which the English writer praised Spain for its championing of Christendom and called the son of Charles V »the last knight of Europe«. However, after the profound socio-cultural caesura of 1968 and the following years, interest in John is now due rather to another dimension of his personality, rarely highlighted in the past: his excluded or marginalised status as a bastard (as in the novel *Stèle pour un bâtard* (1956) by Goncourt winner Edmonde Charles-Roux), or for his many

---

18 »So aber ist diese Welt. Sie reizt den Menschen, alle seine Fähigkeiten zu entfalten: sie treibt in ihm alle Hoffnungen auf. Dann mässigt er sich nicht: seine Kräfte fühlend, jagt er den stolzensten Kampfpreisen der Ehre oder des Besitzes nach. Sie aber gewährt ihm nicht: sie schliesst ihm ihre Schranke zu und lässt ihn untergehen.«

19 This Chesterton poem was translated into Spanish by J.L. Borges in number 1 (1938) of the Argentinean literary magazine *Sol y Luna*.

amorous liaisons. But I can also verify that popular culture of the twentieth century continues to represent him as a heroic defender of Christianity and/or Western Civilisation.

As evidence of the contents of historical culture, my discussion places special importance on the historical novel as a popular narrative genre. But this contribution is also an attempt to capture and synchronously weigh the mediality of history.[20] Thus I also include remarks on the internet, TV and film, as well as newspapers.[21] The internet (with its conditions of linguistic communication and its new *ars scribendi*) exerts an enormous influence in shaping popular historical culture. One could point out, for instance, the creative way in which a large body of people outside the strictly academic area access and use the web. When accessing this information, these individuals act not only as consumers of established knowledge in a persistent and canonical form, but also shape or reshape constantly changing historical representations.[22] ›History in the media‹ and ›media history‹ are not interpretative approaches that can be clearly differentiated. In fact, this case study indicates that the internet phenomenon not only creates access to new content (which was not present in previous platforms for popular historical representation), but new media (or, at least, the new media applications) increase visibility and potential popularity, breathing new life into existing traditional representations that had almost fallen into disuse. I will illustrate this statement with the case of the digital edition of the fictionalised story of John of Austria: *Jeromín* (1903) by Luis Coloma, which was also turned into a popular film in 1953 (fig. 2).

---

20 The work by Crivellari et al. (2004) has been important for the diffusion of the expression ›mediality of history‹.

21 On the names of streets as another source for the study of historical culture cf. Sánchez-Marcos (2002). One possible approach to investigating the image of John of Austria in the historical culture of different countries would be to carry out a comparative study of the street directories of a few cities, well-chosen for their diversity (in terms of membership of different European cultures), and to analyse the presence or absence, and degree of importance, of two such emblematic and closely associated names as John of Austria and Lepanto. Today, both in Barcelona and Madrid, as in Messina, there are streets named after the son of Charles V.

22 This new interaction between ›producers‹ and ›consumers‹ of historical culture is one of the fundamental ideas developed in De Groot (2009).

Fig. 2: The poster for the film Jeromín (1953).

Image credits: Producciones Cinematográficas Ariel

The text of Coloma's novel has been digitised, and fig. 3 gives the numbers of visits until 4 July 2011.

Fig. 3: Information about the book's digital edition (1999).

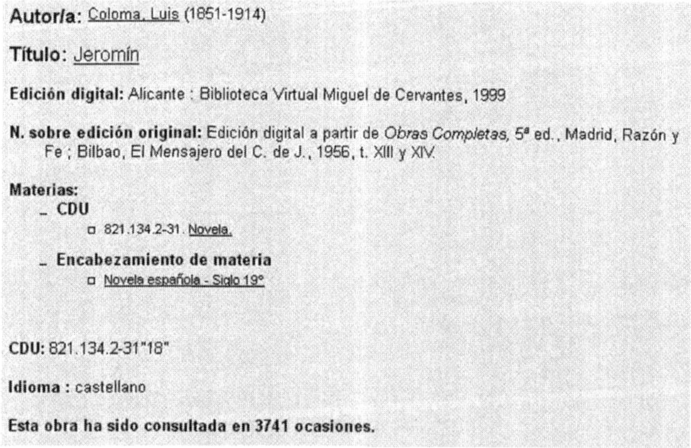

Autoría: Coloma, Luis (1851-1914)

Título: Jeromín

Edición digital: Alicante : Biblioteca Virtual Miguel de Cervantes, 1999

N. sobre edición original: Edición digital a partir de *Obras Completas,* 5ª ed., Madrid, Razón y Fe ; Bilbao, El Mensajero del C. de J., 1956, t. XIII y XIV.

Materias:
 _ CDU
  □ 821.134.2-31. Novela.

 _ Encabezamiento de materia
  □ Novela española - Siglo 19º

CDU: 821.134.2-31"18"

Idioma : castellano

Esta obra ha sido consultada en 3741 ocasiones.

Screenshot. Accessible at http://bib.cervantesvirtual.com/FichaObra.html?Ref=2438 &portal=0. Accessed 4 July 2011.

Jeromín was written in a journalistic style and with moralistic aims (cf. Hibbs-Lissorgues 2007: 147). Coloma emphasises the highlights of John of Austria's life much more than the shadows. Widely read and distributed in Spain, from its publication at the beginning of the century until the 1970s,[23] it had nearly fallen into oblivion in the late twentieth century. But after being digitised, it seems to have sparked renewed interest. This interest can also be explained by the proliferation of historical novels about John of Austria on the occasion of the Fourth Centenary of Philip II's death and the Fifth Centenary of Emperor Charles V's birth, with the whole series of activities promoted by the Government of Spain for their commemoration.[24]

Let us now turn to the articles on John of Austria in two widely circulated Spanish newspapers that were published throughout the twentieth century: *La Vanguardia* (Barcelona) and *ABC* (Madrid). Once again, the increase in accessibility that the digitalisation of content offers for research into historical culture can be observed. Regarding *La Vanguardia*, in order to narrow the search I have currently limited the analysis to the expression ›Juan de Austria‹ and the newspaper's front pages in the course of the twentieth century. The thirteen references that were found are temporally unevenly distributed. The most recent, on Sunday, 3 October 1971, is entitled »On the fourth centenary of Lepanto, Reconstruction of the ›Real‹, Galley of John of Austria« (cf. fig. 4).

There is only one other front page in the second half of the twentieth century, referring to the delivery of a third flag to the Legion in 1951. The other eleven front pages were published in the years 1901, 1902, 1940, 1943 (two), 1944 (two), 1946 and 1947 (three). Thus, out of a total of 13, 11 are concentrated in the time of the Franco regime, and 10 of these in its first decade, when the propaganda for radicalism and National Catholicism reached their greatest heights. As for the months in which such references

---

23 The exaltation of the imperial glories both of Spain and of Catholicism were defining features in the political culture of the early stages of the Franco regime. The life of John of Austria fits easily within that culture, and it is significant that the film adaption of *Jeromín* was also produced during the Franco regime.

24 On the 1998-2000 Memorial Cycle cf. the dossier in *Pedralbes: Revista d'Història Moderna* 2000, no. 20. On the images and commemorations in the remodelling and dissemination of historical culture cf. also Sánchez-Marcos (2000b: 169-175).

appeared, it is not surprising to find that almost half of them occur in October, the month when the Battle of Lepanto took place.[25]

Fig. 4: Front page of La Vanguardia, 3 October 1971, reporting the reconstruction of the Real.

Photograph taken by Alberto Viñals.
(Accessible at hemeroteca.lavanguardia.com/edition.html?bd=03&bm=10&by=1971 &x=58&y=33. Accessed 4 July 2011).

25 The same observation as regards the limited presence of John of Austria in Spanish newspapers in more recent times could be made on the basis of the digital newspaper archive of *ABC*.

Barcelona, the city from which the Real and the other Spanish galleys that fought alongside the Italians at Lepanto set sail, still has a special site of memory of John of Austria: In its Maritime Museum of the *Drassanes* (Shipyards) one can visit a replica of the Real (the flagship galley of the combined fleet of the Holy League) and ›relive‹, through a multimedia show, the roar of battle and the slaves' suffering.

Lepanto is also a prominent feature in the contemporary online presence of John of Austria. As for the specific content created online about John of Austria, I made a first foray into the number of occasions on which the articles offered by Wikipedia with the title »Lepanto« were consulted in a given month, namely May 2009.[26] I chose the term »Lepanto« because it is closely associated with John of Austria and commonly used in different European languages, so that it allows for a comparative analysis, while the name John of Austria experiences greater variations. According to the information obtained from the Wikipedia archive, we have the following number of consultations, in descending order, for the article »Lepanto« in May 2009: English edition: 1940, Italian: 1146, Spanish: 668, German: 610, Polish: 136, Portuguese: 94 (cf. fig. 5).

Fig. 5: Synchronic comparison of visits to »Lepanto« in different Wikipedia editions in May 2009.

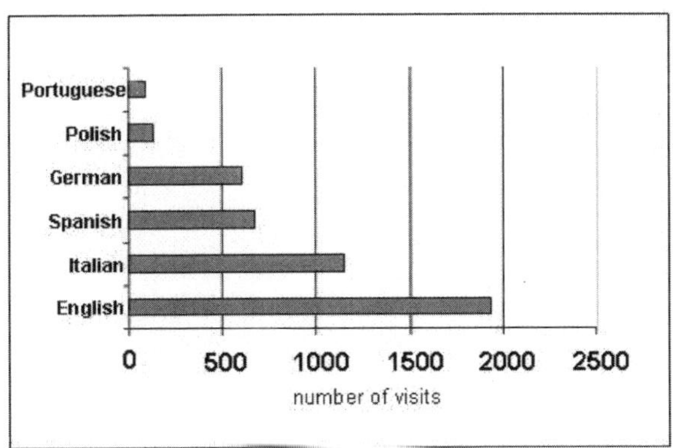

Graph created by the author.

---

26 On Wikipedia cf. Lorenz (2009).

Naturally, this search could be extended to include versions of the article in other languages. However, this limited sample is not random. The versions in Italian and Spanish cover the searches from the two countries most closely associated with the fleet that was victorious at the 1571 battle. I have chosen the German version in order to capture the interest arising from John of Austria's link with the Holy Roman Empire. I have added the English version not only because this language has been the *lingua franca* of the internet since its inception, but also because Lepanto affected all Western civilisation and thus also the kingdoms of the British Isles. The version in Polish has been included because I wanted to explore to what extent the article about John of Austria, the last crusader, continues to be of interest, comparatively speaking, in one of the countries that maintained the spirit of the Crusades for the longest period of time. As for the Portuguese version, I felt I ought to include it in the search as it is another country with a Catholic tradition whose history has been quite closely related to that of Spain.[27]

The comparative dimensions of the above figures can be explained by several factors. The predominance of Lepanto searches in English (1940 hits in May 2009) shows us that, in this case, the mediality of historical culture (the importance of the mediation of a universal communication platform that has been anglocentric since its inception) has been of much greater significance than the specific contents. Lepanto is more directly linked with the history of the Spanish monarchy and that of the Italian powers of the time (Venice and the Papacy) than the British monarchies. When, insofar as possible, the influence of this anglophone mediality is taken out of the equation, and the number of hits in the other European languages is compared, it seems that the weight of Lepanto in certain histories determines the ranking of the number of searches: The versions in Italian and Spanish (far more in the case of the former than the latter; 1146

---

27 Two potentially pertinent versions (the French and the Greek entries) have been left out of the comparative analysis for the moment. In the French entry, the explanation of the course and significance of this battle does not appear in the article under the heading »Lépante« but rather under the entry »Bataille de Lépante«. As regards the Greek version, because of the alphabet used, its analysis requires an additional effort that goes beyond the aims of this work in progress.

and 668) are clearly ahead of the German, Polish and Portuguese entries (610, 136 and 94 searches, respectively).

JOHN OF AUSTRIA: METAMORPHOSIS IN THE POPULAR BIOGRAPHY AND NOVEL

»John of Austria does not belong to history but to legend« (Gonzáles Cremona 1994: 9). With this statement begins the introduction to one of the many fictionalised biographies that have recently been dedicated to him. Although it could seem contradictory, it is a view that complements that made by Juan Rufo, a contemporary of Charles V's son, in his *Austríada* (1584): With a story like that of John of Austria, he wrote, »there is no need for other fictions«.[28] His handsomeness, an unfolding identity, his personal courage, royal blood, the defence of European Christendom in a critical military situation, the fickleness of fortune, his love of women, his frustrated aspirations to a throne, his jealousy of his brother, his courtly intrigues and his early death in a foreign country – the personal characteristics and life story of John of Austria bring together all the ingredients required to build a multiplicity of attractive textual accounts.[29] Here I refer especially to those that have taken the form of historical novels or fictionalised biographies; in particular those which have had a wider distribution. But first I will mention two theatrical works.

One of them, *Don Juan de Austria: Drama in cinco actos* (A Play in Five Acts), was written and performed in Catalonia in the years before World War I. It brought to the stage the intrigues in which our *dramatis persona* was involved, in relation to the murder of Escobedo, his secretary. It was written by an author from Lerida under the pseudonym Aracne. In this drama, the murder starts to take shape in the scene in which the Princess of Eboli, the minister, the secretary and the confident of Philip II Antonio Pérez, and the English ambassador at the Court of Madrid meet.

---

28 Rufo qtd. in Prieto Martín (1999: 725).

29 Merely pictorial representations are not the subject of this paper, but I should point out that John of Austria's handsomeness and his inclination for wearing brilliant costumes have contributed to his iconic status in the history of masculine fashion (cf. http://peter-hug.ch/lexikon/tracht. Accessed 12 July 2011).

Pérez says: »We can speak freely. The three of us hate Don Juan, and all three out of patriotism«.[30] The other play, *Le soulier de satin* (The Satin Slipper), Paul Claudel's masterpiece, appeared in 1929. It is his deepest survey of human and divine love, set in the Spanish empire of the sixteenth and seventeenth centuries. Although not one of the main characters, John of Austria plays a significant role in the fight against Islam and heresy, both assimilated by Claudel. Thus, our dramatist anachronistically places Lepanto (1571) at the same time as the Spanish Armada (1588) and after the Battle of White Mountain (1620), in a synchronic cosmic view, paving the way for Catholicism and its heroes to conquer the world. Applying the prophecy of the Gospel (»There was a man sent from God, whose name was John«, John 1:6) to John of Austria, even if he ambiguously omits the words »sent from God«, and by placing the prediction that »he will die before the age of thirty« on the lips of one of the characters, he makes a sort of a martyr of John, sacrificed for the glory of God.

Let us now review the range of literary historical representations featuring John of Austria, from *Jeromín* (1903) to a recent biography by the German author Marita A. Panzer. My selection is broad enough to analyse the continuities and discontinuities in the literary image of our character that has been projected in Europe and especially in Spain. When Coloma published *Jeromín*, he was already a famous writer, author of such other historical portraits as *The Martyr Queen* (about Mary Queen of Scots). In his note to the reader in *Jeromín*, Coloma indicated that he did not intend to offer a research paper or »unravel deep historical problems« but, more modestly, »only popularise, as it were, among a certain kind of audience, some figures linked to great and momentous events in history, and present them in the light of reason and of the Catholic approach« (Coloma 1903: »Al lector«). According to Rodriguez Villa, an academic historian and

---

30 In the digitised library of the *La Vanguardia* newpaper, I was able to establish that Aracne's work was performed at Barcelona's Apolo Theatre for a number of days. The premiere took place on 22 April 1916 (Easter Saturday) and it was also performed on 4 December 1917. Aracne is today an almost unknown playwright, but he enjoyed some popularity in his time. Escobedo's murder is also the plot in *La conjura de El Escorial*, a Spanish film (2008) by Antonio del Real, and it will surely be a key subject in a recently-filmed series for the Spanish TV channel Antena 3 entitled *La princesa de Eboli*.

contemporary of the author of *Jeromín*, Coloma succeeded, by means of an attractive journalistic style and the use of appropriate sources, in »describing in vivid colours« all kinds of events (Rodriguez Villa 1908: 110). Overall, Coloma gives us a work close to a biography, which constitutes a lively and moralising biographical fresco. This highlights the positive aspects, the virtues, of John of Austria as a Catholic prince and deals with the causes of »his not minor defects« more superficially, both sides serving as a warning for the reader (Coloma 1903: »Al lector«).

A few decades later, in 1934, the short life of the victor of Lepanto interested the American writer Margaret Yeo, who published her fictionalised biography *Don John of Austria* in New York in 1934. She also approaches John of Austria from a viewpoint sympathetic towards the Catholic world at the time of the (Counter) Reformation. In fact, Yeo also wrote biographies of some Jesuits and saints. *Don John of Austria* was promptly translated into French and in 1962 into Spanish.

Even more widely disseminated than Yeo's biography was the one written by a German writer, also a Catholic, who was exiled from the Third Reich in 1935 and fought it from England. This author, best known as Louis de Wohl, published numerous successful historical novels and biographies. The one devoted to John of Austria has received different names in the languages into which it has been translated. In its German original, published in Freiburg im Breisgau, it was entitled *Der Sieger von Lepanto: Roman* (The Victor of Lepanto: A Novel). In other languages, the concept of the title is different, as in the case of *The Last Crusader* (English 1956) or *O último cruzado* (Portuguese 1962). This fictionalised biography has been one of the biggest bestsellers of the Madrid-based Spanish publishing house Palabra. In 2009 it published the ninth edition of *El último cruzado*.

In 1958, László Passuth (1900-1979), the great Hungarian author of historical novels, published his work *Fekete bársonyban* (Black Velvet) in which John of Austria was one of the main characters. In his vivid, precise recreation of John of Austria's life, Passuth, who was very interested in Spanish culture, distanced himself from the policy of world domination and religious coercion carried out by Philip II.[31]

---

31 *Fekete bársonyban* was soon translated into Spanish under the title *El Señor Natural* (1962) and reprinted several times.

After the cultural upheaval of the 1960s, with its connotations of pacifism, anti-authoritarianism, moral relativism and assertion of women's emancipation that culminated in the West in 1968, the literary handling of John and his environment enters a different stage. We observe the tendency to adopt approaches that question the paradigm of the champion of Catholicism as the principal interpretation of the life of John of Austria. This trend also appears in Spain. In this respect, the 1973 publication of the book *La hija de Don Juan de Austria: Ana de Jesús en el proceso al pastelero de Madrigal* (John of Austria's Daughter: Anne of Jesus in the Trial of the Pastry Cook of Madrigal) by Mercedes Fórmica seems to be significant. Anne of Jesus was the daughter of John of Austria (who never married) and his first liaison, Mary of Mendoza, who was the great love of his life. Anne, who had been kept secret as a teenager and entered a convent in Madrigal (Avila), fell in love with the young man known today as ›the pastry cook of Madrigal‹, Gabriel Espinosa. The latter claimed to be the young Portuguese King Sebastian, who had disappeared at the battle of Alcazarquivir. Since the claim of Anne's lover challenged the legitimacy of Philip II as successor to King Sebastian, the ›pastry cook‹ was tried and executed, and Anne of Jesus was closely surveilled. This plot with its novelistic tones is a subplot in the larger pattern of the life of John of Austria, and is treated as such in the vast majority of previous historical novels dedicated to him. But Fórmica makes this subplot the centre of her narrative. The author, a lawyer who had played important roles in the Women's Section of the *Falange,* here shows herself to have been attuned to the emerging demands for women's freedom in Spain. Her research interest focuses not on male heroes like John of Austria, but on the women whose lives were bound and subordinated to them. From a Catholic perspective, Fórmica reports on the subordination of women that took place in the past, in order to overcome it in the future.[32]

---

32 This demand for the freedom of women that Fórmica makes is manifested, for example, in the title of one of the epigraphs: »Female customs in the 16th century. To give birth or to pray. The situation of a young widow« (76-86). Fórmica also writes of Cardinal Borromeo, a well-known reformer of the Catholic Church from John of Austria's time, who also found fault with the expectations of women at the time: He [Borromeo] »preache[d] in Milan harsh sermons

It would be interesting to compare the various editions of the fictional-ised biography of John of Austria, *Stèle pour un bâtard*, written by Edmonde Charles-Roux (1956, 1980, 1990), a prolific, successful French author. However I will focus my attention on the 1980 edition, for which there exists an interview with the author on her interest in John of Austria. What attracted the attention of Charles-Roux was the »marginalité« of John and his mother.[33] Thus, John's being a bastard, excluded and hidden, now became the centre of interpretation. What had been, in previous works, a dark dimension of his character, now became a source of empathy in an effort to overcome unjust social discrimination. From being a champion of Christianity, John of Austria is metamorphosed into a precursor of the fight against morally-motivated social exclusion.

Although this paper is dedicated to European culture, I include a literary recreation of John of Austria written by a Venezuelan author, Arturo Uslar Pietri (1906-2001), because the specific culture of Spain, as a variant of European culture, cannot be understood without its Latin American dimension, and because Uslar Pietri is one of the Venezuelan writers most imbued by French culture. Published in Bogotá in 1990, Uslar Pietri's novel has an enigmatic title: *La visita en el tiempo* (The Visit in Time). It reflects more his literary interests and less a concern for the strict chronological path that other fictionalised biographies of John follow. Its title is in line with the distinctive approach of this work: an exploration of how Jeromín/John of Austria tirelessly seeks his identity and the complex unveiling of the same to himself. One wonders if in this literary reconstruction Uslar Pietri projects back the uncertainty about identity that a culturally hybrid society like his own possesses. In any case, *La visita en el tiempo* proves that recreations of the life of Charles V's natural son have also been made available to the reading public in Latin America.

The introduction of democracy in Spain in 1978 did not interrupt the continuity of interest in the victor of Lepanto and the last crusader. The biography by Louis de Wohl continues to enjoy great success among read-

---

against the parents and guardians of children who lock[ed] the young in convents against their will« (112).

33 »Edmonde Charles Roux sur Don Juan d'Autriche« (Radio Interview). *Antenne 2*, 7 July 1980. Accessible online at www.ina.fr/art-et-culture/literature/video/I000065 48/edmonde-charles-roux-sur-don-juan-d-autriche.fr.html. Accessed 12 July 2010.

ers. A fictionalised biography published in one of the most commercial collections on historical issues, *Memoria de la Historia* by Editorial Planeta, may be classified within this line of continuity: González Cremona's *Don Juan de Austria, héroe de leyenda* (John of Austria, Hero and Legend) (1994). As mentioned before, the holding of several events commemorating Charles V and Philip II in Spain, a Kingdom already integrated into the European Union at the end of twentieth century, undoubtedly favoured the emergence of new books about John. One is Bartolomé Bennassar's *Don Juan de Austria: Un héroe para un imperio* (John of Austria: A Hero for an Empire), a biographical history written for the general public, which offers a balanced and open interpretation of Charles V's son.[34] Moreover, Bennassar also addresses the important issue of the early mystification of the character.

I bring this panorama to a close by discussing a historical novel that is very revealing of the cultural climate in Spain in recent years: the phenomenon of the aestheticisation of culture and the growing role of women as active agents in shaping it. This book is *El Retrato de Don Juan de Austria* (The Portrait of John of Austria) by Lucila Rodríguez de Austria y Giménez de Aragón. The author is an expert on heritage conservation. This background, coupled with her own Austrian heritage, is reflected in her compelling novel with two interwoven plots. One plot involves a professional restorer experiencing the fascinating discovery and restoration of a very special portrait. The other story is of John of Austria's own supposed life, which is narrated ›autobiographically‹ and in a flashback by the character portrayed. One of the first chapters reflects on the perspective with which the life of John is ›restored‹, alluding, as I have attempted to do in this contribution, to the metamorphosis of a popular hero:

»Leader of Lepanto, champion of Christendom, prototype of a Christian man from sixteenth-century knightly Spain. Did you find out something about my fears, my loneliness, my disappointments, my doubts? It is curious how the stigma of being a bastard at the time that I lived has been transformed into sympathy over the centuries. Neither of the two positions, as they are both extreme, have an objective basis for judging people as their starting point.« (Rodríguez de Austria 2000: 16-17)

---

34 On Bennassar's contribution to Spanish history cf. Ribot (2009).

I will end this overview with comments on a (lightly fictionalised) biography of John of Austria published in Regensburg, the city where Charles V lived with Barbara Blomberg: Marita Panzer's *Don Juan de Austria (1547-1578): Karriere eines Bastards* (Career of a Bastard), published in 2004.[35] Panzer dedicates her work to her father: It was he who first spoke to her of John of Austria as the »Sieger von Lepanto« (victor of Lepanto) and »Retter des Abendlandes« (saviour of the West). The author now sees this West (the former Christendom) as a way of life and a geopolitical sphere in confrontation with some Islamic countries. The dedication gives us an indication as to one of Panzer's interpretative angles, but there are others. As suggested in the title, the book also pays detailed attention to John of Austria's status as an illegitimate son. Panzer considers this status to be both an incentive for action and, at the same time, a limit to this incentive as well as to John's dream of achieving a crown.[36] Thus this second interpretative angle is linked to the approach used in Charles-Roux's *Stèle pour un bâtard*. To a certain extent, Panzer's biography, the last to date that is written for a general public, takes up two elements that have marked the twentieth century's take on John of Austria. One is the permanence or continuity (we know that the history of mentalities is a history in the *longue dureé)* of his emblematic figure as a defender of a Christian Europe; the other is the reconfiguration and change which his popular image has undergone in response to new cultural contexts. But it is not only the continued presence of our figure which matters; the increasing absence (or at least the reduced presence) of the same character tells us much about the changing European cultural milieu.[37]

---

35 This author had previously published a similar biography on the mother of John of Austria: *Barbara Blomberg: Bürgerstochter und Kaisergeliebte*, Regensburg: Pustet, 1995.

36 Panzer entitles the penultimate of her eight chapters »In Erwartung einer Krone« (»In anticipation of a crown«).

37 Despite certain variations, the long-term decreasing presence of John of Austria in printed European culture between 1900 and 2000 can be confirmed as a result of a search I carried out, with the help of a new tool supplied by Google labs, Books Ngram Viewer, of the corpuses of digitised books in Spanish and other languages published during the twentieth century.

CONCLUSIONS

The first point that stands out in this diachronic study of the popular image of John of Austria is that our central character has continued to fascinate authors from many European countries throughout the twentieth and the first years of the twenty-first centuries, especially among writers with a Catholic background and/or from the Mediterranean world. Secondly, among those that have made John of Austria the subject of their literary re-creations, there have been a considerable number of women, especially since the 1970s. Thirdly, this study reveals the influence of the different European socio-cultural situations, which can be simplified as those to be found pre- and post-1968, on the viewpoint and axiology with which John of Austria has been represented. Fourthly, this research, while in a limited field, has reinforced my conviction that mediality is acquiring great importance in the creation of and research into historical culture.[38] The fifth and final conclusion is the confirmation of the important role that public undertakings for historical culture have played in the creation and diffusion of textual contents (and also depictions) of John of Austria. More precisely, I here refer to the state-led events that took place in 1971 and 1998-2000 (commemorating the Battle of Lepanto, Philip II's death and Charles V's birth). Derived from a work in progress, this case study thus offers approaches and sources for future research into popular twentieth-century European historical culture.[39]

---

38 This mediality has made it possible for such forgotten works as *Don Juan de Austria: Drama en cinco actos* by Aracne, which premiered in 1916, to be recovered, and has made possible a comparison of internet articles entitled »Lepanto« in different European languages during the same month.

39 Translated from the Spanish by Philip Banks and Enrique Sánchez-Costa. Quotes taken from texts in other languages have been translated by the author and by P. Banks. I wish to express my gratitude to Flavia F. Ramos, Jinhwa Choi, Iva Boitcheva and Gisele Bento for their collaboration. I am also very grateful for the comments on the draft paper offered at the Conference on Popular History (Freiburg im Br., 2010). This work has been financed by means of support for the Research Group HAR2009-08019 from the Spanish Ministerio de Ciencia e Innovación and ENBACH (Ref. 148836) through the Culture Programme of the European Commission.

Works Cited

Aracne [Ramón Ranyer López] (1917): *Don Juan de Austria: Drama en cinco actos,* Bellpuig: Ramón Saladriguero.

Baró i Queralt, Xavier (2009): *La historiografía catalana en el segle del Barroc, 1585-1709,* Barcelona: L'Abadia de Montserrat.

Bennassar, Bartolomé (2000): »Le problème des relations personnelles entre Philippe II et Don Juan d'Autriche«. In: Jesús M. Usunáriz Garayoa (ed.), *Historia y humanismo: Estudios en honor del profesor Dr. D. Valentín Vázquez de Prada,* Pamplona: Universidad de Navarra, 63-71.

Bennassar, Bartolomé (2001): *Don Juan de Austria: Un héroe para un imperio,* 4th ed., Madrid: Temas de Hoy.

Blanco Fernández, Carlos (2001): »Aproximación a la historiografía sobre Don Juan de Austria«. In: Bruno Anatra et al. (eds.), *Sardegna, Spagna e Stati Italiani nell'età di Carlo V* (Studi Storicci Carocci 17), Roma: Carocci, 165-182. (http://www.tiemposmodernos.org/tm3/index.php/tm/article/viewFile/ 18/35). Accessed 4 July 2011.

Braudel, Fernand (1966): *La Méditerranée et le monde méditerranéen à l'époque de Philipe II,* 2nd rev. ed., Paris: Armand Colin.

Cervantes Saavedra, Miguel de (1982 [1613]): *Novelas ejemplares,* ed. and introd. by Juan Bautista Avalle-Arce, Madrid: Castalia.

Charles-Roux, Edmonde (1956): *Stèle pour un bâtard,* Paris: Éd. Mondiales ([1980] Paris: Bernard Grasset; [1990] Paris: Duculot).

Chesterton, Gilbert K. (1911): »Lepanto«. *The Eye-Witness* 12 October 1911, 520-521 [Spanish transl. by J.L. Borges (1938): »Lepanto«. *Sol y Luna* 1, 135-47].

Claudel, Paul (1929): *Le soulier de satin,* Paris: Gallimard.

Coloma, Luis (1903): *Jeromín: Estudios históricos sobre el siglo XVI,* Madrid: Ed. National. Accessible at Biblioteca Virtual Miguel de Cervantes (http:// bib.cervantesvirtual.com/FichaObra.html?Ref=2438&portal=0). Accessed 4 July 2011.

Crivellari, Fabio et al. (eds.) (2004): *Die Medien der Geschichte: Historizität und Medialität in interdisziplinärer Perspektive,* Konstanz: UVK.

De Groot, Jerome (2009): *Consuming History: Historians and Heritage in Contemporary Popular Culture,* London: Routledge.

Del Río, Martin Antonio (2003 [1601]): *Die Chronik über Don Juan de Austria und den Krieg in den Niederlanden (1576-1578)* [*La crónica sobre Don Juan de Austria y los Países Bajos (1576-1578)*], ed. and introd. by Miguel Ángel Echevarría, München: Oldenbourg.

Diputación Provincial de Valladolid (1998): *Dª Magdalena de Ulloa, 1598-1998: Una mujer de Villagarcía de Campos (Valladolid). Su profundo influjo social*, Valladolid: Diputación Provincial de Valladolid.

Fórmica, Mercedes (1973): *La hija de Don Juan de Austria: Ana de Jesús en el proceso al pastelero de Madrigal*, Madrid: Revista de Occidente.

Gachard, Louis P. (1868-1869): »Don Juan d'Autriche: Études historiques«. *Bulletins de l'Académie Royale des Sciences, des Lettres et des Beaux-Arts de Belgique* 26/27.

González Cremona, Juan Manuel (1994): *Don Juan de Austria, héroe de leyenda* (Col. Memoria de la historia 95), Barcelona: Planeta.

Havemann, Wilhelm (1865): *Das Leben des Don Juan d'Austria: Eine geschichtliche Monographie*, Gotha: Perthes.

Hibbs-Lissorgues, Solange (2007): »Jeromín de Luis Coloma: Un sutil equilibrio entre novela histórica y novela de costumbres«. In: Christopher Maurer et al. (eds.), *Prosa y poesía: Homenaje a Gonzalo Sobejano*, Madrid: Gredos, 147-160.

Kahl, Christian (2005): »Juan d'Austria«. In: Traugott Bautz (ed.), *Biographisch-Bibliographisches Kirchenlexikon*, vol. XXIV, Nordhausen: Traugott Bautz, 918-925.

Korte, Barbara/Sylvia Paletschek (eds.) (2009): *History goes Pop: Zur Repräsentation von Geschichte in populären Medien und Genres*, Bielefeld: transcript.

Lorenz, Maren (2009): »Repräsentation von Geschichte in Wikipedia oder: Die Sehnsucht nach Beständigkeit im Unbeständigen«. In: Korte/Paletschek (eds.), *History goes Pop*, 289-312.

Molinié-Bertrand, Anne (2001): »Don Juan d'Autriche, héros de roman«. In: Anne Molinié-Bertrand/Jean-Paul Duviols (eds.), *Charles V et la Monarchie universelle* (Iberica 8.13), Paris: Presses Universitaires de France, 193-203.

Panzer, Marita A. (2004): *Don Juan de Austria: Karriere eines Bastards*, Regensburg: Friedrich Pustet.

Parker, Geoffrey (2010): *Felipe II*, Barcelona: Planeta.

Passuth, László (2000): *Don Juan de Austria, Señor natural*, Barcelona: Noguer y Caralt [Hungarian original (1958): *Fekete bársonyban*, Budapest: Szépirodalmi Könyvkiadó].

Pedralbes: Revista d'Història Moderna 20 (2000). (www.raco.cat/index. php/Pedralbes/issue/view/8336/showToc). Accessed 30 June 2011.

Prieto Martín, Antonio (1999): »La Poesía«. In: *Historia de España Menéndez Pidal*, vol. XXI: *La cultura de renacimiento (1480-1580)*, Madrid: Espasa Calpe, 631-729.

Ranke, Leopold von (1930 [1827]): *Die Osmanen und die spanische Monarchie im 16. und 17. Jahrhundert = Fürsten und Völker von Südeuropa 1,2* (Leopold von Rankes Historische Meisterwerke 25/26), ed. by Adolf Meyer/Horst Michael, Wien: Gutenberg.

Ribot García, Luis A. (2009): »Bartolomé Bennassar y la historia de España«. In: Ricardo García Cárcel/Eliseo Serrano Martín (eds.), *Exilio, memoria personal y memoria histórica: El hispanismo francés de raíz española en el siglo XX*, Zaragoza: Institución »Fernando El Católico«, 47-62.

Rodríguez de Austria y Giménez de Aragón, Lucila (2000): *El retrato de Don Juan de Austria*, Barcelona: Martínez Roca.

Rodríguez Villa, Antonio (1908): »Jeromín: Estudios históricos sobre el siglo XVI, por el P. Luis Coloma, de la Compañía de Jesús«. *Boletín de la Real Academia de la Historia* 52, 109-116. (www.cervantesvirtual. com/buscador/?q=coloma%20jeromin&tab=t%C3%ADtulo&f[cg]=1.) Accessed 4 July 2011.

Sánchez-Marcos, Fernando (1983): *Cataluña y el gobierno central tras la Guerra de los Segadores (1652-1679): El papel de don Juan de Austria en las relaciones entre Cataluña y el Gobierno central*, Barcelona: Universidad de Barcelona.

Sánchez-Marcos, Fernando (2000a): »¿Dos Juanes de Austria en nuestra cultura histórica?«. In: Jesús M. Usuñáriz Garayoa (ed.), *Historia y Humanismo: Estudios en honor del profesor Dr. D. Valentín Vázquez de Prada*, vol. I, Pamplona: Eunsa, 235-242.

Sánchez-Marcos, Fernando (2000b): »La historiografía sobre la edad moderna«. In: Andrés J. Gallego (ed.), *Historia de la historiografía española*, Madrid: Encuentro, 169-175.

Sánchez-Marcos, Fernando (2002): »En revenant sur les identités et les noms des rues en Espagne: Le cas de Barcelona«. In: Christian Amalvi (ed.), *Une passion d'Histoire: Histoire(s), Mémoire(s) et l'Europe*, Toulouse: Privat, 339-349.

Stirling-Maxwell, William (1883): *Don John of Austria: Or passages from the History of the Sixteenth Century, 1547-1578*, 2 vols., London: Longman & Green.

Uslar Pietri, Arturo (1990): *La visita en el tiempo*, Bogotá: Norma.

Van der Hammen y León, Lorenzo (1627): *Historia de Juan de Austria*, Madrid: Luis Sanchez. (http://reader.digitale-sammlungen.de/resolve/display/bsb10362977.html). Accessed 4 July 2011.

Vázquez de Prada, Valentín (2004): *Felipe II y Francia (1559-1598): Política, Religión y Razón de Estado*, Pamplona: Eunsa.

Wohl, Louis de (2000): *El último cruzado: La vida de Don Juan de Austria*, 7th ed., Madrid: Palabra [German original (1956): *Der Sieger von Lepanto*, Freiburg: Walter].

Yeo, Margaret (1934): *Don John of Austria*, New York/NY: Sheed & Ward.

Shifting Imageries

Memory, Projectivity and the Experience of Violence in Northern Côte d'Ivoire

Till Förster

INTRODUCTION

Rebel domination is often thought of as arbitrary and based on an excessive use of violence, not leaving much space for anything beyond the immediate necessities of survival. However, rebels almost always engage in some sort of governance. The provision of public goods grants them a legitimacy that may secure their domination without resorting to the expensive and often ineffective use of violence as their only basic legitimacy.[1] Besides such considerations of a better cost-benefit ratio, rebel governance may also try to establish some kind of cultural affiliation between rebels and civilians. At times, rebels implement cultural policies and fund cultural institutions – refuting common presumptions that military insurgents are not investing in anything except power. They also invest in culture, in particular when they can make use of historical memory to build a closer identification between them and the population under their domination.

---

1   The concept of basic legitimacy is adopted from von Trotha (1995, 2000), who builds on Popitz (1992).

The city of Korhogo in northern Côte d'Ivoire may serve as an example. Military insurgents captured it on 19 September 2002.[2] Since then, the city has been under their domination. In 2005, the newly appointed rebel commander of the city decided to (re-)build a cultural centre – to the surprise of many who had known him only as an arrogant, demanding, if not brutal man. The centre opened in February 2006 after the artists of the city had embellished it with murals that covered the inside as well as the outside walls. They were largely free to paint whatever they thought best. The outcome was a remarkable series of murals that, although painted by fifteen different artists, testified to how the urban population imagined the past, their present situation and a better world yet to come. They turned the popular imagination of the past and the future into a visible imagery that all urban dwellers could appreciate. Many of the murals were cast in conventional genres, but there were paintings that did not fit to any of the existing modes of representation. In 2009, the entire centre was re-painted. The artists gave up some of their old paintings and to some extent developed a new repertoire and a new genre that allowed them to engage in the political articulation of public interests towards both the rebel command and the residing president in the southern half of the country.

This article will explore how the tension between the experience of past violence and the imagination of a better future informed the formation of a new genre in painting and the image of the past. It asks how the iteration of existing genres and their creative transformation in the image programme of the cultural centre generated a cultural space that allowed the artists to address new social and political issues. It concludes with an analysis of the relationship between the visual imagery and the popular imagination, claiming that there is no memory of the past without the projective power of the imagination of a social and political alternative to the present social order.

---

2 On the Ivoirian crisis in general cf. Poamé (2007), who also provides a chronology of the major events.

KEY CONCEPTS: PICTURE, IMAGE, IMAGERY AND IMAGINATION

Before unfolding the history of the cultural centre in Korhogo, I need to clarify my understanding of the key concepts used in this contribution. My basic heuristic instrument is a distinction between material pictures and mental images, building on William Mitchell's ›picture theory‹ (Mitchell 1995). *Pictures*, however, are not merely the material side of mental images. There is a constant tension between the two. The materiality of pictures and their perceptual character endows them with a sort of inner logic that may become visible as ›style‹ and, with regard to content, as ›genre‹. Style and genre both address similarities between pictures. These similarities, however, may also shape the spectator's understanding of how a particular picture should look. As normative expectations, they become part of the image that the spectator has in mind when perceiving a picture.

Usually, *images* are not stable mental representations of something out there – although they are sometimes perceived as such. Images bring a possible future state of the lifeworld to mind.[3] They do not merely recall a sensory perception; images always have a projective element. However, images retain the form of sensory experience; they have a quasi-perceptual character. Because of this quality, images can be very persuasive, at times even seductive. Unsurprisingly, the power of images is a well-established trope in art history, though less so in the social sciences.[4] They may acquire a certain stability because human actors make use of them – implicitly or explicitly – in social life to communicate with others. A constant reversal of shared images would render regular communication almost impossible. As social beings, we rely on shared images of how the shared lifeworld appears to us as members of society. However, images are also subject to the mental activity of those who ›see‹ them. Because an image does not exist as

---

3   An appropriate phenomenological term for this capacity is *Appräsentation* in German, usually translated as ›appresentation‹ in English. The term was introduced by Edmund Husserl in his *Phänomenologie der Intersubjektivität* and later elaborated by Alfred Schütz (1966). From a sociological and anthropological perspective, cf. also Soeffner (2004).

4   An outstanding, seminal work was Freedberg (1989). A more recent influential publication is Mitchell (2005).

a material object, it can be modified and transformed at will. Images grow out of subjectivity and intersubjectivity. I will call this continual process *imagination*. This process has two aspects, one individual, the other thoroughly social. Artists, for instance, may focus on their individual subjectivity to generate images and pictures that mirror their own projectivity, their ›visions‹ which then turn into pictures and artworks. Imagination, however, also emerges from intersubjectivity, the encounters with others. It often embraces large parts of a society – and it can move entire societies. A utopia, for example, is perhaps best understood as a persuasive alternative image to an unsatisfying social order.

In general, an image does not exist in isolation. It competes with other images, or more precisely, the process of imagination breeds more than one image. Due to the power of images, the process of imagination has a political dimension. It is not separated from other political processes, though its precise relationship to other discursive formations requires further theoretical clarification. To address the multifaceted societal formation of images, I will use the term *imagery*. Imageries consist of images that occupy a particular place in the social world. Imageries are not closed systems; they are embedded in ongoing processes of social, political and cultural articulation. It does not come as a surprise that a cultural centre, and in particular one that was founded by a rebel movement, engages in the formation of an imagery that addresses the past, the present and the future.

KORHOGO AS THE HEART OF SENUFOLAND

Korhogo was a fast-growing city until the military insurgency of 2002. Because of the division of the country, it was cut off from the southern parts of Côte d'Ivoire and from Abidjan with its harbour. Though the rural hinterland still viewed Korhogo as the dominant market place in the region, attracting traders from all over West Africa, the city's population actually stagnated since the outbreak of the violence.[5] This was less due to the fact of the local population fleeing than it was to the city's loss of significance

---

5   There are no reliable figures. The present population is estimated at 170,000 to 212,000 inhabitants (cf. http://www.populationdata.net/index2.php?option=pays &pid=51&nom=cote_d_ivoire. Accessed 26 May 2011).

as a hub for the national government of Côte d'Ivoire. Too many well-paid civil servants and their families left Korhogo when the state administration ceased to function. The loss of their buying power was a severe blow to the city's economy until it was replaced by other businesses, for instance the trade in inexpensive motorcycles from China.[6]

Until the turn of the century, however, Korhogo was much more than a provincial town with a few offices and a market. It was perceived as the cultural stronghold of the Senufo, by far the biggest ethnic group in northern Côte d'Ivoire. The mayor of the city was always a direct descendant of Péléforo Gbon Coulibaly, one of the most powerful intermediary rulers of the French colonial empire and himself a Senufo. The French made him the *chef suprême Sénoufo*, a position that did not exist in pre-colonial times. It was intended to provide some cultural legitimacy to the intermediary of the white colonial administration. *Le vieux Gbon* (Gbon the Old), as he was called locally, dominated urban and regional politics to a degree that left little space for the ambitions of others. Cooperating closely with the French administration, his entire family became very wealthy and many Coulibalys held influential positions in various parts of the administration. When it became apparent that the French would give up their colony, Gbon forged an alliance with the coming strong man of Côte d'Ivoire, Félix Houphouët-Boigny. He became a member of the Parti Démocratique de Côte d'Ivoire – Rassemblement Démocratique Africain (PDCI-RDA), which later became the single party of post-colonial Côte d'Ivoire until 1990. His successors engaged in political careers on that ticket and were repeatedly elected as members of parliament or ministers in PDCI governments.

The Coulibalys claimed that they represented the entire North with the Senufo as the rightful first settlers of the area. Though Gbon the Old had converted to Islam as a child when he was brought up at the Muslim court of Kénédougou in Sikasso, today a provincial town in Mali, he was always tolerant toward local religious beliefs – like the majority of the Muslim

---

6   The trade in motorcycles was perhaps the most visible aspect of the economic transformation. Many other commodities were imported from China, India and other Asian countries through the ports of Guinea, Ghana and Togo and sold to residents of other neighbouring countries. As there were no customs fees, the North attracted many traders who profited from the low prices in that stateless area.

traders who, for centuries, had respected the rites and ceremonies of the peasant Senufo. Indeed, many Muslims were initiated into the local secret society, although they did not accept the same duties as the Senufo. The Coulibalys were able to sustain an image of their family as the chief, even ›royal‹ dynasty representing the entire North, deeply enrooted in local Senufo culture as well as in Islam as the genuine religion of the North. There was no contradiction between the two. The many Muslims of foreign origin, living as traders, carriers or for some other business in Korhogo, also accepted both claims (Launay 1992). They confirmed the Coulibalys' status as Muslims and integrated them in their communities while they in turn were integrated into the far-flung patrimonial network that the Coulibalys maintained with the various groups living in the city and in the wider area.[7]

This cultural unity was, however, largely a construction. It was staged at ritual and ceremonial events, for instance at funerals in the area that once had belonged to the dominion of the colonial ›supreme chief‹, i.e. where he was authorised to act on behalf of the French administration. If an elder died in a village, the Coulibalys sent delegates to participate in the mourning rites and to distribute small amounts of money and a few condolence gifts among the family of the deceased (Förster 1995). Such acts renewed the patrimonial ties that were threatened by the death of the elder. But they also re-produced the image of the Coulibalys as both conscious of what was cast in French terms as ›tradition‹, and as pious believers of the one true religion.

KATANA – THE OLD FESTIVALS

In 1983 and again in 1992, the mayors and dignitaries of the family decided to organise a festival that would bring the entire population of the region together in Korhogo as the capital of the Senufo. The mayor Lanciné Gon Coulibaly, who was later dismissed for tax fraud, held the first festival

---

7   While the local religious scholarly families, the *mory*, had to observe all of the rules and regulations of Islam, the other groups were not expected to do the same. The only group that questioned the ›good faith‹ of the local political elite were the few reformists such as the Wahhabis (Launay 1992: 121-125).

(Coulibaly 2004: 330-332), introducing the name Katana, which means ›good thing‹ in the language of the Senufo.[8] It had many faces, being a feast for the urban population of Korhogo and at the same time a highly political event that aimed at making claims at the national and even at the international level.

For the ordinary population, it was a kind of trade fair accompanied by a lot of entertainment. There were stalls of companies presenting their products such as agricultural engines, TV and stereo equipment, and household appliances. Besides the officially invited companies, there were countless stalls held by small business people, trying to sell bits and pieces of whatever they had to offer. Musicians from the region performed more or less spontaneously wherever they could find an audience. The mayor himself addressed the national and international levels. He had invited foreign embassies and ambassadors to attend the festival, which took place at the end of January when the Harmattan, a seasonal dry and dusty trade wind, was slowly coming to an end. Each nation was offered a special day and invited to celebrate the festival with contributions from their own country. Besides France as the former colonial master still keeping a close watch over his former child, the mayor asked Canada, Belgium, Japan and neighbouring Guinea to send delegations and to participate in the performances of the day. The choice was built at least partially on his existing social networks.

This first festival served as model for the second in 1992. Again, it was scheduled for the end of the Harmattan season, now in mid-February, and again it had a commercial side. This time, however, the cultural aims were much more prominent. The former two-storeyed house of Péléforo Gbon Coulibaly – his ›palace‹ in popular opinion – was refurbished and transformed into a museum. It was integrated into a programme that aimed at endowing the major provincial cities of Côte d'Ivoire with museums where the cultural heritage of the region would be preserved and displayed to tourists and the local audience. In addition, the museum was included in the West African Museums Programme funded by the International African Institute (Savané 1994). The building in Korhogo was no longer inhabited since the death of the patriarch in 1962 – or more precisely, it was occupied by homeless people and lunatics. The choice of Coulibaly's former resi-

---

8   The term has a subtle connotation in Senari, the vernacular language, as it may also mean ›sweet thing‹ or ›joyful thing‹.

dence was nonetheless a direct reference to the former glory of his kingdom. When the national minister of communication and culture at the time, Henriette Diabaté, decided to incorporate the dilapidated building in her programme of Musées Regionaux, it was clear that its renovation would be a tribute to the mayor and his family, too.

The mayor, again Lanciné Gon Coulibaly, tried to profit as much as he could from the external funding and opened the museum together with the minister. In addition, three days later, while the festival was still going on, he received the official visit of Henri Konan Bédié, then president of the national assembly and promising successor to the senescent residing president of the nation. Together they visited the workshops of local craftsmen in the entrance courtyard of the museum. It was an occasion to renew the alliance between the two families, the Coulibalys and the Houphouëts, as the two pillars of PDCI power after independence.

Foreign embassies were once more invited to contribute to the event. Their participation was, however, not as prominent as in 1983. The most spectacular contribution came from another neighbouring country, Mali. As Guinea had done almost ten years earlier, they sent their National Ballet. The site where the Mali ballet performed was an unroofed but walled multipurpose courtyard known locally as *Centre de la Jeunesse* (Youth Centre).[9] When the National Ballet of Mali performed, the courtyard was filled with plastic chairs and the platform was used as a stage. While the mayor, the minister and their special guests from abroad were sitting in the first rows, the Korhogo youth in the back preferred to dance to the rhythms of the Malian sounds. However, the director of the ballet, who had accompanied his troupe to Korhogo, made it clear that this was an official event and that there was no space for any political subversion in the programme. There were good reasons to warn the younger spectators dancing behind the official guests.

In 1992, the university crisis in Côte d'Ivoire had already gone into its third year, leaving many students without any chance to complete their studies as the national university in Abidjan declared one *année blanche*

---

9 Youth in Ivoirian French does not necessarily mean that a person is young in physical age. It rather suggests that the person has not lived up to his or her social ambitions. An unmarried man who does not have a family is still considered young even at the age of forty or over.

after the other.[10] Bands such as Les Parents du Campus or Sur-Choc had created a novel musical style, the Zouglou.[11] The term was borrowed from the local Baule and tellingly meant ›mixture‹ or ›trash‹. Unlike former Ivoirian music, it depicted the suffering of the students, their difficulties in making a living in the midst of underfunded institutions and harassment by state authorities. One of their battle cries made it crystal clear what they were aiming at: »Ceux-là, Houphouët ne pourra pas les commander!« (»Houphouët will not be able to boss these guys around!«).[12] The unruly texts were not sung in the ›good‹ French that was a marker of bourgeois identity in the postcolony; they were sung in the street slang spoken by Ivoirian youth. For the first time in history, they were proud of deviating from the dominant French culture that had informed the post-colonial identities since independence (cf. Touré 1981). Zouglou was also a dance that developed its own movements called *coupé décalé* (cut and shift). It soon spread over most of West and Central Africa and was also appropriated by the African Diaspora in Paris. When the director of the Malian ballet moved on stage, one of his first words was that he would never wrench his arms and legs as the ›Zouglouists‹ would do. He raised laughter at the rear of the courtyard. In 1992 the Malian ballet was already engaging in an invisible competition with the urban youth that had started to articulate its own history of the post-colonial nation state – one that was far less positive than the official story.

FROM KATANA TO WOMIENGNON

In 2002 the civil war brought all remaining activities in the youth courtyard to an end. The iron entrance gate had disappeared and the walls were partially demolished. The debris filled the yard together with shrubs and gar-

---

10 Literally ›white year‹, it meant that no courses were offered. Officially, the university never closed completely and continued to organise exams – which the students regularly failed because there was no teaching.

11 Other bands were Magic System, Les Garagistes, Mercenaires, Yode et Siro and Espoir 2000. For a general overview cf. Konaté (2002).

12 Unfortunately, the rhythm of the French slang does not translate into English. The sentence sounds almost like a song and invites the listeners to join in.

bage from the surrounding houses. However, the avenue in which it was located never lost its representative role in the city. In 1964, on the occasion of the fourth anniversary of independence, it was one of the first streets to receive a bitumen surface. The former French offices became the new prefecture, but the avenue remained the central axis of the city.

Rebel governance in Korhogo was heavily influenced by one powerful man, the *comzone* Fofié Kouakou Martin. In 2005 he was appointed commander of Zone 10 – hence the short form *comzone*.[13] Unlike most of his peers, he had a long-term political agenda, which was not solely aimed at maintaining the dominant position that he had acquired through the disorder of the first year after the beginning of the insurgency on 19 September 2002. Being in charge of the second-largest city under rebel control was more than a challenge; it was also a chance to show that the rebellion could do more than the former state administration.[14] Fofié developed a programme to rebuild the city.[15]

His plans to renovate the city went beyond the economic agenda and included popular as well as cultural goals. There were public gardens, a space already covered by acacia trees but abandoned for decades, where he established a bar and a restaurant, and himself planted a tree. Musicians and actors were invited to perform under the soft shade of the acacias. He also organised feasts for the children of Korhogo and their mothers. His most visible achievement in the field of culture was, however, the reconstruction of the cultural centre where the dances of the last Katana were once performed. It was more than a mere renovation as Fofié decided to construct a new, entirely roofed tribune on one side of the courtyard and to enlarge the existing small rooms on the other. The construction material

---

13 Fofié was in charge of security in Korhogo between 2002 and 2005. The territory under rebel domination was, until summer 2010, divided into ten administrative zones. Cf. Heitz (2009) on another mode of rebel domination in the West of Côte d'Ivoire.

14 Sapéro, personal communication, 5 February 2009. Sapéro was heading the group of artists that negotiated with Fofié on the renovation of the cultural centre. According to him, Fofié stated repeatedly that he wanted to show that the rebels were performing better than the former ›functionaries‹ of the state.

15 Cf. http://www.fansara110.com. Accessed 19 May 2011. The site displays visual and verbal documentation of Fofié's works and his biography.

was officially ›donated‹ by the big merchants and businessmen of Korhogo. In actual fact, however, the material was requisitioned from them, often under dubious circumstances. Whoever wanted to do business in Korhogo at the time had to contribute – and if the person did not do so voluntarily, Fofié could become quite unpleasant.

The new centre to some extent built on the old one, but it was also a break with the past. Fofié gave it a new name, Womiengnon. The term was borrowed from Senari, the language of the Senufo. Literally translated, it means ›good for us all‹ or ›beautiful for us all‹.[16] The rebels preferred a more figurative translation and understood it as *le bien commun* (the common good).[17] The opening of the new centre on 18 February 2006 was a public event.[18] After an inaugural speech, the *comzone* took his guests around to have a look at the centre and in particular its walls. All of them displayed murals commissioned from artists in Korhogo that were, as Fofié claimed, related to the history of the North, the Senufo and the City of Poro, as Korhogo was often called because of the Senufos' famous secret society.[19]

2006 – THE FIRST IMAGE PROGRAMME

The murals had all been painted in the two or three weeks that preceded the opening of the new cultural centre. The rebel leader contacted Issa Koné, an artist whose works he had already collected earlier and with whom his administration cooperated from time to time. Issa Koné is better known as

---

16 Senari does not distinguish between ›good‹ and ›beautiful‹. The modern autonomy of the arts and aesthetic experience does not exist in their culture (cf. Förster 1997).

17 Cf. http://www.fansara110.com/l_inauguration_du_centre_culturel_915.htm. Accessed 25 May 2011.

18 The opening ceremony is still documented on the website of the former rebel leader, cf. http://www.fansara110.com/l_inauguration_du_centre_culturel_857.htm. Accessed 26 May 2011.

19 Sapéro, personal communication, 10 January 2010.

Sapéro de Farafina,[20] his stage name. He has a weekly radio programme and an occasional TV show on the local, private SRTV station. He also spells his name as Sap-Héro (the hero of Sap), referring to SAPE, the Société des Ambianceurs et Personnes Elégantes in Brazzaville (Martin 1995). To Sapéro, the movement represents a truly African way of being modern, and it has created a contemporary African culture.[21] His own way of dressing, however, does not fit to SAPE: He has long dreadlocks and often wears the very wide ›traditional‹ trousers or the short, brown shirts of the peasants with pockets on all sides. Sapéro was and still is an eye-catcher in Korhogo. Because of his radio show and his unusual appearance, he is known all over the city.

Sapéro calls his studio ›Safarim Maison‹[22] and sees it as a centre for the promotion of all crafts and arts in the North. He regularly invites other artists to come to his place and reflect about the (few) possibilities to launch new projects, to attract clients, to win new patrons and to advertise their activities in the city and beyond. In order to obtain the status of an NGO, Safarim Maison has a written programme that defines its purpose as an association of artists fostering development, including capacity building, efficient training, etc. The reference to development discourse was a means to get access to possible funders.

Sapéro received the commission to cover the walls of the cultural centre with murals less than four weeks before the inauguration. Partly because he would not be able to do all the paintings himself, but also because he saw an opportunity to advance his plans for the association of Korhogo's artists, he invited all of the artists of the city to join and do the murals together. Some who happened to be in Abidjan were even sent messages to come back and participate in the joint effort. In all, fifteen painters and five sculptors participated.

The choice of the subject was largely up to the artists themselves. However, Fofié had told Sapéro that he wanted them »to respect« the purpose of the place, i.e. culture. Besides, he said, he would like to see something

---

20 Farafina means ›land of the blacks‹ or, freely translated ›black Africa‹ in Dyula, a dialect of Manding serving as a market language in Korhogo.

21 All personal information on Sapéro and his studio was collected in January and February 2009, and in January, February and August 2010.

22 Safarim stands for Sap-Héro Farafina Images.

about the new Korhogo, the new era that had begun with the rebellion of 2002. The rebel leader did not intervene directly in the execution of the paintings. He inspected the progress of the work regularly but, with exceptions, kept silent on what the painters were depicting.

The walls were covered with murals on both sides. As the structure was on Main Street, it was a prominent place in the city and no artist refused to join the project. The most visible panels were to the right and left of the entrance. The first panel left of the entrance showed a typical scene from Senufo culture. It displayed a *kpoye* group, an ensemble of three xylophone players with two drummers. The drummer carrying the lead instrument was dancing as the players usually do when they praise somebody. Every village and even every quarter of bigger villages and towns has such an ensemble of musicians that perform whenever there is an event that is related to the identity of the village. The *kpoye* bands articulate belonging and simultaneously generate social space – the social space of a settlement in its unity. They are seen by many as a primordial expression of Senufo culture.

Other panels also displayed scenes from Senufo culture and rural life, which was widely understood as the source of all Senufo culture. There were scenes depicting circular huts with thatched roofs. Masked and unmasked dancers were performing in front. These pictures were obviously borrowed from a genre in easel painting on canvas, »the village in the times of old«.[23] As a narrative genre, it was embedded in a discursive formation about the past and the present, answering widespread expectations about ancestral life: In the old days, elders were still respected, and life was based on the values of mutual understanding and reciprocity; it stood in stark contrast to the selfishness that now penetrated all spheres of contemporary urban life. It was this selfish attitude that had, as many people claimed, brought Côte d'Ivoire to the brink of the present economic, social and above all political disaster. Depicting idyllic scenes of village life was a political statement – and not a retreat from the public sphere, as a Western spectator might have suspected.

As a visual genre, the landscapes and scenes from rural life shared some characteristics: They displayed crafts and well-known masks and dances, in particular those that had once been performed for tourists. Though tourism had already ceased to exist before the outbreak of the civil war in 2002, it

---

23 I adopt the term from Fabian (1996: 17, 193-211).

had left its traces in the collective visual memory. For instance, the holy dance of the *boloi* and the *wãbele* masks were depicted as performances in a village setting. The masks are actually not a central element of Senufo culture and do not belong to the Poro society, which is the most important institution of the segmental social order. They exist only in a comparatively small part of Senufoland where they hunt witches. Indeed, they are more a sign of how the villagers tried to cope with the malcontents of modernity than a living testimony to the peaceful ›times of old‹. The imagery of tourism also shaped the pictorial style. The masks were displayed in the foreground and from an angle that allowed the spectator to see all of the iconographic details. To a certain degree, they reproduced the way the masks were depicted in coffee-table books and on posters for the tourist market. In the local setting, the masks perform only late in the day and at night, and the spectators cannot see much more than a fuzzy shape moving through the village. Similar paintings and their reproductions were often displayed in places accessible to many, for instance in restaurants, big hotels, pharmacies and sometimes offices. There was a shared visual awareness of how such paintings should look, and the murals in the centre were no exception. Knowledgeable visitors who passed while the painters were still working on their respective panels brought their opinion on the scenes into play. They also pointed at features which they would have associated with an ancestral lifestyle. The main and much more precise criticism came, however, from the other artists working on their panels close by. Sapéro remembers animated debates about how to depict a particular figure and how to design a panel so that it would fulfil the purpose of the centre at large. There was a certain tension between their own knowledge of the genre and their anticipation of what the centre was meant for. Because there were no clear instructions by the rebel leader, they chose a combination of different genre paintings.

Pictures of sportsmen and women formed a second genre. Unlike the first, however, it was not appreciated by tourists or other outsiders, such as expatriates working for development agencies or international NGOs.[24] Football, handball and other games were most prominent. Wrestling and the martial arts came next as they were very popular in the city which accom-

---

24 They were once an important clientele for the artists living in Korhogo but had also left in 2002.

modated five big clubs promoting these sports. Like the ancestral genre, the sports genre also had its roots in urban visual culture. Unlike the former, however, it was seldom reproduced on canvas. Rather, such paintings were displayed in public places such as schoolyards and the municipal baths[25] as well as in private sports clubs. The artists reproduced pictures of that genre because they assumed that the centre would primarily house sports events after its completion.

PICTURING THE EXPERIENCE OF THE PAST

Though the two genres were not known by name to the ordinary urban populace, most visitors to the centre and also the passersby were familiar with what the pictures showed and related them to their experience of urban visual culture. However, several artists produced paintings that did not fit one of the conventional genres. Sapéro, the most courageous among them, painted the most prominent panel inside the court, right opposite the entrance and the tribune of honour. All visitors entering the centre would first look at this mural before becoming aware of the others to the left and right.

The mural showed a cityscape with a broad street in the foreground and a skyline of modern houses in the background (fig. 1). On the right side of the road stands a troop carrier marked FANCI. The acronym stands for Forces Armées Nationales de Côte d'Ivoire, the former national army of the first republic and the Gbagbo government. It clearly identifies the soldiers on the street as representatives of the oppressive regimes of the 1990s and the years before the 2002 insurgency. Three scenes are depicted in the street, all three showing interactions between national soldiers and local people. Both are easy to recognise; the soldiers wear uniforms while the others are dressed in *boubous*, the long caftans that Muslims usually wear in northern Côte d'Ivoire, or in ordinary clothes. The first scene on the left of the panel depicts a soldier with a gun grappling a young man on the shoulder while the terrified man tries to hold the soldier off by pushing him back with his hand. The second scene in the background of the tableau shows a fleeing man in a light yellow *boubou* being

---

25 In 2006, the municipal baths were dysfunctional and had been closed for many years. For the artists, who were all in their twenties and early thirties, the municipal baths were not much more than a story from a distant past.

pursued by a soldier, again with a gun in his hand. The fleeing man drops a tiny card behind his back; the small rectangle in the upper left corner identifies it as a national identity card. The third scene is more brutal than the others and catches the attention of the spectators depicted in the middle of the entire tableau. It shows a soldier battering a man and a woman. The man is old, with white hair and a white beard. While falling backwards on the ground, losing one of his sandals, he is still trying to apologise by saying »padon misié« [sic] (»excuse me, sir«). The two words are written in Ivoirian French, showing that the old man does not have a formal education. With his left hand, the same soldier is battering a pregnant woman who appears to be passing by behind the two. The soldier's hand is touching the woman's belly while her face is contorted with pain. Like the old man, she is dressed in ordinary clothes; a wrap-around skirt and a simple yellow blouse.

Fig. 1: Identity crisis. Mural by Sapéro, wall paint, 2006.

Photograph taken by the author.

The fourth and last scene in the foreground to the right depicts a soldier with a machine gun who is inspecting an identity card which he holds in his right hand. The passport photo is clearly visible. The owner of the card is another old man wearing a white *boubou*. He is also terrified and, with a gesture of despair, lifts his right hand to his chin, still looking at the soldier in front of him.

In the background of the four scenes and close to the houses stands a crowd of people, apparently not daring to approach. Above the city in the background, a white thundercloud hovers and lightning descends on the houses. Larger than life, another soldier appears in the upper right corner of the tableau, shaking his fist and shouting »Stop!«. He wears a cap with a star – an emblem that identifies him as a rebel soldier. The man has a long black beard and can be identified as Fofié Koakou Martin, the chief rebel of Korhogo. In his left hand, he holds a Kalashnikov. To the left of the »Stop!«, one reads »ya na marrrr!!« – the sound of a firing gun. The picture is a plain and unequivocal image of what fuelled the rebellion of 2002: the constant harassment of the ordinary populace in the North by arrogant and brutal men in uniforms from the South. It is an image of the collective experience of being second-class citizens. As such, the tableau is not a depiction of an actual event, but casts the collective experience into a visible picture.

Sapéro signed the panel in the middle, right behind the sound of the machine gun. He selected the panel, and it was also he who decided on the subject of the tableau. However, while he was still working on the picture, the rebel commander showed up to supervise the progress of the artists working in the centre. Sapéro did not notice his arrival and kept on painting until another artist standing next to him gave him a sign. When turning around, Sapéro noticed that Fofié was attentively observing what he was doing. He had not said a word until Sapéro became aware of him, but now he asked, »Who is the man in the back?« Sapéro, who had not asked for permission to portray the rebel commander, was scared because Fofié was known for his arbitrary and rude way of dealing with people who did not do what he wanted them to do. Sapéro told me later that he believed that he saw Fofié frowning but »there was nothing«. He answered: »This is a man who wants to re-build the city.« Fofié told him to continue and to come when the centre would be opened.[26]

This was not the only panel with political content. The head of Ernesto Che Guevara filled the panel to the left. It adopted the usual style of Che Guevara portraits: plain black and white surfaces that reduced the facial features to a few essential traits.[27] Like the insurgents in northern Côte d'Ivoire, he waves a cap

---

26 Sapéro, personal communication, 2 February 2009.

27 Like most of the posthumous portraits, it was based on the iconic photo taken by Alberto Korda on 5 March 1960.

with a star on the front. When talking to the artists of Safarim Maison, I was told, »this was a man who fought for the poor – in some other part of Africa«.[28] The name of Che Guevara was unknown, and when I mentioned the name and that he was a Latin American revolutionary who had mainly fought in Cuba, they said that it did not change anything as long as he was fighting for the rights of the suppressed. His iconic portrait stood for the will to give a voice to those who suffered from an unjust regime.

Fig. 2: French officers and Senegalese Rifles arresting villagers.
Mural by SAM, wall paint, 2006.

Photograph taken by the author.

Closer to their own past were two other panels. The first showed a scene from colonial life (fig. 2): two French officers and six *Tirailleurs Sénégalais*, the African auxiliary troops of the colonial army, arresting three men in a rural village.[29] The style is much more naturalistic than in the other paintings. According to Sapéro, it was inspired by pictures in schoolbooks on the country's his-

---

28 Group discussion on the occasion of a guided visit to the centre on 14 January 2009.

29 Despite the name, the Senegalese Rifles were not only recruited in Senegal. They came from all parts of Africa under French domination (cf. Michel 2003).

tory.[30] The tableau shows the French officers dressed in blue uniforms and the African soldiers in dark green with white caps. The French officers are trying to separate the captured men from their wives and families, and the African auxiliaries assist them and push the captives on a truck. Remarkably, one of the two French officers is supported by an African soldier who presses his hands on the officer's back to withstand the pressure of the captives. The French colonial army did not allow such an act; no African soldier was allowed to touch his superior in such a way.

Fig. 3: The Tower of Babel. Mural by Sapéro, wall paint, 2006.

Photograph taken by the author.

---

30 As the artist was not living in Korhogo, I was unable to inquire directly but had to rely on what I was told by the members of Safarim Maison.

Another panel is dedicated to the more recent, post-colonial history of Côte d'Ivoire. It shows a meeting hall with well-dressed men sitting on the right and a tall person in a black suit on the left (fig. 3). In the middle is a table with a kind of bowl on it showing the national emblem of Côte d'Ivoire, the contour of the country and two Ivory tusks. In the background, a painting on the wall depicts a crowd of people around a pyramid. It is subtitled »Tour de Babel« with the name of the artist in the upper right corner. The man standing on the left is easily recognisable as Félix Houphouët-Boigny, the founding father of the nation. He carries medals on his chest and raises his left hand. Sapéro explained that the men sitting on the right are talking to each other but not listening – everybody is talking a different language. The first president, this picture suggests, did not found a nation but only confusion. He constructed a Tower of Babel that was bound to crumble, Sapéro added. Such a statement against the founding father was exceptional – even under rebel domination. The reputation of the ›old man‹, as he was usually called by ordinary people, was sacrosanct, and even after his death in 1993, many politicians still legitimated their own ambitions by claiming that they would just do what the ›old man‹ would have done. The tableau was also a statement about the continuity of political attitudes. It suggested that many politicians who were arguing with each other at the time when the picture was painted still did not want to listen. This meaning was, however, not immediately obvious to the spectators, as Sapéro admitted. Some just saw the former president and assumed that the painting was honouring him – a fact that would affect the later destiny of the painting.

IMAGERIES OF A BETTER FUTURE

A third group of panels addressed the future of Korhogo as a modern and ›developed‹ city. On the outside wall of the centre, the rebel commander was depicted with a hammer and a chisel working hard rocks (fig. 4). Behind him on the left, a few thatched houses were visible, indicating that he worked for a Senufo village »community«. On the other side stood a basket with utensils and a small figure on a pedestal. It resembled the wooden Senufo statues, although it was somewhat distorted. However, the figure clearly looked toward Fofié working on the »foundations« of a new Senufo village, as the artists explained.

Another mural, again by Sapéro and also on the exterior wall, showed Independence Square, not far away from the cultural centre. Every person living in Korhogo knew the square as a place where important ceremonies were held since the days of colonial domination, with the prefecture on one side and the town hall on the other. Both buildings were now part of the administration put in place by the insurgents, and the former prefect's office had been turned into an office for the rebel commander. In the middle of the square was a small traffic island with a high flagpole. The French had hoisted their Tricolore here, and after 1960, the post-colonial administration had done the same with their own tri-colored flag. In an attempt to show that times were changing, the *comzone* had invited the visual artists and architects to submit plans ›to develop‹ the city. The competition had two aims: One was to refurbish the buildings around the square and other prestigious places in town; the other was to endow Korhogo with monuments in honour of the rebellion. Unfortunately, the funding for the second part was insufficient, and apart from a monument for the unknown rebel soldier, most of the monuments remained unfinished. Some pedestals and bases for future monuments were constructed, but then the rebels ran out of money.

Fig. 4: The rebel commander re-building Korhogo.
Mural by Sapéro, wall paint, 2006.

Photograph taken by the author.

Sapéro had submitted plans for a monument too. He had presented drawings and a small model to Fofié, but this did not lead anywhere. Now, on
the exterior wall of the cultural centre, he painted his vision of how Independence Square should look in the future. In the middle, he painted his
monument, on the left, the building of the prefecture and on the right, the
town hall. The square itself was a fine black tarmac. Sapéro also included
elements that had been put into place already or that were planned for the
immediate future, namely walls to separate the two buildings from the
square. The monument in the middle looked like his model, but Sapéro had
added two elements: The date of the military insurgency, 19 September,
figured prominently on the cube above the pole that would support the
monument and a man was climbing the pole above the cube. The figure was
disproportionately small and was only dressed in a waistcloth. The artist
commented on this detail only very briefly, stating that the man represented
the old way of living while he was already in a new environment.

Fig. 5: La renaissance. Mural by Kassem, wall paint, 2006.

Photograph taken by the author.

Other murals addressing contemporary life and the future depicted men sitting in offices equipped with various business devices, in particular com-
puters, phones and mobile phones. There were also a few paintings com-

menting on the present situation of the country. A mural by Kassem showed Côte d'Ivoire as an egg with ivory tusks on either side. Elephants were sitting on them, blowing their trunks (fig. 5). A hand arose out of the egg, and the picture was subtitled »La renaissance«. Other murals showed the contours of Côte d'Ivoire with a bleeding heart, or the country carried by a sweating elephant. Another painting was titled »L'afrique se meurt« (»Africa commits suicide«). The seemingly more critical attitude of the artist, who signed the mural as Cooless, was not well received by the public. It was the only mural that was obviously damaged deliberately.[31]

THE RENEWAL OF 2009

Since the paints used in 2006 were not of the best quality, the murals of the centre were badly affected by weather and, to a lesser degree, also by visitors who did not pay attention and touched them when walking past the walls. When the rainy season of 2009 ended, the rebel leader urged the artists to re-paint the entire centre. After some discussions about the materials, Sapéro was asked to bring the artists together. As an intermediary between the rebel command and the artists, he could decide who would participate and who would not. Some of the artists who had participated in 2006 were no longer in town; others refused to join the group this time because they were not promised a payment. The group was significantly smaller than three years earlier.

The social and political setting had also changed. Fofié Kouakou was still commander of Zone 10, but he was now in charge of organising the transition from rebel governance to state-run public services. The rebel command very reluctantly engaged in this process, suspecting that this transition was meant to give the Gbagbo regime better chances in the upcoming elections. Still in mid-2010, when the ten zones of rebel administration were officially dismantled, Fofié controlled most of the public services provided in and around Korhogo. His space of manoeuvring, however, was much more restricted by written and unwritten agreements with other stakeholders. In the second half of 2009, a strong majority believed that the time

---

31 At the time of my documentation in January 2009, the picture had almost vanished, but the title was still visible.

of rebel governance would soon come to an end. Another widely shared conviction was that the country, at long last, needed some kind of reconciliation.

The genres of 2006 were maintained, but the content had shifted. The most stable genre was that of the ›old Senufo culture‹. The existing murals showing masks and dances were renewed or, more often, replaced by new paintings on the same topics. The xylophone players were now praising an old man sitting in front of them, the *boloi* dancers now performed in front of a long row of thatched houses, while another mask replaced the *wãbele* performance. Yet there were differences in how such images were framed.

A bucolic landscape, a sunset over the sea with trees in the foreground and birds in the sky, caused a debate among the artists. The painters, Florent and Alf Décor, were accused of plagiarism and it was argued their painting did not mirror what was really at stake in Korhogo at the time. The two unconnected allegations came from an artist who had specialised in landscape painting. Landscapes, however, were an unspecific genre and closely related to ›the village in the times of old‹. Many artists in Korhogo produced such paintings, and in the end, Sapéro as the intermediary patron decided that the allegation was invalid. The mural remained in place. More interesting was the artists' reaction to the second allegation. They claimed that the idyllic landscape, which did not show any traces of human beings, was actually a statement on what had been lost in the present and that the painting suggested that there had once been a better world.[32] At times visual references to ›the times of old‹ were combined with new, contemporary elements. *Kora* harps were displayed in front of multi-storey buildings and electric guitars in ›traditional‹ village environments. The sports genre did not change much either. The wrestlers were still there, but now they had an audience. The Kung Fu fighters did not change either, except for the colours, which became brighter. Footballers still played ball, and the athletes were running and jumping as they did back in 2006.

What really changed were the murals about history and the present political situation. Many of them disappeared. President Houphouët-Boigny constructing the Tower of Babel was replaced by an old man playing the *kora*. The colonial scene was also covered by another painting, this time a

---

32 Unfortunately, I was unable to inquire among possible visitors to the centre as to whether they interpreted the landscape painting in that sense.

sports event. Much more interesting, however, was the fate of the big mural facing the entrance where Sapéro had depicted the roots of the Ivoirian conflict (fig. 1). He went over it and gave it a completely new meaning. He kept a few figures and scenes from the old mural but replaced other scenes (fig. 6). The entire tableau is now divided into two parts. The right half of the mural still displays the grey background of the former tarmac street and the light, nearly white colour of the clouds above. It also continues to depict the scene of the national soldier checking the identity card of the terrified old man in the lower right corner. The artist went over the old man's face and painted it more realistically, but also added another soldier standing behind the old man and grabbing him by the throat. In his other hand, the soldier holds a gun and shoots into the air. The other scene of a soldier beating an old man and a pregnant woman has also changed. The soldier now holds a pistol in his right hand, targeting the heart of an old man dressed in a blue *boubou* in front of him. Sketches of other scenes of violence are depicted behind the two soldiers on a light background. Two tusks and the shade of a third surround the light space in the middle above the scenery. Between the tusks, Sapéro wrote in big letters »Hier!« (»Yesterday!«).

Fig. 6: Transitions de l'histoire. Mural by Sapéro, wall paint, 2006-2009.

Photograph taken by the author.

The left side of the tableau is completely different. It is titled »Pour 2Main« (»for 2morrow«) on the upper margin of the wall. The violence is over. Instead, Sapéro painted two scenes of compassion, each of which involves a soldier. One is a member of the rebel army, marked by the letters FAFN (Forces Armées des Forces Nouvelles) on his cap. The other soldier belongs to the troops loyal to the Gbagbo regime, FANCI. Both are helping civilians. The FAFN soldier supports an old man with a stick who apparently cannot walk anymore. The FANCI soldier arrests a young man who has stolen the bag of a young woman standing behind the soldier. The thief raises his arms while the soldier threatens him with a gun. In the background, other people are reacting joyously, also raising their arms and shouting. Some parts of the former cityscape with high-rise buildings are still visible, but the sky has turned into a dark grey. The face of the rebel commander is no longer visible. The message of the renewed painting is clear. After a time of violence and civil war, everybody is longing for a better, more peaceful future that brings the people of Côte d'Ivoire together. What has been painted here is an image of a possible future. It does not yet exist – but there is a chance to attain this state of a just and non-violent social order. Though still wishful thinking at the time, the imagery of that social order has had an impact on the imagination of others, the visitors of the centre. The visitors who had a closer look at the murals almost always stopped in front of this particular one, sometimes commenting on it.[33] Some voiced doubts: »Will that ever happen?« Others saw it as a normative statement: »Yes, it should be like this.« Still others complained about the lack of social cohesion in the recent history of their country. Later, Sapéro told me that it was because of such comments that he became interested in the question of social cohesion. He put it on the agenda of his Safarim Maison.

The cohesion of the postcolony was an issue that figured prominently in what emerged as a new genre, the murals addressing the present state of Côte d'Ivoire. In a literal sense, it was depicted in a tableau showing an old woman spinning and weaving a long narrow strip of fabric. It was meant to show how one common thread should run through the society, uniting all

---

33 This statement is not based on my own observation. I was told so by the apprentices of Safarim Maison who had helped Sapéro during his work on the tableau (personal communication, 12 January 2010).

the people. Another tableau showed how three men sewed the three coloured bands of the Ivoirian flag together while an elephant watched over them. The most impressive mural was, at least for the members of Safarim Maison, a broad panel that showed two rows of people holding a giant egg in their midst. SAM, the artist, explained that the egg stood for Côte d'Ivoire – simultaneously precious and fragile. Only when everybody joined, and only when the people became aware of the enormous task ahead of them, would the egg survive.

Fig. 7: The future of the city. Mural by Samson, wall paint, 2009.

Photograph taken by the author.

Not all artists subscribed to these positive imaginings of the future. There were darker, sinister views, too. A tableau by Samson depicted a cityscape late in the day (fig. 7). The houses are high-rise as in the other pictures, but here the focus is on three young men in the foreground. All three are dressed in local varieties of hip-hop fashion. The young man on the right is a muscled singer, holding a microphone is his hand. The man in the middle wears a jacket with a hood that partially covers his head. »Donys'LX« is written across his belly, the name of a Parisian rapper.[34] On the left, a young man rides on a skateboard, also hiding his head under a hood. The atmosphere is quite sombre as all three are painted in dark shades of grey. When I visited the centre together with the artists of Safarim Maison, they did not want to comment on the painting. Only Chigata said that the mural was about the future of Korhogo as a modern city.

SHIFTING IMAGERIES

Comparing the murals of 2006 and 2009 raises some basic questions about their character as pictures, as popular imagery and as imagination of an alternative social order. Before addressing these questions, however, a word must be said about their status as artworks. The majority of the painters saw themselves as artists, not as mere craftsmen. All of them were running workshops that also executed purely decorative works. Many of them made a living as painters of signboards and other advertisements.[35] Nonetheless, most of them aimed at more, complaining that there were just no connoisseurs and art collectors in Korhogo – with the notable exception of the rebel commander. They said that doing the murals in the centre might help them to attract new customers and perhaps a patron from the international artworld. On one panel close to the entrance, they all painted their stage names followed by their mobile phone numbers for visitors who would want to come to their studios. The ›real‹ artworks were those painted on canvas in their studios – not the big murals. It did not matter much to them whether they would last five or ten years as everybody knew that they had to be renewed regularly. Nobody saw a need to preserve the initial paintings of 2006.[36] What seemed to be a disregard for their former artwork, however, opened a space for a review of what they had done three years

---

34 His stage name is actually Dony S. He is the founder of the Rap Contenders. Cf. http://www.rap-contenders.com/dony-s and http://www.youtube.com/watch?v=a SCSIGblD5Y. Accessed 31 May 2011.

35 Some mainly painted words in big letters on cars, lorries and public buildings. The other painters did not consider them to be artists.

36 Almost nobody understood my surprise when I saw the repainted centre in January 2010.

earlier – and it allowed them to follow the popular imagination. The process of imagination became visible only through the shifting imagery, the painted and re-painted pictures on the walls of the cultural centre.

A closer look at the murals reveals not only a shift in the imagery; it also points to a few highly persuasive images. In 2006, these were, first of all, the images of the past. The brutality of French colonial domination is a conventional pattern of thought, promoted by schoolbooks and in many other media. What was new was the critique of Houphouët-Boigny, the once sacrosanct *père de la nation.* The respective picture on the wall imbued the past with a new meaning and it related the other murals to a new image of the past. The fact that this chapter of Ivoirian history was no longer cast into a fixed image meant that other chapters could be more ambiguous, too. The prominent tableau, showing national soldiers harassing ordinary people and the rebel leader ending this outright discrimination, had no dislocating effect. It was approved by the commander himself and promoted an image that the rebellion was keen to foster among the general populace: the insurgency as a legitimate act against oppression. The tableau did not raise any debate about its content. It was seen as an accurate picture of the injustice that everyone had experienced in the old regime under Gbagbo.[37]

The imagery of 2009 had changed, however. What was an outright statement about the political legitimacy of the rebellion became a statement about a possible future state of society: rebels and national soldiers working hand in hand – an image that was hard to believe in at the time. It had simply not happened until then – regardless of all of the attempts by the United Nations and other international actors to bring the two militaries together. The spontaneous comments I witnessed at the centre were telling: Many people doubted that such cooperation would ever become reality. On the one hand, the spectators judged the situation very appropriately as »pas encore mûre« (»not ready yet«). On the other hand, the image of an alternative social order was not rejected. Nobody said that they did not want a peaceful society to emerge. The projective element in the image became a

---

37 When I used photos of this painting at a conference on the experience of the past at the Goethe Institute in Abidjan in February 2009, many listerners in the audience jumped up and exclaimed that the picture showed how they had suffered under the old regime. It demonstrated how powerful images are.

problematic but attractive element of the picture on the wall. Between 2006 and 2009, the popular imagination had worked on the political imageries. The images that were then transformed into pictures had increasingly turned into normative statements on how the social world should be. They articulated societal aims – aims that were perhaps still unrealistic, but that increasingly informed the political agenda.

WORKS CITED

Coulibaly, Lanciné Gon (2004): *Côte d'Ivoire: Au cœur du bois sacré*, Paris: Harmattan.

Fabian, Johannes (1996): *Remembering the Present: Painting and Popular History in Zaire*, Berkeley/CA: University of California Press.

Förster, Till (1995): »Die Darstellung neuer Herrschaft: Die Entstehung repräsentativer Öffentlichkeit in einer akephalen Gesellschaft Westafrikas«. *Anthropos* 90.2, 377-390.

Förster, Till (1997): *Zerrissene Entfaltung: Alltag, Ritual und künstlerische Ausdrucksformen im Norden der Côte d'Ivoire*, Köln: Köppe Verlag.

Förster, Till (in print): »Dialogue direct: Rebel Governance and Civil Order in Northern Côte d'Ivoire«. In: Zachariah Mampilly et al. (eds.), *Rebel Governance*, Cambridge: Cambridge University Press.

Freedberg, David (1989): *The Power of Images: Studies in the History and Theory of Response*, Chicago/IL: University of Chicago Press.

Heitz, Katharina (2009): »Power-Sharing in the Local Arena: Man a Rebel-Held Town in Western Côte d'Ivoire«. *Africa Spectrum* 44.3, 109-131.

Konaté, Yacouba (2002): »Génération Zouglou«. *Cahiers d'Etudes Africaines* 42.4, 777-796.

Launay, Robert (1992): *Beyond the Stream: Islam and Society in a West African Town*, Berkeley/CA: University of California Press.

Martin, Phyllis (1995): *Leisure and Society in Colonial Brazzaville*, Cambridge: Cambridge University Press.

Michel, Marc (2003): *Les Africains et la Grande Guerre: L'appel à l'Afrique (1914-1918)*, Paris: Karthala.

Mitchell, William J.T. (1995): *Picture Theory: Essays on Verbal and Visual Representation*, Chicago/IL: University of Chicago Press.

Mitchell, William J.T. (2005): *What Do Pictures Want? The Lives and Loves of Images*, Chicago/IL: University of Chicago Press.

Poamé, Lazare M. (ed.) (2007): *Penser la crise ivoirienne*, Paris: Meniabuc.

Popitz, Heinrich (1992): *Phänomene der Macht*, 2nd ed., Tübingen: Mohr Siebeck.

Savané, Yaya (1994): »Le musée regional Péléforo Gbon Coulibaly à Korhogo, au centre nord de la Côte d'Ivoire: Œuvre de toute une communauté«. *West African Museum Programme Bulletin* 5, 34-38.

Schütz, Alfred (1966): »The Problem of Transcendental Intersubjectivity in Husserl«. In: *Studies in Phenomenological Philosophy* (Collected Papers 3), The Hague: Nijhoff, 51-83.

Soeffner, Georg (2004): »Protosoziologische Überlegungen zur Soziologie des Symbols und des Rituals«. In: Rudolph Schlögl et al. (eds.), *Die Wirklichkeit der Symbole: Grundlagen der Kommunikation in historischen und gegenwärtigen Gesellschaften*, Konstanz: UVK, 41-72.

Touré, Abdou (1981): *La civilisation quotidienne en Côte d'Ivoire: Procès d'occidentalisation*, Paris: Karthala.

Trotha, Trutz von (1995): »Gewalt, Staat und Basislegitimität: Notizen zum Problem der Macht in Afrika (und anderswo)«. In: Heidi Willer/Till Förster/Claudia Ortner-Buchberger (eds.), *Macht der Identität – Identität der Macht*, Münster: Lit, 1-16.

Trotha, Trutz von (2000): »Die Zukunft liegt in Afrika: Vom Zerfall des Staates, von der Vorherrschaft der konzentrischen Ordnung und vom Aufstieg der Parastaatlichkeit«. *Leviathan* 28, 253-279.

Seeing the Past 1800 – 1900 – 2000

History as a Photo Album

Susan A. Crane

Popular enthusiasm for history is a distinctively modern phenomenon. Not coincidentally, technologies of vision have developed rapidly over the past 200 years, particularly photography. But even as photography offered a novel means to preserve the presence of the passing present, it challenged the nature of historical experience by ›freezing‹ the past, no longer allowing it to decay or fade away. The paradoxical quality of photography's relationship to historical consciousness deserves closer analysis – as preserver of the past, producer of presence and resister of historical time. Modernity's peculiar ability to ›see the past‹ through photography enabled a new mode of historical visualization which left traces in historiography as well as in the popular culture of memory. As a result, popular conceptions of history have become visually motivated, visually mediated and visually experienced in ways which have transformed the meanings of the past and the nature of historical consciousness.

As historians, we always begin our work *in medias res*, that is, ›from the middle‹: If we were entirely ignorant of the past, we would not recognize what we encounter as having existed before our perception of it; we would have no historical consciousness. But we also begin *in medias res* in another sense: We are always already in the midst of media which mediate our relationships to the past. And when we respond to these traces of the past interactively, the common metaphor we use to express the sense of distance between past and present is that we hear it ›speak to us‹. But the language the past uses is not universal. Before we can read a text or view an object, it requires interpretation and contextualization, which the historian must already have some sense of before s/he can begin. The trace of the past represented by the object, which we refer to as our ›source‹, can then illuminate or refine our understanding of that past. But the past only ›speaks‹ through a reader's mental ventriloquism – the voice we hear in our heads when we read. Visual means are always necessary to facilitate what we then say we ›hear‹. Historians are primarily viewers, especially as readers, and we produce historical narratives which are then viewed (read) by other readers.

And yet historians have been slow to acknowledge the role of the visual in historical study, or to take the same responsibility for photographic or other visual sources, as they do for their textual sources. When it comes to the visual, a curious passivity emerged in nineteenth-century historical narrative that has stubbornly persisted, virtually unnoticed. In what has become a canonical text for the history of photography, Roland Barthes' *Camera Lucida* (1981), Barthes suggested that the simultaneous emergence of professional history and photography in the nineteenth century was no mere coincidence: »the same century invented History and Photography«. Barthes' notion of history is devoid of historians, even of historical actors: His nineteenth century is »also the age of revolutions, contestations, assassinations, explosions, in short, of impatiences, of everything which denies ripening« (Barthes 1981: 93-94). The passive voice achieves agency with Barthes' denotation of the capital H for History and capital P for Photography: No one caused the explosions but events happen, in a hurry, without due consideration for the exquisiteness of flavor which can only be found in that which was not forced in a greenhouse but left to mature on the vine. Crediting an invention to an era rather than its historical actors might not strike us as more than a charming or appropriate metaphor but, as John Tagg points out in his essay »The Pencil of History«, those capitalizations overburden the camera as an agentless tool of representation (cf. Tagg 2009: 212). Nineteenth-century historians tended to see the photograph as merely an illustration offering exact replicas of the past.

It is striking how many twentieth-century historians and critics followed suit. Barthes was no positivist, but he spoke of photographs as possessing an undeniable historicity and extraordinary empirical value, offering a »certain testimony« – not of that which it represents, but of Time (with a capital T) (cf. Tagg 2009: 226). The affinities between structuralism and historicism are significant, because they have contributed to the denigration of the photograph as evidence, limiting it to the indexicality of the image. The nineteenth century, as Mary Ann Doane writes, was obsessed with a desire to believe that photographs could record and exactly duplicate conditions of material reality for posterity, in defiance of the natural processes of decay and death (cf. Doane 2002: 220). One expression of this obsession might be seen in the work of historical-photographic surveyors. Both Barthes and Tagg discuss a British book called *The Camera as Historian* (Gower/Jast/Topley 1916), which offered advice and training in the methods of historical-photographic surveyors. Tagg, in fact, joked that the authors of *The Camera as Historian* »might better have titled their work ›The Filing Cabinet as Historian‹« (Tagg 2009: 223) because they hoped that dedicated historian-cameramen would use the camera for inventory purposes, to record historically significant data, from surveying topography to recording significant landmarks and objects. As photographic documents of local sites and buildings, these records would illustrate an encyclopedic scope of historical knowledge about the English landscape for posterity. They also spent a great deal of energy outlining the proper methods of organizing and storing the photographic data, hence the suggestion that the filing cabinet is the real hero of the preservation story. But if the photograph is understood merely as a means to authenticate a past as having existed – that is, to preserve a record of the present as the future's past – then the camera acts not like a historian, who of course must provide interpretation and produce narrative about the significance of the past; instead the camera, or rather the photographer, acts like a curator. The camera becomes the archivist of the photographic image – still blurring the agency of the photographer and the camera. Just as Barthes removed the photographer and the camera maker from the invention of Photography with a capital P, so too *The Camera as Historian*'s authors metaphorically removed the agency of both the photographer and the historian in favor of granting agency to the technological process of photograph making.

To remedy the misleading metaphor, the social anthropologist Elizabeth Edwards is undertaking the vast research project of investigating precisely the kind of survey work promoted by *The Camera as Historian* (cf. Edwards 2009). Edwards describes looking at over 75 surveys produced by amateurs and members of the photographic sections of natural history, archaeological and antiquarian societies. Not only did these amateurs fulfill their intentions to create an archive, they also succeeded in promoting a morally informed historical narrative. Edwards insists that the materiality of photographs and cameras, which make them tools in a historical trade, permit users to invest their historical consciousness into their work. Edwards has made an important contribution to the discussion of nineteenth-century visual culture, and photography in particular, by insisting that the material culture of photography – the camera, the printing process, the photograph as print – enables historically conscious subjects not only to reflect on the indexical nature of the past, but to invest their historical desires into an active means of producing presence. By putting the people back into the metaphors, Edwards succeeds in highlighting the materiality of the photographic process, because she calls a tool a tool, and lets the historically conscious individuals actually make their histories. And clearly, in the German context, Timm Starl's work and the scholarship published in the journal *Fotogeschichte* have made a serious case for paying attention to the material aspects of photographs and their interpretation as historical sources (cf. Starl 2009). A new generation of historians can now look at photographs as historical evidence in ways less burdened by the critical debates about indexicality.

The obsession with indexicality, it should now be clear, which persisted into twentieth-century structuralism and therefore into a canon of texts on how to interpret photographs, was only one marker of an incredibly vital era of visual culture. In *The Culture of History*, Billie Melman depicts the long-term British fascination with the material culture of the Tudors as an expression of a popular historical consciousness that gravitated towards the fashion, décor and depiction of that earlier time. Melman argues that it is impossible to »overstate the centrality of the visual aspect of history and its social dimension throughout the nineteenth and twentieth centuries« – indeed, that in that era, »men and women in the modern city were living ›in a frenzy of the visual‹« (Melman 2006: 11). It is crucial to understand the scope of visual culture as being more than two-dimensional documents or merely indexical. What if, as the critic Geoffrey Batchen suggests, photographs are not so much »static objects from the past that represent it« truthfully, but rather, »dynamic modes of apprehension« (Batchen 2009: 33). Dynamism is active and insinuates actors actually doing something. The collector's insertion of photographs into albums constitutes one avenue of a dynamic interaction between photographic production and visual-cultural reception, and, not surprisingly, the photo album and the photo essay book were also inventions of the nineteenth century. As a broader public gained access to photography, they created a demand for means of display and preservation. These genres of popular history offer insight into the ways in which the presence of the photograph, not only its indexicality but its flexible capacity for historical representation, could be manipulated in the interests of historical consciousness. The popularity of the photo album transcended personal use, leading to the rise of mass-produced photo books. I will focus here on three distinctive twentieth-century examples of this genre which take the nineteenth and twentieth centuries as their objects, and consider how popular historical works can make distinctive use of photographs as »dynamic modes of apprehension« modeled on the personal photo album.

As a twentieth-century British feminist and writer, Rebecca West's historical consciousness figured prominently in her novels as well as her non-fiction. West (1892-1983) had not written about photography, however, before she undertook the creation of a historical photo album called *1900*. Published in 1982, at the very end of her life as West turned ninety, *1900* is a photo-essay book which uses the centenary marker as a pivot for reflection on the century that had passed. With her characteristic wit and political acumen, West reviewed what she considered the significant events of the century which gave birth to modernity and shaped her life. She does not come right out and say why she is doing this, now, or why she chose to use photographs, but West highlights the photographic record of the century that invented the camera, and quite strikingly, the album's introduction opens with West family pictures (the photo captions, however, are written in the third person and suggest that the family photographs were inserted by someone else, perhaps an editor).

The images illustrate an anecdote about the death of British Prime Minister William Gladstone, which occurred when West was six years old. She remembers hearing about his death while in Richmond Park, whose grounds lay in a well-to-do London suburb, where her family often took walks (depicted representatively in fig. 1, since West's own family is not present in this scene).

Fig. 1: »The Terrace, Richmond, at the turn of the century; the walk up this hill, lined with neo-classical mansions, was a favourite with Rebecca West and her family.« (West 1982: 8)

Image Credits: The Francis Frith Collection.

West recalls a precociously mature discussion with her parents about the fate of national leaders, which struck her particularly because it involved a neighbor, making the national event locally relevant. Although she was only six at the time, it is perhaps not entirely unlikely that she could have remembered such a politically charged conversation, given West's proclivity for politics and her youthful career as a radical feminist. For the purpose of the photo album, the conversation is recalled because it occurred in 1898 as the century was drawing to a close, and from it West derives the moral that the nineteenth century was the last time that the British people could rely on their prime ministers to act as paternal guardians: »Since 1900 we have had no certainty at any time that there was somebody who would take care of us. We were going to have to look after ourselves.« (West 1982: 8)

Fig. 2: »The six-year-old Rebecca West being fed blackberries on a country outing with her sisters Letitia and Winifred (left) and two cousins.« (West 1982: 6)

Image Credits: Rebecca West papers, Coll. No. 1986-02. Department of Special Collections and University Archives, McFarlin Library, University of Tulsa. Tulsa Oklahoma.

A family photo (fig. 2) shows six-year-old West being fed blackberries by her sisters and cousins. West neatly mixes several layers of historical consciousness into this story which motivate the album's production. A child's perception of the larger, global forces intersecting with her smaller, local world of family and home is rendered against the backdrop of nationally significant events. The grown woman remembers her own childhood within ninety years of lived experience and the right she has earned to evaluate political history from the perspective of personal experience. The album proceeds with a chronology of significant events in 1900, selected to represent the then-powerful British Empire, and a photo gallery of portraits and hallmarks of nineteenth-century culture, technology and science. From page 48 to the end of the book, West writes short essays to accompany a selection of historical images which she uses to illustrate her sense of the people and moments that shaped modern identity. The essays are nothing if not eclectic and personal, with no apologies offered for idiosyncrasy, and many generalizations made on behalf of a ›we‹ or ›us‹ in whose voice she claims to speak. This is not meant to be a definitive history, nor is West a trained historian. But *1900* is also more than just one of the so-called coffee table books that end up filling discount bins at the bookstores. Her choice of the photo-essay book genre permits her historical consciousness a fuller expression; she literally cannot remember or represent the year 1900 or the nineteenth century without photographs.

In 1997, members of the Department of History at the University of Illinois at Urbana-Champaign collaborated on a photo-essay book entitled *Imagining the Twentieth Century* (cf. Stewart/Fritzsche 1997). Each historian chose photographs which they felt were most emblematic of some aspect of twentieth-century history, and wrote a personal essay to accompany the images. The photos were not captioned in the conventional manner, with information about the photographer, date of first publication, title or source of archival image; instead, the essays themselves functioned as commentary-captions which designated the images only generally, as depicting some aspect of a historical event. While this is similar to Rebecca West's approach, it is more unusual, I think, to see this coming from professional historians. Many of the essays ground their discussion in the author's subjective historical experience, using personal memories, sometimes related to historical research, to motivate photo selection and broader historical analyses. The historians speak from their geographical and chronological areas of expertise but draw conclusions about the significance of twentieth-century events as much from the position of intelligent readers of images as from nationally trained professional historians. The editors, German historian Peter Fritzsche and African historian Charles C. Stewart, asserted that »the photo album or scrapbook is perhaps the best way to introduce the twentieth century. Recent history is inescapably autobiographical because the reach of political catastrophe, technological innovation and economic pressure is so great.« (Stewart/Fritzsche 1997: vii) They jump very quickly from asserting that the photo album is the most appropriate mode of representing the twentieth century, to stating that recent history is autobiographical because moderns cannot escape the reach of industrialized, globalized society. They imagine history as a photo album because the events they wish to describe in narrative are personally significant. Historians, like anyone making an album, choose the images they like and tell stories about them.

Fig. 3: The Birth of a New Age.

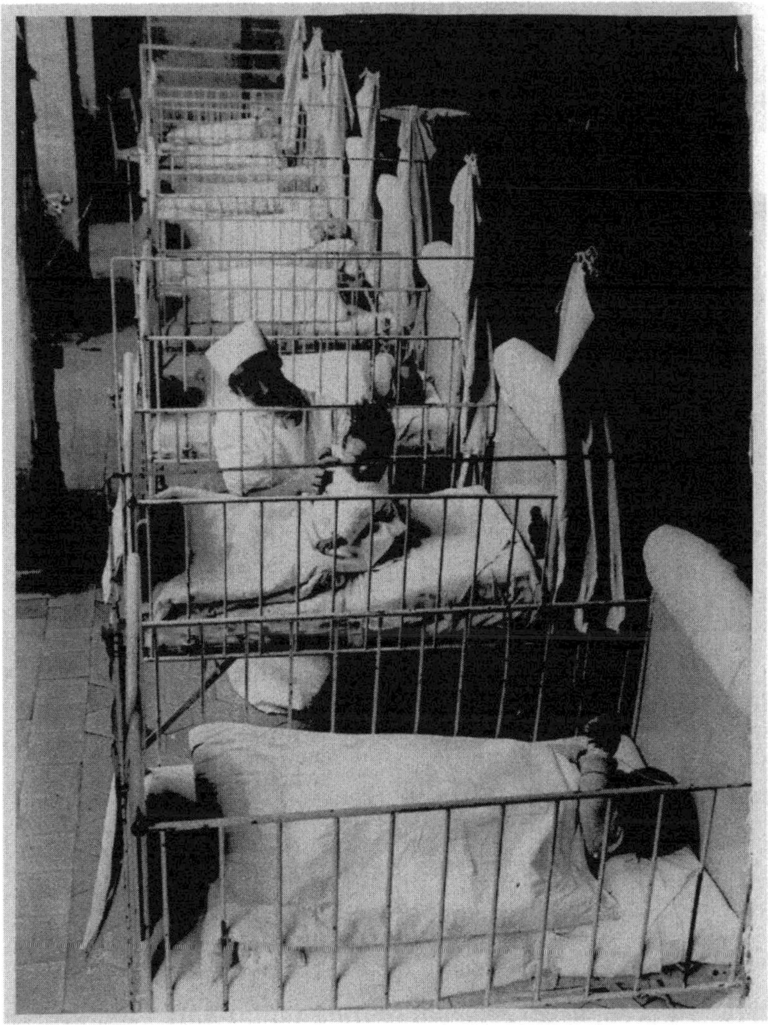

Image Credits: Courtesy National Archives, photo no. 306-NT-533-13.

Both West's album and *Imagining the Twentieth Century* open with images of babies and children signifying the »birth of a new age« (fig. 3). In both albums, the authors choose not to directly refer to the selected images in their accompanying essays. The images lack captions. In *Imagining the Twentieth Century,* the only information provided to identify the photographs is a minimal designation of the archive from which the image is reproduced. These images merely illustrate the larger theme and do so in an often witty manner, which I appreciate. But the fact is, we have no idea who these babies are, nor does this concern the authors; what matters more is the visual metaphor. According to a newspaper clipping associated with this photograph in the National Archives, the babies were in the Kaiserin Auguste Viktoria Home in Berlin, where they recieved exemplary care regardless of »the birth or origin« of the child. The essay accompanying the image in the book, however, makes no mention of the historical context, although that information was available, nor attempts to identify the children (which would likely have been almost impossible to ascertain). Whether because of this difficulty, or a genuine lack of interest, historians have long felt entitled to use photographs merely as illustrations, in the same manner that, for generations, people have put together photo albums: idiosyncratically, choosing the images that please them and bring to life some aspect of the story they want to tell. And since the photographs are chosen presumably with a great deal of familiarity with the subjects, captions are not required in order for the producer, or those they choose to share the album with, to understand the significance of their choice or to appreciate the chosen images. Historians have been treating their own histories like photo albums in this way for well over a century: *sans* caption, *sans* numbering, *sans* reference in the text to the accompanying figures. Even John Tagg, a pre-eminent scholar of historical photographs, uses photographs this way in »The Pencil of History« – he numbers the figures, but nowhere does the text allude to the presence of the photograph on the page (cf. Tagg 2009). The images are sometimes, but not always, mentioned in the narrative, and their presence is otherwise absolutely neglected, when it would have been very easy to insert textual reference. By offering this critique, I am merely pointing out that even among the best historians, there is a tendency to be more lax with visual evidence than with textual evidence. Do we ever allow quotes (other than perhaps an epigraph) to stand alone on a page? Would this not be considered irresponsible or inept scholarship? The author is implicitly counting on the image to do some of the work of making an argument or stating a case. But as I pointed out earlier, photographs cannot speak for themselves. Photographs render their subjects mute; they remove agency from their subjects, and cause them to be depicted in a format which literally takes away their voices. What we know of them, we know from other sources – from contingency, analogy, memory and context. And all this, without even mentioning the fact that the past did not happen in black and white.

When a scholar selects a quote from a source text, or when anyone selects a photograph to place in an album, we are choosing illustrative content which is one piece of the larger narrative. The image, however lovely or intact, is a fragment of the temporal context from which it was ›taken‹. As anyone who has worked in an archive knows, when you get a box of miscellaneous items, whether documents or images or both, you often really have no idea where most of them come from. Archivists have regularly removed photographs from the albums they arrived in unless the album itself is deemed significant (as was recently the case with the photo album of SS officer Karl Höcker from the summer of 1944 at Auschwitz, which the United States Holocaust Memorial Museum scanned in its entirety and posted on the museum website for viewers to flip through, page by virtual page). The fragmentary nature of evidence is a given for historians, and it is equally untroublesome to amateur photographers, most of whom probably do not think of themselves as ›being photographers‹ when they are ›taking pictures‹ with their cell phones. You take what you can, and those are your photographs. Modern historical consciousness, whether among historians or within popular culture more generally, has accommodated itself to the photograph as a fragment of experience, without that painful sense of loss or nostalgia which characterized pre-camera, early nineteenth-century historical consciousness.

In this sense, we can usefully compare photographs to potsherds or any other fragment of the past. Each photograph is a shard of both Time and the Past; each photograph is an entire fragment, but only a fragment, and histories, like photo albums, are intended to piece the broken wholes back together. Nineteenth-century observers of a famously fragmentary statue, the Venus de Milo, similarly tried to imagine restoring the object to its intended, whole form.

Fig. 4: Attempts to reconstruct the Venus de Milo, photographs, artist unknown.

Image Credits: Archaeological Institute of Heidelberg University. Reprinted in Dolf Sternberger (1977): *Panorama of the 19th Century*, New York: Urizen Books, n.p.

Several renditions of the imaginary, original statue were included in a book which was itself originally intended as an unusual kind of photo album: Dolf Sternberger's *Panorama oder Ansichten vom 19. Jahrhundert* (1938). The book is admittedly something of an oddball. Sternberger is better remembered for his postwar advocacy of democratic values or his journalism, than for this funky cultural history, although Suhrkamp has kept it in print. Like Rebecca West and the Illinois Department of History, Sternberger wanted to create a depiction of an era, and like them, he found a visual metaphor the most appropriate trope. His narrative panorama intended to present German culture from 1860-1910 in order to show the direct links between his own era and the nineteenth century as he defined it, by those dates. Sternberger had also intended to have the book illustrated, but despite several postwar reprintings, only the American translation, *Panorama of the 19th Century*, which was instigated by Erich Heller, appeared with images in 1977, and those were chosen by an art historian, Hortense von Heppe, rather than by the author himself.[1] Her selections included this image of imaginary whole Venuses (fig. 4). Even in the absence of the images, the book works like a photo album, offering snapshots of cultural history tied together by a narrative thread which itself invokes visual metaphors.

Panorama of the 19th Century opens with a discussion of Anton von Werner's panorama of the Battle of Sedan, which received thousands of visitors in Berlin after opening in 1883. Sternberger's allegory of the panorama proceeds on at least two levels. First, the physical attributes of the panorama are contrasted to its ability to create an illusion of reality. Sternberger refers to the »alchemy« of panorama artistry, its ability to create the deliberate illusion of historical reality in the »crucible« (an allusion to the alchemist's tools) of the rotunda and the craftsmanship of lighting technique (Sternberger 1977: 13). The alchemist's skill is always visible, yet the successful panorama belies the artistry in the apparent illusion of reality. It offers, as Sternberger wrote, »a mirage of nature, admittedly: for everyone – the industrious creator and the admiring observer alike – is from the very outset aware of, and agreeable to, being deceived« (ibid.: 11).

---

1 Cf. Sternberger's book proposal, 14 April 1935, Nachlass Sternberger 1989/ 10/9783, Deutsches Literaturarchiv Marbach (DLM).

The allegory of the panorama continues in Sternberger's discussion of the »seamlessness« of panorama representation. The panorama developed in the same era as photography, and Sternberger suggests that both formats responded to the new viewing experience provided by railway travel. Landscape seen from a train, instead of remaining in the static position presented by landscape paintings, literally rolled by, offering a mobile terrain viewed by an observer who is both stationary (because seated in the train) and in transit (as a passenger on a train). The seams of the panorama canvas, almost but not quite invisible, reminded the viewer of artifice and included him or her in the joke, as it were; one expected to be duped, and was relieved or satisfied by the reassurance of human handiwork. The dynamics of modern vision inform Sternberger's analysis of visual modes of representation. The seamless narrative skill informing the panorama is analogous to the historian's skill in translating the meanings of fragments and photographs into coherent historical narratives.

Sternberger then makes a rather startling leap to a discussion of genre painting and how exoticism became a popular theme in nineteenth-century art and literature. He connects these discussions through the trope of panoramic viewing. The experience of railway spectatorship, he argues, transformed viewers' conceptions of what could be known: The extension of railroads brought the world closer as a »procession of tableaux« which could reach an audience at home (ibid.: 39-40). Situated as he was on the cusp of the information technology revolution that would globalize access to knowledge, Sternberger already saw that »the view from European windows had lost their depth« (ibid.: 46). Greater access to foreign realms, such as the mythical Orient now connected from Berlin to Baghdad, produced a passive viewer of exoticism who expected art and literature to represent that newly mediated access. Orientalist art and genre painting, which today are widely regarded as a kind of ground zero for modern kitsch, are for Sternberger evidence of how viewer expectations were met by mass culture. Where others might see a suffocating preference for cheap sentimentality in the representation of anthropomorphized animals, particularly dogs, Sternberger argued that the same kinds of expectations drove genre painting as well as panorama viewing:

»The target of expectation is not in the picture – it is the viewer [...who] has a need for an arranged, expectant scene – in short, genre. [... T]he impact of genre on the thoughts and feelings of this age can scarcely be overestimated: that is to say, genre not in the sense of a special branch of art or learning, but as a form of viewing, a form of human condition, of life itself.« (Ibid.: 53)

Viewers desired a vicarious experience of reality – in the case of genre, they sought passion; in the case of the panorama, they sought an experience of historical reality. Even the desire to restore the recently discovered statue of the Venus de Milo becomes for Sternberger evidence of genre mentality: In the various suggestions of what the original statue might have looked like, he finds a preference for ›filling in the gaps‹ or seamlessness that cannot be reconciled to an armless female figure. Panorama viewers expect their kitsch to be complete, whole, and yet illusionistic. Genre scenes examined by Sternberger include those produced by animal rights activists who decried the practice of vivisection. He is acutely sensitive to tensions within the nineteenth-century desire for scientific ›progress‹ – those proponents of technology who drove the modern chemical and steel industries to become avatars of the German economy as well as those who feared its human costs. If the anti-vivisectionists appealed to the public's expectation for anthropomorphic identification through the depiction of animals' suffering, they also completed the panorama of species co-existence. The most stunning chapter of this almost breathless articulation of the panorama allegory comes under the heading »Evolution«. »One might almost think«, Sternberger writes, »that this word itself indicated the long, unfolded picture [...] of what Natural Selection (quite properly capitalized) leaves behind on its battlefield during its both ruthless and solicitous advances« (ibid.: 83). Sternberger focuses on the way that Darwin understood the exclusionary aspect of natural selection: Only the fittest are included in existence, and the rest expire, in a ruthlessly destructive process that ends up producing existence as we know it – quite properly, this force of Nature is capitalized; its agency is distinctive and distinctly non-human. Sternberger briefly discusses contemporary challenges that Darwin could not account for the absence of visible »transitional forms«, but in the evolutionary panorama nothing is left out and everything must be accounted for:

»half natural force, half tool (if closely examined, both at once), serviceable and yet demanding admiration if not veneration, but at least submission, natural selection accurately performs the task of joining together the previously separated forms of organic nature into an unbroken gliding sequence of changing images and at the same time offering this whole of evolution as its own work to the scientist, a further traveler on the railroad.« (Ibid.: 87)

The scientist, like the railroad passenger, passively observes and records what he sees – the panorama of evolution, with its only apparently unbroken series of stages, like the seams in the panorama canvas.

Genre and panorama viewing reappear simultaneously in Sternberger's elaboration of evolutionary theory. Recognizing Darwin's inability, indeed unwillingness, to separate human agency from its embeddedness in the process of natural selection, Sternberger once again sees a desire for seamlessness, for filling in the gaps between what is understood and what cannot be known with certainty. Morality's role in evolutionary theory, itself a topic of great debate and discussion ever since, is to fill in those gaps. Sternberger reiterates Darwin's assertion that moral sensibility could evolve within other animal species, because it had evolved in human animals (cf. ibid.: 105-106). Therefore humans could retain the position of »the lofty observer« of evolution (as the species capable of this higher level of knowledge), and yet also be caught up in the panorama they observe (ibid.: 109). For example, animal rights activism which garners support for the monkeys and baboons used in experimentation, or the dogs flayed by vivisectionists, risks nothing of humanity's status as victors in the battle of natural selection. Survival of the fittest, understood in social Darwinist terms as a validation of racial superiority, instead figures in panorama representation as the selection of survivors – as Sternberger notes, Darwin and his followers »regarded not so much the war as its issue, not so much the destroyed as the survivors, not so much the extinction as the selection« (ibid.: 80). And his chillingly ironic commentary sums up the implications of natural selection for the present: »An unerring power! And selecting exclusively for the good of each being! How remote now lies the field of destruction, how brilliantly the myriads of deaths are rationalized! [... D]eath serves only for the best of life.« (Ibid.: 81) This abrupt apostrophe to power, stridently appearing with exclamation points, articulates the synergies of evolution and Nazism in an uncanny fashion. Both mimicking Nazi rhetoric and tellingly repeating out of context its genocidal intentions, while simultaneously ironically challenging its claims, Sternberger managed to walk the fine line past the censors.[2] The book was published in 1938, prior to the onset of the Second World War and the atrocities of the Holocaust, but the implications of violence were everywhere apparent in Nazi propaganda and rhetoric, if anyone wanted to take it seriously, as Sternberger did.[3] Sternberger's *Panorama* rewards twenty-first-century reading by illuminating continuities linking the short nineteenth century to his present-oriented, 1930s-nineteenth century through its visual culture.

Both the panorama and the photo album, products of the nineteenth century, shaped the dynamic modes of apprehension used by historically conscious individuals in the twentieth century. We historians are readers of the visual, and the popular genre of the photo album offers the best analogy for our work because it is the most appropriately autobiographical form for twenty-first-century historical consciousness. As such, we are all children of nineteenth-century visual culture, for whom photographs illustrate the passive agency we assign to Reality.

WORKS CITED

Barthes, Roland (1981): *Camera Lucida*, New York/NY: Farrar, Straus & Giroux.

---

2   The book was in fact denounced by the Reichsstelle zur Förderung des deutschen Schrifttums for its ›liberal handling‹ of the historical subject, but published and reviewed nonetheless. Cf. the *Gutachten* of 15 July 1938, DLM Nachlass Sternberger, 1989/10/9788/1938.

3   Walter Benjamin famously accused Sternberger of bad faith and collusion with the regime, as well as plagiarism of his own Arcades project. Sternberger was in contact with Benjamin, but mainly familiar with his work through conversations with Theodor Adorno, and certainly both scholars shared a fascination with late nineteenth-century visual culture. I am suggesting, however, that Benjamin missed the point: Sternberger was not celebrating Nazism but revealing its nineteenth-century affinities. What Benjamin saw as the demerits of the book were actually signs of its successful critique. Cf. Benjamin's review of *Panorama oder Ansichten vom 19. Jahrhundert*, originally published in the *Zeitschrift für Sozialforschung* in 1939 (Benjamin 1972), and Sternberger's account in »Sternberger über Sternberger: Panorama.« In: *FAZ* 11 May 1988.

Batchen, Geoffrey (2009): »Saying and Seeing: A Response to ›Incongruous Images‹«. *History and Theory* 48.4, 26-33.

Benjamin, Walter (1972): »Dolf Sternberger, Panorama oder Ansichten vom 19. Jahrhundert«. In: *Gesammelte Schriften* III, Frankfurt am Main: Suhrkamp, 572-579. [English translation (2003): *Selected Writings: 1938-1940*, vol. 4, Cambridge/MA: Harvard University Press, 145-152].

Doane, Mary Ann (2002): *The Emergence of Cinematic Time: Modernity, Contingency, the Archive*, Cambridge/MA: Harvard University Press.

Edwards, Elizabeth (2009): »Photography and the Material Performance of the Past«. *History and Theory* 48.4, 130-150.

Gower, H.D./Louis Stanley Jast/William Whiteman Topley (1916): *The Camera as Historian*, London: Sampson Low, Marston & Co.

Melman, Billie (2006): *The Culture of History: English Uses of the Past 1800-1953*, Oxford: Oxford University Press.

Starl, Timm (2009): *Bildbestimmung: Identifizierung und Datierung von Fotografien 1839-1945*, Marburg: Jonas Verlag.

Sternberger, Dolf (1977): *Panorama of the 19th Century*, transl. by Joachim Neugroschel, New York/NY: Urizen Books.

»Sternberger über Sternberger: Panorama« (1988): In: *FAZ* 11 May 1988.

Stewart, Charles C./Peter Fritzsche (eds.) (1997): *Imagining the Twentieth Century*, Champagne/IL: The University of Illinois Press.

Tagg, John (2009): »The Pencil of History: Photography, History, Archive«. In: *The Disciplinary Frame: Photographic Truths and the Capture of Meaning*, Minneapolis/MN: University of Minnesota Press, 209-233.

West, Rebecca (1982): *1900*, New York/NY: The Viking Press.

Afterword: Past, Present, Future

Jerome De Groot

Is Popular History Obsolete?

As this collection of articles demonstrates, and the work that contributed to it in terms of conference papers, discussion, seminar work, doctoral research and international conversations, the investigation of popular history is thriving and constantly developing. It is no longer possible for historians to dismiss popular culture or ignore the ways in which the past is represented, rewritten, reordered, versioned, disrupted and fragmented in multiple ways in television, film, drama, novels, re-enactment, advertising, games, museums, newspapers, architecture. As a way of concluding, then, without closing off, I want to suggest mildly some new avenues for popular history and our scholarly investigation of it.

When preparing *Consuming History*, my book about popular history, for publication in 2008, I would joke that I wanted the opening line to be »This book is obsolete«. Whilst I never took this provocative step, it maybe would have been fair, for several reasons, which I offer here as a way of thinking about the limits of what we do as scholars of popular history and as a way of thinking about what we might think about doing in the future.

The first reason was the continuing hybrid development of popular historical tropes. As a mode, genre, trope, form, whatever you wish to term it, popular history continues to evolve and develop profile and audiences in new and complex ways, and at seemingly exponential speed. Some good recent examples of this in the anglophone world would be: the worldwide mainstream success of Hilary Mantel's revisionist Tudor novel *Wolf Hall*

(2009); celebrity scientist-cook Heston Blumenthal's historical cooking show *Heston's Feasts* (including Victorian, Roman, Medieval and Tudor) and the 2011 opening of his fashionable London restaurant *Dinner* (featuring a scholarly menu with numerous historical dishes from as far back as 1630); the invocations of various historical paradigms in the 2008 American Presidential Election (such as Barack Obama's use of Abraham Lincoln as a comparative figure or the genealogical investigation into both candidates which showed Obama's family had owned slaves); the continuing development of docudrama techniques and re-enactment models in mainstream historical television; the complexities of remaking historical timeslip (the 2008 American version of BBC's *Life On Mars*); the heritage television mini-boom in the UK in 2010 (*Downton Abbey*, ITV and *Upstairs, Downstairs*, BBC); the success of challenging American drama series such as *Spartacus* (Roman antiquity), *Mad Men* (the 1960s), and *Boardwalk Empire* (the 1920s).

Work on popular history is always, it seems, doomed to look out of date as producers, writers, audiences, practitioners, artists, re-enactors, historians and readers shift the paradigms, interrogate the form, twist and reconfigure the ways in which we think about pastness. Any final word on the contemporary would be immediately out of date. At the same time, investigation into popular history is pushing backwards, with important work being undertaken on the Tudor period, Victorian periods, radical heritage and modern Medievalism. Undertaking to audit popular history in its many forms, and the ways in which it is being produced, researched and reconfigured is a task seemingly doomed to failure.

The second reason was more precise – actual, technological obsolescence. As my book went into production, Facebook was not even being talked of in any sense as a software (whilst it had some market penetration, the key period of its emergence was 2008-9); similarly social networking media such as Bebo and Twitter were not used by many people at all while they are now mainstays of news coverage and the online presence of anything from museums to supermarkets. New media forms are proliferating at such a rate – and their use is diversifying so fast – that gaining a discursive foothold appears impossible. New research techniques, broadcasting forums, accessibility media and ways of accessing, versioning, reworking and interrogating the past online will develop increasingly innovative ways of encountering the past.

The third problem is breadth of coverage, as indicated by my loose term ›anglophone world‹. Whilst increasingly media forms are part of a globalised system, as I will discuss further below, and therefore any sense of historically national specificity is going to have to be reconciled with different audiences (How do Polish viewers engage with *Mad Men*? How do American viewers understand *El Labertino del Fauno/Pan's Labyrinth*?), it is the case that popular historical practices have a local meaning and iteration, and the relation between globalised media flows and intercultural, localised practices is still not clear in any coherent way. We need to think using international or globalised or cosmopolitan frameworks, particularly as, in the future, much popular historical product is going to lose its national identity (through being part of a globalised non-specific cultural imaginary), its ideological impetus, its local heft.

The next two sections will discuss briefly two examples (made by the same production company) to show the current paradoxes inherent in contemporary comprehension of the past: a central concern with, and innovation in, rendering pastness on television; similarly a problematic tendency for this to be part of capitalist cultural imperialism, drawing the national sting of history. Both these examples seem to demonstrate a closing down of histories but ultimately suggest the thriving quality of popular history and its ability to disclose authoritative historical narratives and undermine them, the ability of the popular historical text to deconstruct, destabilise and challenge orthodoxy, conservatism and authority. In this challenge, it seems, lies the continuing value of the phenomenon.

EFFECT INTO AFFECT: PASTNESS IN THE PRESENT

My first example is from an unusual source and suggests the prevalence of history (quite literally as a popular practice) in culture, and that we might profitably investigate the ways in which pastness (and the modes of identity this invokes and transforms) is used in texts that are not resolutely ›historical‹. This latter would open up a model of thinking about the ways in which memory, flashback, criminality, ghosts and revenants of all kinds and much more contribute to a sense of history/historicity (particularly in relation to – and maybe this is the point – a fragile and composite definition about what contemporariness or ›now‹ means).

Set in Bon Temps in rural Louisiana, the American television series *True Blood* (HBO, 2008-present) imagines a contemporary world in which vampires have been legalised, freed from their desire for human blood by synthetic blood substitute. Vampires have been recognised and are beginning to demand rights as citizens. (The series echoes very deliberately the civil rights movement, but it also relates to the American Civil War. Bill, the central vampire figure, had been a soldier during the war and was turned into a vampire – and hence became undead – during the conflict). In series 1, episode 5 Bill has been persuaded by the grandmother of his human lover Sookie to address the meeting of the »Descendants of the Glorious Dead«, i.e. a society commemorating the Confederate side of the Civil War. The interest in Confederate history (the Confederate flag is raised in the church) is seen to be both innocent (the joy that the grandmother has in the past) and distasteful (the black character Tara stares at the flag in disbelief; she has already asked Bill if he owned slaves). The past is still very much alive and problematic in this Southern community.[1] The »Descendants of the Glorious Dead« model of remembrance of course suggests a direct link to those that took part in the Civil War or the Revolution, a sense of historic racial purity that has affinity with, but is much more heightened than, general genealogical interest. It suggests a link that echoes through the ages, like the vampires themselves, and recalls, surely, Thomas Jefferson's famous line »The tree of liberty must be refreshed from time to time with the blood of patriots and tyrants.« The Descendants' meeting is itself popular history, the local community coming together to remember in certain amateur ways (and to celebrate their link with the past). Bill's involvement makes the past to them (and us, through flashback) more real – his body and his story (rather than a textual narrative or written version of history) make the past live, because it is still alive in him. He demonstrates the way that popular history returns the viewer/audience/genealogist to the body of and in the past.

The use of a vampire in this way to transcend time and disrupt linearity is not unusual. Anne Rice's *Interview with the Vampire* (1976) begins in Louisiana in the eighteenth century (*True Blood* has many connections with this now classic novel) and the central figure is doomed to walk alone through time. Similarly there are various jokes in the *Twilight* series about

---

1   For the general context cf., for instance, Horwitz (1999: in particular 275-280).

how the vampire family have gone to college multiple times. The use of Bill's experiences in *True Blood*, though, contributes to a queering element that the series undertakes more generally. It is interested in blurring boundaries of sexuality, anthropology and identity throughout, using its status as Southern Gothic to do this (and to add in layers of ghostliness, haunting and revenants throughout). Its use of history is no less complex. The vampire is literally a relic, something which lived then and lives now; anti-historical longevity combined with true, authentic historicalness.

Bill tells a story about the death of one of the congregation's ancestors during the Civil War. He was fighting for the Confederates and attempting to save a boy (whose ancestors are also in the hall). It is a moving story and the shifting of viewpoint from Bill to his memory, to the dying boy and then into the head of his drugged ancestor both contributes to this account (Bill's voice in voice-over renders the sequence diegetically recalled into the present) and makes it clearly resonant and effectual in the present. Bill is the conduit for the past, a witness and participant who despite his claims to be human is very much not so – and the thing that defines him as such is his ability to stand outside history, or, perhaps, to stand in historicity and not care. The show thus argues that death is what makes us human and the point of death is to recall us to memory and history. Without this and the ineffable sense of poignancy and fleetingness that it invokes, we are above – or outside – humanity.

What happens next, however, shifts the tone. In the same way that the vampire in Rice's novels is lonely (a trope that harks back to Byron and echoes through vampiric writing), Bill's isolated state historically is recalled. The Mayor of the town gives him a picture of his family taken just before he went to war. The pain in his face demonstrates how it affects him, and he sees and comprehends his loss – the loss of his humanity and his history. Bill weeps. Being outside of history is possible but you can still, even if you are undead, be brought back in (and the conduit for that is the memory of death, the recollection of the death and loss of his family, friends and comrades). Later, Bill has visions of his family (children, wife) in his house. The vampire who made him a vampire appears in a flashback sequence outside his family home telling him, »You can never enter ... do you wish to see them grow old and feeble, year after year? [...] They are as good as dead.« Being human means being in history which means being mortal; popular historical texts have this at their heart. Popular history, or the manifestation of the past in the cultural text, reconciles us to at the same time as repelling us from death. We recognise the otherness of the past and its complete difference from now – that otherness allows us to control our reactions to it. But the vampire stands outside this, queering the linearity and smoothness of history and disrupting our understanding and comprehension in the same way that they complicate our notion of humanness, sexuality and science. The vampire queers the linearity of history, by disavowing the otherness of the past (and hence demonstrating the falsehood of our narrativising of that past into history), by not allowing death to make a binary of then and now.

The manifestation of the past in the present in *True Blood* demonstrates a malleability of trope, an ease with the ways in which a kind of history might be iterated in the now (and hence a new way of comprehending ourselves as contemporary figures). Georg Lukács argued that Walter Scott's historical fiction allowed, for the first time, a popular sense of historicity, of the individual in history of some description (and of history as process): »Hence the concrete possibilities for men to comprehend their own existence as something historically conditioned, for them to see in history something which deeply affects their daily lives and immediately concerns them.« (Lukács 1962: 24) The versions of the past that are presented to us allow a new conceptualisation of the contemporary self through a renewed/reanimated/renovated modelling of the engagement with the ways in which history might be seen to work (or how it might be undermined).

AFFECT INTO EFFECT: HISTORY AS BATTERING RAM

In February 2011 the satellite and cable television channel Sky launched Sky Atlantic in the UK. Sky Atlantic is a channel dedicated to drama and American imports. Previewing media material emphasised the importance to the new channel's identity of *quality* programming, particularly by pointing out the awards given the keynote shows:

»In one sense, Sky Atlantic is no gamble at all. Its roster of programmes, the lion's share made by the US cable network HBO, is impressive. These new shows include

Boardwalk Empire, which recently won the Golden Globe for Best Television Drama, and the fifth series of *Mad Men*, itself a serial award-winner.« (Pettie 2011)

The channel opened with the first episode of the 1920s-set *Boardwalk Empire* (HBO 2010-present), which every critic noted was directed by Martin Scorcese; it also controversially outbid the BBC for the UK rights to screen the upcoming new series of AMC's hit show about the lives and loves of advertising executives, *Mad Men* (2007-present) (cf. De Groot 2011). Historical television, then, is part of the new configuring of British television culture and it is a key element in Rupert Murdoch's new ›battering ram‹ for the expansion into middle-class homes. In 1996 he had used sport – mainly football – as a means of achieving a huge market share.[2] Now the past and ›quality‹ imported television takes the place of sport in Murdoch's strategy to achieve the same market saturation (and content ownership) for bourgeois audiences used to watching import drama on niche channels such as BBC 4 and Channel 4. Future shows on Sky Atlantic include the fantasy-medieval *Game of Thrones*, the war series *The Pacific* and possibly a show about the Borgias featuring classy British actors such as Jeremy Irons and Derek Jacobi. Sky Atlantic uses glossy fictions of the past to sell the channel (and, by implication, Sky TV more generally) and to associate it with the gravitas of the past. Costume drama, hitherto the province of the BBC, is now firmly the purview of the non-mainstream, non-public broadcaster. In British culture, the BBC is now outflanked by Sky and, implicitly, America – the ›Atlantic‹ of the channel's title reminding all viewers that the history and drama that is unfolding is not domestic. Where the BBC has partnerships with American channels to sell product in the USA and elsewhere around the world, these are often sold as ›Masterpiece Theatre‹ (PBS, USA). Similarly the BBC was outflanked by its domestic rival ITV, whose thoughtful 2010 costume drama *Downton Abbey* was a global hit.

However, the masterstroke of Sky Atlantic is to suggest that costume drama is as valid and as important as, for instance, key sitcoms and classic dramas (such as *The Wire* and *The Sopranos*, which the channel showed in

---

2   »Rupert Murdoch yesterday signalled his plan to take an even more aggressive approach towards buying television rights for leading sports when he announced that he intended to use sport as a ›battering ram‹ for the expansion of his global pay television network.« (Milliken 1996)

entirety). The liberal newspaper *The Guardian* ran a debate asking, »Is Sky Atlantic bad for British Television?« in which Imogen Carter argued: »For millions, just as high quality US drama has become as much a part of our culture as American pop music, films and fast food, the supply across our core TV channels has, in the main, been cut off.« (Carter/Anthony 2011) Carter's point is that Sky had decided to restrict access to something that was as important to the cultural identity and social self-representation of the middle-class audience as Sky owner Murdoch had gambled that sport was to a working-class one. Implicit, too, in Carter's argument is the resonance of a cultural transference of historical modes of thinking and a transcultural identity; American historical television aids the penetration into the British historical imagination of a past that is not native, a cultural or historical globalisation effect in which the product becomes both something alienated from its origins and also a commodity shorn of signification for those consuming it. All renderings of the past – whether they be fiction or ›History‹ – are translations of an othered chaos into a form comprehensible to the now, so nationality might make little difference (hence the *Borgias* series, or the global success of the American-made *The Tudors*). What is key now is the way in which global media groups and companies materially control the making and distribution of such programmes, and the ways in which they are marketed and comprehended as a consequence.

Terence Winter, writer of *Boardwalk Empire*, argued that the key was its relative familiarity:

»People looked different and sounded different and the music and pop culture were different, and yet it was still accessible [...]. It was still modern enough that it felt like you and I could watch it and could relate to these people. They still had the telephone and they rode on trains and ate dinner and they went to movies and they did all the things we do, but it's still almost 100 years ago. I think if the show was in 1910, I don't think you'd watch it and feel the same way.« (Ryan 2010)

The past must be comprehensible somehow. This idea of representing something as the same but different, familiarly ›modern‹, argues for an audience familiar with historical difference so long as it is still clearly part of a comprehensible modernity, part of the now (or at least part of the evolutionary, teleological, positivist movement of history from then to the contemporary). Winter points out quite how difficult it is to achieve authenticity: »HBO did roll the dice in a really big way on this show. It was very, very expensive to do.« (Ibid.)

Historiographically *Deadwood* (HBO 2004-6, also shown on Sky Atlantic) and *Rome* (HBO 2005-7) showed the way: unflinching, violent, iconoclastic shows suggesting the grim reality behind two of the most enduring historical identity myths (American pioneering and Roman civilisation).[3] *Boardwalk Empire* similarly imagines the American past through the lens of Scorcese – literally in the case of the first episode – and the *Sopranos*, televisually emphasising a perverted, familial sense of community but also seeking to highlight the grim, violent, perverted ways in which the nation has formed itself and created its own myth. The use of Scorcese allows the series to claim his artistic integrity and a certain cinematic or textual authenticity, attain gravitas and echo the interrogative historiography of his own series of films. *Boardwalk Empire* contributes to the ›telling‹ of America undertaken in Scorcese's historical projects such as *Raging Bull* (1980), *GoodFellas* (1990) and *Gangs of New York* (2002). The historiography of these films and the new TV series, then, is to demonstrate the violence of the past rather than to construct a nostalgic echo. America, the films suggest, was built on crime and violence rather than idealistic acts – something demonstrated most famously in the speech of Bill the Butcher, draped in a torn American flag, in *Gangs of New York*:

»I'm forty-seven. Forty-seven years old. You know how I stayed alive this long? All these years? Fear. The spectacle of fearsome acts. Somebody steals from me, I cut off his hands. He offends me, I cut out his tongue. He rises against me, I cut off his head, stick it on a pike, raise it high up so all on the streets can see. That's what preserves the order of things. Fear.«

This key sense of the foundational moment of history being grounded in violence echoes contemporary critiques of modernity, modern historiography and neo-liberal models of the state. As Terry Eagleton (2005a) points out, the first usages of the term ›terrorism‹ date from the 1790s in response to the atrocities occurring in France.[4] Terror and violence is complicit in the first manifestation – as Eagleton argues – of the bourgeois state,

---

3   Cf. De Groot (2008: 199-201) and Landsberg (2010).

4   Cf. also Eagleton (2005b).

and is if not foundational at least influential in the creation of the modern nation. »Terror and modernity were twinned at birth«, Eagleton asserts, before going on to consider the lawlessness of the modern capitalist state (ibid.: 18). Eagleton's work is in the main a critique of America (or the West) and its inability to »discern an image of its own monstrous visage in the raging fury at its gate«, leaving it only capable of »fear rather than pity« (ibid.: 19). His key point is that »capitalist modernity [...] could survive only by perpetual transgression« (ibid.: 18).

Much contemporary historical fiction is interested in exposing this, critiquing the neo-liberal models of statehood through undermining idealistic creation narratives and positivist teleologies, iconoclastic if subtle interrogations of nationhood and capitalism. The adaptation of David Peace's *Red Riding Trilogy* by Channel 4 in 2009 similarly refutes the easy nostalgia tropes of the 1970s for a bleak rendition of the horror and violence of past periods (historical difference actualised and defined, as in *Mad Men*, by the constant smoking, a physical difference with diverse presence in the body and in the air, signifying a difference between then and now). *Red Riding Trilogy* covers the years 1974-83 in Yorkshire, particularly focussing on police brutality and corruption during the hunt for Peter Sutcliffe, the ›Yorkshire Ripper‹. In the films news reporters become historian-detectives looking in the archives for information about the present, searching for a ›truth‹ that is either not there or never revealed fully. Edward Dunford in the opening film is told by a paranoid colleague to look for comprehension in the present via the lessons of the past: »You're ignorant Dunford. Try carrying an history book along with that notebook of yours.« (*Red Riding* 2009). The past might allow us to understand the present. Yet in these films the past is violent and unrelentingly grim, nightmarish, poor and traumatic, constantly a source of horror in the present. To even attempt to present it as coherent is impossible, despite our attempts to do so. History is what is narrated in order to obviate or avoid the fear that this might be all there is, that society is built upon horror rather than idealism. As Eagleton argues, the barbarian at the gate that has destroyed the social order is the ravening capitalist nation-state. This has often been the historiographical undertone, particularly of crime narratives; the models for these modern grim nightmares are *Chinatown* (Roman Polanski, 1974) and *The Godfather Part II* (Francis Ford Coppola, 1974), but the manifestation of such paranoid and iconoclastic versions of the past in mainstream television series is relatively new.

Boardwalk Empire's opening credits show Enoch ›Nucky‹ Thompson smoking and looking out to sea. The camera lingers on the waves, a motif of time being inscrutable, perhaps, but also invoking a sense of endless fluidity that the viewer – both Thompson and the TV viewer – attempts to control or order into something comprehensible. The camera also concentrates on tropes of authenticity in close-up – costume, action (smoking, particularly), props and location. Thompson is situated as historical but a pioneer, individual but prepared to define himself against the chaos out there. He then turns to walk to civilisation. Yet the music is a modern guitar-based song, »Straight Up and Down«, by The Brian Jonestown Massacre. From its opening, then, the series prioritises a kind of cultural clash, a trope of subtle anachronism.[5] This paratextual moment positions the entire show at an acute angle to the now, echoing the ways in which *True Blood* plays with historicity, contemporariness and linearity. This sophistication of historiographic engagement, and the concomitant intelligence of the textual entity as a consequence, is common to much contemporary historical drama – and, one might argue, is a keynote of *all* representations of the past. Fictions of the past are *de facto* illusory and ›fictional‹; they cleave to an aesthetics of authenticity and realism whilst always constantly acknowledging and (to use a term from literary critical theory) deconstructing their own ability and authority.

The way in which the past is represented in renderings of the past itself demonstrates how shows like *Boardwalk Empire* conceptualise their own complex relationship to the contemporary audience. *Mad Men* and *Boardwalk Empire* deal themselves with memory in very interesting and metafictional fashion. For Don Draper, a central figure in *Mad Men*, his childhood is something revealed as traumatic, violent and unpleasant; something he flees in order to create a new identity for himself. Nucky Thompson in *Boardwalk Empire* obliterates his childhood even more, burning down his family house in empty vengeance over the way his father treated him as a child (Episode 7, »Home«). In both examples the past has a difficult and complex hold over the figure in the present, and their relationship to it is

---

5   Similarly *Mad Men*'s credits are soundtracked by an electronic composition, »A Beautiful Mine« by RJD2.

vexed. Both Draper and Thompson are at once defined by and simultaneously attempt to avoid being trapped into models of behaviour imposed upon them from within their personal histories. The obvious motif-shift here is for the audience to consider how the past informs the contemporary moment, imposing meaning and resonance whether consciously appreciated or not. The fact that both Draper and Thompson are haunted by violence meted out to them by their fathers suggests that history is a revenant in the present of something repressed or a traumatic event contributing to a damaged and possibly vengeful identity in the now. Nucky's father burned his son's hand with a poker; he still carries the scar. The past is physically resonant in the present, and this motif of scarring is developed in the same episode as Nucky's young protégé Jimmy spends time in hospital due to a wound he took during the 1914-18 war. He befriends a man with extensive facial scarring. Their experiences are literally written on their bodies, and scars thus become the textualised, externalised evidence of their patriotism, their bravery and their propensity to violence (a kind of violence, state-sanctioned, that is allowed in the way that their criminal violence is not). They are scarred by the past and thus they act in the present; they cannot escape what has happened to them. Thus the show demonstrates a similar sophistication about pastness and internal memorialisation to most other popular historical texts. It has metafictional moments, a sense of the importance of connection; internal signifier and metatextual, paratextual elements point out the sophistication of its engagement with the past but also its falsehood.

CONCLUSIONS

What is key, here, and unprecedented, is the global reach of these programmes. It seems clear that, whilst international links and the histories of other cultures have always been part of popular historicity, the issues associated with new globalised forms and increasingly profit-driven, unregulated media markets (as well as the influence of new digital and online environments, softwares and interfaces) allow a *de facto* global reach whilst simultaneously constructing a single narrative (American history, the history of nation and capital, the move to liberal democratic nowness). Whilst these shows are productions of a capitalist globalised media market, and represent purely commodified history in the sense that they are constructed within industrial frameworks and reified according to economic models, they also hold within them the ability to query, trouble and challenge. They suggest through their revelation of the mythos of state and nation that history is simply the narrating of a set of convenient facts, a construction of an ordering narrative (and they suggest the chaos beyond this) by an authority with vested interests in controlling the present. They point out the fallibility of the archive, the fact that inserting the human back into the past can tell us as much if not more than the raw data we attempt to comprehend.

We might point out, too, that the histories that are being presented here are resolutely nationalistic, western and (mainly) white, male, positivist and liberal. Much historiographical thinking in the past decades (by feminists, poststructuralists, queer theorists and postcolonial theorists) has rejected the construction of such history as simply replicating, in the versions of the past, the structures of inequality and problematic power relations of the present. Dipesh Chakrabarty argues:

»So long as one operates within the discourse of ›history‹ produced at the institutional site of the university, it is not possible simply to walk out of the deep collusion between ›history‹ and the modernizing narrative(s) of citizenship, bourgeois public and private, and the nation-state. ›History‹ as a knowledge system is firmly embedded in institutional practices that invoke the nation-state at every step.« (Chakrabarty 2000: 14)

How might popular history contribute to a challenge on this (or attempt to sustain such nationcentric, problematic narratives of the past)? How much has the global historical imagination been constructed by a centre (and is that dominant culture one that is national or shared)? Lukács argued that Scott allowed a new history because of an innovative sense of national identity through relationship to the past: »The appeal to national independence and national character is necessarily connected with a re-awakening of national history.« (Lukács 1962: 25) Seemingly popular history is fundamentally nationalistic at some level. Yet it can also challenge these narratives and present new ways of thinking about a non-national past, a past which belongs to everyone and that all might partake of. The past is other, and the ways in which it is manifest in the present (through fiction-history) should reject modelling themselves upon repressive measures, avoid attempting to colonise, domesticate, oppress or control; they should open up comprehension and point up empathy. We need to investigate the nexus of power that creates our popular cultural texts and think about how history works within and without this. We need, most pressingly, to think about how audiences use such texts (and to invoke Michel de Certeau's work, as has been done by some historians, to think about resistance and usage).[6] We need to think internationally and to work together as much as possible (for whilst *Boardwalk Empire* only works if one considers its international iteration, the same could be said for the novels of Walter Scott – read from Brazil to Russia in the nineteenth century). We need to be alive to the ways new technologies open up innovative ways of thinking about our past. Most importantly, we need to think about how versions of the past enact the present, contribute to our contemporaneity and our current identity, and how we might audit, challenge and study that.

WORKS CITED

Boardwalk Empire (USA 2010-present, Creator: Terence Winter).

Carter, Imogen/Andrew Anthony (2011): »Is Sky Atlantic Bad for British Television?«. In: *The Guardian* 6 February 2011 (http://www.guardian.co.uk/tv-and-radio/2011/feb/06/sky-atlantic-boardwalk-empire-mad-men). Accessed 19 February 2011.

Chakrabarty, Dipesh (2000): *Provincializing Europe: Postcolonial Thought and History*, Princeton/NJ: Princeton University Press.

De Certeau, Michel (2002): *The Practice of Everyday Life*, Berkeley/CA: University of California Press.

De Groot, Jerome (2008): *Consuming History*, London: Routledge.

De Groot, Jerome (2011): »›Perpetually Dividing and Suturing the Past and Present‹: *Mad Men* and the Illusions of History«. *Rethinking History* 15.2, 269-285.

Eagleton, Terry (2005a): »Terror – It's a Truly Bourgeois Tradition«. *Times Higher Educational Supplement* July 15, 18-19.

---

6   De Certeau's model in *The Practice of Everyday Life* (2002) of the small resistances and scope for dissidence available within mainstream culture and/or society is increasingly attractive to those writing about popular culture.

Eagleton, Terry (2005b): *Holy Terror*, Oxford: Oxford University Press.

Gangs of New York (USA 2002, Director: Martin Scorsese).

Horwitz, Tony (1999): *Confederates in the Attic*, New York/NY: Vintage.

Landsberg, Alison (2010): »Waking the *Deadwood* of History: Listening, Language, and the ›Aural Visceral‹«. *Rethinking History* 14.4, 531-549.

Lukács, Georg (1962): *The Historical Novel*, transl. by Hannah and Stanley Mitchell, London: Merlin.

Mad Men (USA 2007-present, Creator: Matthew Weiner).

Milliken, Robert (1996): »Sport Is Murdoch's ›Battering Ram‹ for Pay TV«. In: *The Independent* 16 October 1996 (http://www.independent.co.uk/sport/sport-is-murdochs-battering-ram-for-pay-tv-1358686.html). Accessed 8 March 2011.

Pettie, Andrew (2011): »Sky Atlantic: Will BSkyB's Gamble Pay Off?«. In: *The Telegraph* 1 February 2011 (http://www.telegraph.co.uk/culture/tvandradio/8 296088/Sky-Atlantic-will-BSkyBs-gamble-pay-off.html). Accessed 19 February 2011.

Red Riding: In the Year of Our Lord 1974 (UK 2009, Director: Julian Jarrold).

Ryan, Maureen (2010): »An Interview with *Boardwalk Empire* Creator Terence Winter«. In: *Aol TV* 10 September 2010. (http://www.tvsquad.com/2010/09/10/boardwalk-empire/). Accessed 7 March 2011.

True Blood, Series 1, Episode 5 (USA 2008-present, Creator: Allan Ball).

Dyke, Greg (2002): »Diversity in Broadcasting: A Public Service Perspective«. In: *BBC* 3 May 2002 (http://www.bbc.co.uk/pressoffice/speeches/stories/dyke_cba.shtml). Accessed 26 October 2011.

List of Contributors

Stefan Berger is Professor of Social History at the Ruhr University Bochum and Director of the Institute for Social Movements and the House for the History of the Ruhr. Between 2003 and 2008 he was head of a research programme funded by the European Science Foundation entitled *Representations of the Past: The Writing of National Histories in 19th and 20th Century Europe* (NHIST), the findings of which were published between 2006 and 2012 in 14 volumes. His current research focuses on the history of social movements in Europe and the history of historiography. His latest monograph is *Friendly Enemies: Britain and the GDR, 1949-1990* (2010; together with Norman LaPorte).

Susan A. Cranc is Associate Professor of Modern European History at the University of Arizona. A graduate of Smith College, she received her MA and PhD in History from the University of Chicago. She is the author of *Collecting and Historical Consciousness in Early Nineteenth-Century Germany* (2000) and editor of *Museums and Memory* (2000). Her recent publications have focused on historical subjectivity and the ways historians use photographs as evidence, particularly the historical reception of atrocity photography.

Frédéric Döhl studied Musicology, Ethnomusicolgy and Law in Berlin and wrote his doctoral thesis on the origins and development of barbershop music. He is currently a researcher at SFB 626 at the Free University Berlin. His current research interests include composing with referential material in contemporary art music and popular music; copyright law and music; Beethoven; *fin de siècle* chamber music and crossover artists in music (in particular Bernstein, Jarrett, Kreisler, Previn).

Birte Förster teaches History at Darmstadt University of Technology. Trained at the University of Cologne and the University of Bologna in History and German Literature, she received her PhD from Justus-Liebig University, Gießen. Her research focuses on the intersection of gender and national history, as well as media and transnational history. She is the author of *Der Königin Luise-Mythos: Mediengeschichte des Idealbilds deutscher Weiblichkeit, 1860-1960* (2011) and has co-edited *Mädchenliteratur in der Kaiserzeit* (2003). She is currently writing a book on British and French infrastructure projects in Africa, 1930-1970.

Till Förster holds the chair of social anthropology and is founding director of the Centre for African Studies at the University of Basel, Switzerland. He has specialised in visual culture and political transformations in West and Central Africa where he also conducted field research for many years. His recent publications focus on questions of governance and social creativity in northern Côte d'Ivoire and on urban visual culture in Cameroon.

Jerome de Groot teaches in the department of English and American Studies at the University of Manchester. He is the author of *Royalist Identities* (2004), *Consuming History* (2008) and *The Historical Novel* (2009). He works on popular history, the 1640s, the historical novel, manuscript culture and identity.

Leslie Howsam received her PhD in Modern British History from York University in Canada and teaches at the University of Windsor. She is president of SHARP, the Society for the History of Authorship, Reading and Publishing. Her research addresses problems in the history of the book in nineteenth-century Britain. Her Lyell Lectures at the University of Oxford were published in 2009 as *Past into Print: The Publishing of History in Britain 1850-1950*. Her current work expands on that project, moving into popular history to examine the presentation of the past in the Victorian periodical press.

Barbara Korte is Professor of English Literature at the University of Freiburg, and co-speaker of the DFG research group *History in Popular Cultures of Knowledge*. Recent publications include work on the British short story, English travel writing, Black and Asian British culture and the cultural reception of the First World War in Britain. Her current research focuses on British periodicals of the nineteenth century.

Stefanie Lethbridge is Lecturer in English Literature and Cultural Studies at the University of Freiburg. Her major research interests are in eighteenth- and nineteenth-century Book History and in popular culture. She is the author of *James Thomson's Defence of Poetry* (2003). She is currently completing a monograph on British poetry anthologies from the Renaissance until the twentieth century.

Billie Melman is Professor of History, Henry Glasberg Chair of European Studies and Director of the Graduate School of Historical Studies at Tel Aviv University. She is author of *The Culture of History: English Uses of the Past, 1800-1953* (2006) and *Women's Orient: English Women and the Middle East, 1718-1918* (1992) and co-editor, with Stefan Berger and Chris Lorenz, of *Popularizing National Pasts 1800 to the Present* (2012).

Philipp Müller is Lecturer at University College London. Following his graduation in History and Modern Literature at the Ruhr Universität Bochum, he obtained his PhD at the European University Institute in Florence with a thesis on the dramatisation of crime in imperial Berlin. His research focuses on the history of media, crime and police, the history of archives and historical knowledge. In his current project, he investigates the historical use of archives in Central Europe and the transformation of governmental archives into sites of historical research in the long nineteenth century.

Sylvia Paletschek is Professor of Modern History at the University of Freiburg, and co-speaker of the DFG research group *History in Popular Cultures of Knowledge*. She studied History, German Literature, Geography and Educational Studies in Munich and Hamburg. Her research interests include university history, women's and gender history, and historical culture.

Fernando Sánchez-Marcos studied Philosophy and Humanities (History section) at the Universities of Madrid (UCM) and Barcelona (UB). He has held a Chair in Early Modern History at the University of Barcelona since 2003. He served (1990-99) at the bureau of the International Commission on Theory and History of Historiography (ICHS) and created an international website on historical culture, the theory of history and historiography (http://www.culturahistorica.es). His main fields of research are the history of Baroque Europe, historical writing from the seventeenth to twentieth centuries (from a socio-cultural approach) and the formation of historical culture.

Antonie R. Wiedemann is currently a PhD student at the graduate school of Visual Arts, Performing Arts and Multimedia Technologies of the University of Genoa. In her PhD thesis she explores the work of the art historian William E. Suida. Antonie Wiedemann studied European Cultural History, Italian Studies and Contemporary History in Augsburg, Pisa and Genoa. Her main interests are the cultural history of the nineteenth and beginning twentieth century, the history of art criticism and new technologies applied to research in the humanities.

Index